1992

W9-CFQ-982

Anatomy of a Nursing Home

A New View of Resident Life

Anatomy of
a Nursing Home

A New View
of Resident Life

Mary Elizabeth O'Brien, RN, MSW, PhD

National Health Publishing
A Division of Williams & Wilkins

Published by
National Health Publishing
99 Painters Mill Road
Owings Mills, Maryland 21117
(301) 363-6400

A Division of Williams & Wilkins

Printed in the United States of America
First Printing

Designer: Sandy Renovetz
Compositor: National Health Publishing
Printer: Edwards Brothers

ISBN: 0-932500-96-x
LC: 88-063447

This book is dedicated to the study group of Bethany Manor residents,
their families and friends and their caregivers,
who generously and lovingly shared their joys, their sorrows,
their successes, and their concerns in the hope of helping others
who might one day tread a similar path.

CONTENTS

Appendix B

Study Instruments

FOREWORD

This book comes at a time when the United States, for the first time in history, has released information on the quality of more than 15,000 nursing homes caring for disabled and elderly Americans. These data are part of a growing effort by the U. S. Government to provide consumers with more information about the facilities that care for them and their families.

The Health Care Financing Administration, in its third annual report, focused on the quality of hospital care, providing the public with specific data on the number of deaths in each of the 6,000 hospitals caring for Medicare patients. In addition, the nursing home data covered 32 separate areas including cleanliness, prescription drug delivery, food service, and staffing. Information was provided on two types of nursing homes, skilled nursing facilities (SNFs) and intermediate care facilities (ICFs). Such data can be useful to the consumer as a "screening tool" in choosing a home (American Public Health Association 1989).

The release of this book coincides with multiple major public health policies and public initiatives addressed to the needs of the elderly. Few consumers really understand the nursing home. What makes it tick? Who works there? What is important? In addition to consumers of care, the targeted audience of this book is practitioners of all professions, particularly physicians, nurses, social workers, administrators, gerontologists, and mental health specialists.

The author does not offer simple solutions to these very complex long-term problems, but she does raise the issues that should be considered and possible approaches to their solutions. The book will also be of interest to those who are not currently working in the field of aging. Hopefully, they will be encouraged to not only understand what goes on in the nursing home, but might select this as a career providing great satisfaction.

By understanding the residents who are in nursing homes, by looking at every phase of that nursing home, one can shatter many prevalent and negative myths and stereotypes about the aging. Many people feel that once they reach 65 they are old. It's the end of life. Some believe that most people who are old are in poor health. Many do have chronic, controlled health problems as they age, but they are not limited by these. Some believe that as one grows older the mind also grows old. Dr. Robert Butler, the first director of the National Institute on Aging, has stated many times that "the belief that if you live long enough you will become senile is just wrong." Some believe that older people are unproductive. Yet the evidence shows that they are, if anything, more productive, have better attendance records, are better educated, and are contributing members of society. Many think of older people as unattractive and sexless. Research shows that men and women continue to feel sexy and sensual in later life.

By understanding what goes on in a nursing home, we will predict what we will be like in later years. Major breakthroughs in medicine and public health have changed the whole picture of the future—the eradication of smallpox, the possible eradication of measles, and hopefully the control of the deadly disease, AIDS.

The good news is that nearly 80 percent of Americans will live to be past age 65 (Dychtwald and Flower 1989, 6). New technologies are discovered every day. We see a major drop in individuals with stroke and heart disease. Major strides are being made in terms of understanding the contributuing factors of cancer. We will begin to see a major shift in the attitudes, style, and the meaning of the social revolution referred to as the "age wave" (Dychtwald and Flower 1989, 21). The way old people are treated contributes to their loss of intelligence. If they are isolated, kept in wheelchairs, or confined to bed, within a very short time they will act "senile, become dependent, antisocial, irrational, and unintelligent" (Dychtwald and Flower 1989, 39).

The power of older Americans is becoming evident. They are becoming more articulate, they control more wealth than younger people, they are willing to fight for their causes and make their viewpoints known. Older Americans want to make their own decisions to direct their own lives. They want to be involved in life and not perceived to be in a wheelchair. Most of all, they want to be treated with dignity and provided an assurance that the later years will provide a quality of life to which they are entitled.

Having worked some 25 years in the field of aging, and as former director of the Office of Long Term Care within the Public Health Service, it became quite evident to me that the most important thing that made the difference in relation to nursing homes was the quality of care. We defined quality of care as that which the patient/resident needed and no more. The key word was "need" and in pursuing the definition of need this made it quite evident that we needed to find out much more about the characteristics of the residents of nursing homes, their care needs, the circumstances and settings in which the care is provided, and expected outcomes.

Quality of life, in essence, is an outcome goal. Of course, it is related to the quality of care provided. The author, in dissecting the anatomy of a nursing home, has provided the reader with the very essence of the quality of care. Studies show that many aspects of nursing home life that effect a resident's perceptions of quality of life—and therefore a sense of well being—are intertwined with the quality of care (Committee on Nursing Home Regulation 1986, 51).

It is not sufficient just to show that the quality of care is based on the level of nursing services provided. One must look at the level of restoration of function following such events as hip fractures, the number of new strokes, the number of indwelling catheters, infection rates in residents with indwelling catheters, the number of incontinent individuals who can be helped, skin breakdowns in at risk bedridden residents, and improvements in depressed patients (Committee on Nursing Home Regulation 1986, 61).

The use of a standard instrument increases the power of interpreting and using information for quality assurance purposes. Standard information obtained from the use of these instruments is basic to making comparisons and determining the level of quality care provided.

In my own pursuit to strengthen regulations for Medicare and Medicaid, it became evident that a major weakness in the current Federal regulations is that they do not address quality of care nor quality of life. An Institute of Medicine study has made a strong recommendation that a new condition of participation on quality of care be added to the certification regulations (Committee on Nursing Home Regulation 1986, 130).

An underlying problem in the assessment of nursing homes is that the current criteria have to be made more resident-centered and outcome-oriented. In 1976, the Public Health Service developed and introduced a new assessment tool called PACE, Patient Assessment and Care Evaluation. A more recent generation of this tool has been introduced by the Health Care Financing Administration to be included in part of the survey protocol. This is called PaCS, Patient Care and Services. HFCA developed PaCS to direct the survey process away from facility-structure and theoretical care to more emphasis on the actual delivery of care and its outcomes.

The PaCS survey includes the evaluation through direct observation of certain aspects of physical environment, including cleanliness, space, equipment, infection control, and disaster preparedness; a review of a sample of the residents through observation, interviews, and record review;

evaluation of meals, dining and eating assistance; and an observation of drug administration for a sample of residents. What is missing is the lack of inclusion of quality of life factors.

The author has documented through her research the empirical data of the life career of the nursing home resident. It is through this documentation that we can truly understand the quality of life factors. The unique qualifications of the researcher, the combination of experience as a nurse gerontologist and a sociologist, make an ideal combination in conducting this research. Researchers wishing to replicate this study will find the study instruments particularly helpful. These are all included in the appendix. The reader will also find very helpful the description of how a teaching-nursing-home concept can be implemented.

The researcher has adhered rigorously to meeting the essential components of quality research and has included a section on the protection and involvement of human subjects. Just as one can carefully follow through the anatomy of a nursing home, the researcher has also provided an anatomy of her methodological approach and data analysis.

The author has brought us closer to identifying those factors which contribute to the quality of life. The leadership provided by the author in this book will help many other leaders in the field of aging to make a decision and help to prepare others to select a career in the field of aging. The author will help us to make quality of life a reality and guide policy-makers to make more realistic decisions about caring for our aging population.

Rear Admiral Faye G. Abdellah, R.N., Ed.D., Sc.D., F.A.A.N.
Washington, DC

References

American Public Health Association. Nursing Home Data Report is Released to the Public 1989. *The Nation's Health*, XIX:1:5.

Committee on Nursing Home Regulations, Institute of Medicine. 1986. *Improving the Quality of Care in Nursing Homes*. Washington, DC: National Academy Press. p. 51.

Ibid., p. 61.

Ibid., p. 130

Dychtwald, K. and J. Flower. "The challenges and opportunities of an aging America," in *Age Wave*. 1989. Los Angeles: Jeremy P. Tarcher, p. 6.

Ibid., p. 21

Ibid., p. 39

Medicare and Medicaid; Long-term Survey. 1987. Federal Register. 53:22850.

FOREWORD

Most of the nursing homes that exist today have been built since the mid-sixties. Over these decades, nursing homes have changed from quasi-hotels or apartment-like dwellings to settings that more closely resemble hospitals, or acute care facilities.

Initially, many residents in nursing homes were retirees. Often they held part time jobs as employees or volunteers outside the nursing home. Some engaged in volunteer activity within the home. A small percentage of the residents experienced some type of health problem. A reverse situation exists in the nursing home today. Few, if any, residents are employed or volunteer outside the home and few engage in volunteer activities within the home. Most of the residents experience some type of health problem and many are increasingly dependent on the services of care givers.

Professional nurses and social workers were among the employees in those early nursing homes; however, these professionals have experienced major role changes in the present nursing homes. The nurses continue to be responsible for directing the auxiliary personnel who are direct caregivers for the residents. These auxiliaries have increased in number and in level of preparation; for example, there are licensed practical nurses, nurse aides or nursing assistants, geriatric aides, medication aides, and others. The nurses, social workers, and other professionals are responsible for coordinating the many levels and disciplines necessary in providing care. Both nurses and social workers have obtained increased education and advanced professional degrees; hence, they bring additional knowledge and skills to the nursing home residents' care. Nurse practitioners and clinical nurse specialists are frequently among the nursing home employees as well as recreation therapists, physical therapists, occupational therapists, and others. With the increase in employees in the nursing home, there has been a proportionate increase in challenges to maintain communication among all persons, to coordinate the care giving goals, and to provide leadership in achieving quality of care.

As more and more of the elderly have become increasingly dependent due to frailty, society has become more knowledgeable about quality care

xvii

as well as more vocal in requesting and demanding quality care. Society's expectations have been realistic, yet they have also been colored with the guilt that families experience when faced with the need to see a family member enter a nursing home.

Since the mid-sixties, the needs of the nursing home residents have undergone noticeable changes resulting in the increase in and preparation of nursing home personnel. The structure of the nursing home is different today as are the lives of those who live and work in the nursing home. Despite these recognized changes, the perceptions by the public about life in a nursing home have not changed appreciably. Many fallacies and misconceptions still abound about the nursing home.

What then is the reality? What is the true picture of the nursing home and its inhabitants?

Without any intention of generalizing about the findings in this one setting, Dr. O'Brien has presented a report of observations and discussions that should provide in-depth insight into one nursing home setting. Life in the nursing home is filled with complexities. It is not possible to extrapolate each element and place it in a discrete package, column, or paragraph, despite the urge to do so. In *Anatomy of a Nursing Home,* cross references of related data are made within the report to assist the reader to identify the multiple facets in the system. These "key actors" include the residents; their families; nursing home administrators; nursing, social work, and medical staff; support disciplines such as dietetics, occupational, physical, and recreational therapists; maintenance personnel; and others. The interpersonal relations and contacts among people are tremendous.

Dr. O'Brien presents an appropriate blend of sociology and nursing. Over the two year period that data were collected, a wide variety of responses and observations were obtained. To provide a focus on the psychosocial adaptation to the nursing home, there are descriptions of the many "actors" in the situation as they coped with the "multiple and complex demands and stresses of nursing home life."

Specific instances are cited to illustrate resident needs. Situations are described, using quotes from the "actors," to show the positive response of residents to hugs from caregivers, to attention, to hand-holding, and other demonstrations of interest and caring. The vital role of the family in the care of the nursing home resident is illustrated by reporting the verbatim comments of the involved persons. Clinical challenges are reported by the professional staff members. There are clearly described accounts of frustrating and heartwarming encounters that will stimulate and encourage caregivers to continue their determined efforts to provide quality care.

Professional nurses, specifically, will be convinced that gerontological/geriatric nursing is the specialty of the future. Indeed, it is the specialty which permits the use of critical decision making, enables the professional use of clinical judgement, and pleads for nursing expertise to be used to the maximum.

With outstanding skill, the author stresses the inherent right to respect what abides in every elderly person. There are citations to demonstrate to readers that these rights are respected, yet there are also instances to suggest these rights are easily, often inadvertently, violated. An awareness of the importance of literary documentation has resulted in the inclusion of a wide variety of gerontological/geriatric references about long-term care.

The "hope" of the author is praiseworthy: that the reader can "walk" in the world of the nursing home, if only for a brief period. In addition to the walk and reflection upon incidents that are described, a model of study is suggested by which other persons can identify the same type of information in another setting. All or part of the pattern can be followed to identify macro or micro dimensions in other nursing homes with other "actors."

This examination of the complexity of resident life in one nursing home for two years is exemplary. The publication makes a significant contribution to nursing home literature. Careful consideration of the information reported here will benefit the residents, families, and employees whose lives are molded and enriched by the environment of the nursing home.

Mary B. Walsh, D.Sc., R.N., F.A.A.N.
Retired Associate Professor
The Catholic University of America
School of Nursing

PREFACE

Anatomy of a Nursing Home is the result of a three-year research effort to identify and describe the attitudinal and behavioral patterns operating in the adaptation and care of the institutionalized elderly. A number of earlier nursing home studies exist in the literature. The distinction of the present work lies in the comprehensive and in-depth nature of the observations and discussions, which were carried out over a two-year period. Data were collected through both formal and informal conversations with key actors—the residents, their family members, the medical and nursing caregivers, and the ancillary care providers—in or about the nursing home milieu. Observations were made regarding all of the major processes and activities of nursing home life.

The study design was given direction by the conceptual orientation of social system analysis. The ultimate goal of the research was to document through empirical data the life career of the nursing home resident. A secondary aim was to understand whether the nursing home is indeed a "home," an "institution," or an amalgam of the two. It was learned that a multiplicity of unique and creative patterns of attitude and behavior were adopted by the residents, their families, and their caregivers in coping with the multiple and complex demands and stresses of nursing home life.

The research study on which this book is based, entitled "Anatomy of a Nursing Home: Behavior Patterns in the Adaptation and Care of the Institutionalized Elderly," was supported in part by a grant from the Robert Wood Johnson Foundation (grant #7606), as well as by several Biomedical Research Support Grants awarded by The Catholic University of America, and by a Dean's Research Award granted by The Catholic University School of Nursing.

In preparing the manuscript for *Anatomy of a Nursing Home,* an attempt was made to be totally faithful to the study data as recorded. The home is given a pseudonym, as are all individuals where naming is warranted, in order to preserve confidentiality. Demographic variations (e.g., in age, sex, or length of time at the home) have been introduced in several case examples to guarantee the residents' anonymity. Grammatical inconsistencies in respondents' comments have not been edited out but remain as transcribed from tape-recorded or handwritten notes.

This research was the effort of a sociologist attempting to "walk" in the world of gerontology. However, the study was by no means a one-person endeavor. The author's deep gratitude is expressed to those who encouraged, supported, and assisted with the research over the three-year period of study. Thanks go first to the residents, their families, and their caregivers, who shared lovingly and generously their thoughts and feelings about the nursing home experience. Appreciation goes also to the nursing home administrators—several during the course of the study—who graciously welcomed the intrusion of researchers into the many and varied dimensions of their world.

A cadre of baccalaureate and master's nursing students assisted with data collection, and numerous colleagues provided invaluable advice and support; notable in this regard were Dr. Mary H. Burke, Dr. Helene M. Clark, and Ms. Gaie Rubenfeld. Professor Doris Schwartz provided expert consultation in the area of gerontology; Mrs. Mary Mariani advised on working with the cognitively impaired residents. Dr. Denise Korniewicz assisted with quantitative data collection and analysis; Mrs. Carol Ann Cairns was instrumental in processing much of the study's qualitative data and in facilitating preparation of the manuscript. S. Rosemary Donley's vision supported the author's affiliation with the home.

Most sincere thanks go to Mrs. Mary B. Walsh, who in her role as director of the home's Teaching Nursing Home Project taught, encouraged, supported, and advised the author from the study's conception to its completion, gently guiding, never intruding, ever available, and always keenly astute. She also read and critiqued the manuscript, as did Ms. Helen Walsh and Ms. Rose Fennell, to whom a special debt is also owed.

Finally, deepest appreciation goes to Dr. Faye G. Abdellah, whose interest and concern, especially during the study's initiation, provided the author with much-needed inspiration and fortitude to complete the endeavor.

Presentation of the research data is organized around two foci: first, the key actors in and about the social system of the home, namely, the residents, their family members, the medical and nursing caregivers, and the ancillary care providers; and second, the major stages in nursing home life, namely, admission and early adaptation and long-term adaptation to the home. Certain concepts such as religion, death, family support, friendships, and staff-resident relationships are addressed in several chapters, as they have been examined from differing perspectives and are supported by data provided by a diversity of respondents.

In Chapter 1, a brief introduction to the world of long-term care is presented together with an overview of the research problem and design, including a description of the study facility under its pseudonym, Bethany Manor Nursing Home.

Chapter 2 explores who the Bethany Manor residents are, why and how they came to reside in the home, how they relate to other members of their social environment, and what constitute their activities of daily life. Family members of the residents are profiled in Chapter 3 in terms of both their own needs and their provision of needs for an older loved one.

Chapter 4 focuses upon early adaptation to life at the home, describing in detail the admission process with its unique stresses as well as the fears and anxieties that may beset a new resident. The health caregiving system is addressed in Chapter 5 from the perspective of nurses, nurses' aides, physicians, and nursing students. The roles of ancillary care system members—administrators, spiritual caregivers, social workers, therapists, dietitians, maintenance and security staff, and volunteers—are described in Chapter 6.

Chapter 7 analyzes the nursing home as a social system and examines both the structure and the processes involved in the maintaining of Bethany Manor's physical, technical, and psychosocial environments. In Chapter 8, long-term adaptation to nursing home life is described and analyzed with the presentation of a typology of resident attitudes and behaviors under the labels "socialite," "guardian," "single-room occupant," and "free-lancer." Appendix A contains an expanded version of the study protocol, including a discussion of methodological issues, and Appendix B presents the actual study tools used, which may be useful in replication or extension of this effort.

CHAPTER 1

The World of
Nursing Home Care

We must afford the individual the opportunity to withdraw from
the demands of life, as needed, with honor, comfort and dignity.

Bethany Manor Credo

The Nursing Home: A Contemporary
Health Care Challenge

It is suggested that by the year 2010 a large proportion of our population,
the baby boom generation, "will reach retirement age and become dependent on society for support" (Goeldner et al. 1983, 1). During the 1970s and
1980s, the provision of long-term care for these elder citizens became a
significant concern "among public policy makers, advocates for aging
services, and older people themselves" (Melemed 1983, 4). Approximately
5% of the elderly who require long-term care reside in nursing homes
(McConnell 1984, 193); however, 25% to 40% of the older population enter
a nursing home at some time for health care services (Lewis et al. 1985). As
members of our population live longer, they accumulate a greater number
of health deficits, many of them of a serious and chronic nature. The
presence in nursing homes of residents with a multiplicity of health
problems compromising both physical and cognitive functioning puts
tremendous strain on the caregiving system as well as on the home's
administration. The modern nursing home no longer resembles the early
domiciliary-type residences where the majority of individuals could carry

1

out basic activities of daily living under the supervision of minimally trained staff. At present, most nursing homes require a significant number of skilled and semiskilled nursing care beds as well as the services of such care providers as physicians, pharmacists, physical therapists, social workers, and dietitians. The sophistication of long-term care for the elderly has grown tremendously in the last 15 to 20 years. This is reflected by the fact that "approximately 26 percent of all health care expenditures for the elderly is for nursing home care" (Lanahan 1982, 13).

Long-Term Care

The 1980s expression "long-term care" refers to a "continuum of interrelated health and social services" and may encompass "both institutional and non-institutional services" and requires co-ordination of public policies, funding, and care management to provide appropriate options for service to individuals whose needs inevitably change over time" (Koff 1982, 1). Long-term care services are described as directed toward "helping the recipients successfully master the activities required for daily living while improving their personal satisfaction and the quality of their lives" (Kaufman 1980, 133).

In discussing the role of the nursing home in long-term care, the Committee on Nursing Home Regulation of the Institute of Medicine asserts that, in most places in the United States, elderly individuals may be placed in a nursing home when they require "more assistance in the activities of daily living than can be provided by the immediate family or friends" (Institute of Medicine 1986, 8). The committee's report notes that an older person may also require nursing home care for a convalescent period following surgery or an acute illness, if neither a rehabilitation facility nor home health services are available in the local community. Nursing homes are called upon to provide care for residents possessed of a multiplicity of physical and cognitive deficits, from minor difficulties or anxieties revolving around successfully coping with life activities, such as shopping trips outside the home or visits to the physician, to severe physical and cognitive impairment requiring complete bed rest and skilled care.

The Institute of Medicine study reports general agreement that present governmental regulation of nursing homes is unsatisfactory, as manifested by the plethora of substandard homes. The study asserts, "The implicit goal of the regulatory system is to ensure that any person requiring nursing home care be able to enter any certified nursing home and receive appropriate care, be treated with courtesy, and enjoy continued civil and legal rights" (Institute of Medicine 1986, 2).

Further determinants of the need for nursing home care are related to the elderly individual's "housing, income, and social support conditions" (General Accounting Office 1983, 15). Frequently a resident enters a home because most of his or her family and friends have died or are themselves incapacitated and the resident can no longer maintain a home alone.

Contemporary nursing home care presents a significant challenge because of the variety of physical and psychosocial needs associated with health deficits in old age. The fragility of both body and mind confronts the caregiver with many treatment dilemmas not ordinarily encountered among a younger group. Coupled with these unique care requirements is the older person's need to adjust to the concept of productive life (if possible) parallel to that of institutionalized long-term care.

The Study Problem: The Life Career of the Nursing Home Resident

Prospective demographic trends for the older population and their health care needs point out the rapidly increasing numbers of fragile elderly: "The age group 65 and over is expected approximately to double in size between 1976 and 2020, moving from 23 million in 1976 to 32 million in 2000, to 45 million in 2020. In this period all age segments of the elderly population are expected to grow rapidly, particularly in the extreme age" (Siegel 1977, 289). Of particular concern is the problem of physical relocation or uprooting: "A special type of mobility in later life is movement from private households to group quarters such as nursing homes and rest homes. We still do not know what living arrangements for the elderly will produce the lowest morbidity and mortality and the greatest measure of life satisfaction" (Siegel 1977, 311). Kasl et al. (1977, 214) report, "The general literature on housing and health would seem to suggest that the elderly as a group are more susceptible to the adverse effects of the social uprooting experience accompanying residential change." Concern about both the physical and psychosocial adaptation and care of the institutionalized elderly is a topic of notable interest among both social and behavioral scientists and health care personnel involved with the aged. Vladeck, in his work *Unloving Care* (1980), reports on a major analysis of the nation's nursing home problem, which found "tragic mistakes in policy." In a related report, *Tender Loving Greed*, Mendelson (1974) asserts that in many nursing homes the function of the home itself may have damaging effects upon the elderly resident population.

A limited number of studies, however, have examined the individual nursing home facility in detail. One of these is the work of Gubrium (1975), who examined "how care in a nursing home is accomplished by those who participate in its everyday life"; a related work is Kayser-Jones' (1981, 3) comparative evaluation of two long-term care facilities, one in the United States and one in Scotland. In the present study an in-depth examination and analysis of the inner workings of the world of the nursing home resident were carried out. Through the research a profile has been developed of the structure, function, and processes of the home as a social system. As anticipated, dominant themes emerged from observation and discussion of data that reflect the significant attitudinal and behavioral patterns operating in the adaptation and care of the institutionalized elderly.

The Research: Behavior Patterns in the Adaptation and Care of the Institutionalized Elderly

Specific Aims

This study centered on the broad arena of psychosocial adaptation required of an elderly individual when relocating from a private home to the institutional setting of a long-term nursing care facility. It has long been observed and reported in the literature that adaptation and care of the aged in the nursing home setting vary notably both within and among institutions. Some of these differences relate to institutional variables, such as staff education and orientation, management strategies, and the philosophy of care espoused by the facility's administrative personnel. Also of influence are individual patient variables, such as physical and psychological integrity, degree of cognitive functioning, and effective social support. To more clearly understand the complex interweaving of the myriad variables involved in the world of the nursing home requires an in-depth case study or ethnographic approach. The purpose of this research was to examine and describe the overall institutional nursing home setting, as well as the patterns of attitude and behavior exhibited by the actors: residents, family members, medical and nursing caregivers, and ancillary staff involved with the adaptation and care of the institutionalized elderly.

Conceptual Orientation

The research effort was organized according to the broad conceptual orientation of social system analysis. In an exploratory qualitative study such as this one, the investigator adopts only a general conceptual orientation highlighting the "principal or gross features of the structure and processes in the situations that he will study" (Glaser and Strauss 1967, 45). The underlying orientation for this research consisted of an eclectic base composed of social system function as described by Loomis (1960) and the stress-coping-adaptation process of Scott, Oberst, and Dropkin (1980). In the social system framework, elements, processes, and conditions of action of social systems are identified and described in the "Processually Articulated Structural Model" described by Loomis (1960, 8):

Processes (Elemental)	Elements
1. Cognitive mapping	Belief (knowledge)
2. Tension management	Sentiment (feeling)
Communication of sentiment	
3. Goal attaining activity	Goal (achievement)
Concomitant "latent" activity	
4. Evaluation	Norm (standard)
5. Status-role performance	Status-role (position)
6. Allocation of status-roles	Rank
7. Decision making and action	Power (control)
8. Application of sanctions	Sanction
9. Utilization of facilities	Facility

The stress-coping-adaptation model of Scott et al. (1980) supports the study of the stress-coping process through variable entry points, including the nature of the stressor, coping responses or modes of coping, behavioral responses to stress, and adaptive outcomes. The model suggests that responses move from the more general to the more specific, and continued appraisal and reappraisal of an event are advocated, thus supporting the in-depth case study approach used in this research.

Method

The research employed an exploratory case study approach in order to provide a "narrative description and analysis of the individuals [and] institution" under investigation (Abdellah and Levine 1979, 692). The board case study subject is a private metropolitan long-term geriatric care facility (i.e., nursing home) providing three levels of patient care: domiciliary, intermediate (semiskilled), and skilled. Subgroups of subjects within or related to the home included residents, family members, health caregivers, and other support personnel within the facility (e.g., physicians, social workers, dietitians, chaplains, recreational therapists, physical therapists, and clerks). The nursing home is a 230-bed residential facility with a health caregiving staff including registered nurses (MSN, BSN, AA, and diploma), licensed practical nurses, and nurses' aides. The initial study foci included those variables identified as central to social system analysis, which include beliefs, sentiments, goals, norms, status-roles, rank, power, sanction, and facility (Loomis 1960). The analytic methodology chosen was a modification of that articulated for the discovery of grounded theory (Glaser and Strauss 1967).

Procedure

Data were collected by means of observation and focused discussions conducted by the principal investigator and a number of research assistants over the course of approximately 24 months.

The research was initially conceived as a case study of the nursing home, to be carried out by one individual through informal observation and interviewing during a period of approximately six to nine months of immersion in the life of the home. During the early weeks of the study, however, consultants both within and outside the facility provided advice and suggestions that notably expanded the original protocol. These included specific methodological strategies, such as following several residents and their families through the admission process; accompanying Manor physicians on patient rounds; attending all of the home's standing committee meetings, (the Admission Committee, the Department Heads Committee, the Utilization Review Committee, and approximately seven others); participating in patient care conferences on all floors; developing a profile of the resident population's physical and psychosocial deficits, employing data from the home's Assessment of Patient Progress records; and constructing a profile of the admission status of the resident population through analysis of social history data. It was also suggested that a specific sampling design be operationalized for the conduct of discussions with both cognitively alert and cognitively impaired residents.

These extensions of the original methodology were justified by the increased complexity of contemporary nursing home life and its caregiving strategies. To accomplish the work required by the expanded protocol, a cadre consisting of one baccalaureate and ten master's-level nursing students and one doctorally prepared RN was enlisted to assist with various facets of the data collection process. Eleven baccalaureate nursing students who had educational experience at Bethany Manor also shared their "student logs," providing additional data for the study's profile of nursing home life. All baccalaureate and master's students employed formally as study data collectors were trained by the principal investigator in the use of the focused discussion and observation guides, and were oriented to the grounded theory methodology of Glaser and Strauss (1967). (Data collection activities are detailed in the Appendix.)

Direct observation was carried out on all three care shifts (7 a.m. to 3 p.m., 3 p.m. to 11 p.m., and 11 p.m. to 7 a.m.) and on five nursing units within the home. Residents were observed during meals, recreational periods, and other general activities. Observations were also made during such activities as staff meetings, physician visits, nursing rounds, and shift-change reports. Formal discussions were conducted with sample subpopulations of residents, family members, caregivers, and other support personnel within the home. Discussion and observation guides to focus the initial phases of data collection were developed based upon the broad conceptual orientation of social system functioning (Loomis 1960) and the stress-coping-adaptation model described by Scott, Oberst, and Dropkin (1980). Additional foci in the discussion and observation guides were derived from the gerontological literature on physical and psychosocial adaptation among the institutionalized elderly. The tools were submitted to a panel of experts in the area of gerontology and geriatric nursing to determine content validity.

Data Analysis

Following the initial semistructured phases of observation and discussion, a modification of the analytic methodology of Glaser and Strauss (1967) for the discovery of grounded theory was initiated. Theoretical sampling and the constant comparative method were employed: Dominant themes emerging from data obtained through earlier observation and focused discussions were pursued in follow-up discussions and observation sessions, and emerging categories of attitude and behavior were then established. As these categories became more clearly defined, through comparing the properties of individual actors' attitudes and behaviors comprising a category, the process moved on to the stage of determining a construct or bit of theory (Glaser and Strauss 1967; Glaser 1978).

The Facility: Bethany Manor Nursing Home

"Bethany Manor" is a pseudonym used to protect the true identity of the study facility. The home might, however, be said to be not atypical of other moderate-sized, religiously oriented nursing homes in the urban United States.

History of the Home

As there are many Catholic nursing homes administered by religious women in the United States, some details of the home's founding and about its community of sisters may be presented without compromising anonymity.

Bethany Manor Nursing Home was dedicated by the local Catholic archbishop in 1957. It is reported that approximately 6,000 people attended the inaugural "open house," and residents soon began being admitted to the Manor. The home, with a capacity of 230 residents, is situated on a pleasant 26-acre site surrounded by a modest suburban neighborhood. The building is set back approximately a block from the main street and is surrounded by wooded areas on three sides, giving the residents privacy to walk or sit on the grounds. A Bethany Manor newsletter of 1957-1958, published by one of the residents, described the home as being characterized primarily by the "inspiring spirit of Catholic faith" and "the heart-warming spirit of charity among the residents."

The religious sisters who assume primary responsibility for administration of and care provided in the home are a group of women whose lives are dedicated to the care of the frail elderly. The congregation, which was founded in the late 1920s, has as its primary purpose "to tend to the aged of both sexes." It is written that the sisters of Bethany Manor are committed to the "total care with dignity and independence" of those who choose to make the Manor their home; it is added further that the sisters are concerned for both the "physical and spiritual" well-being of their residents.

Administrative Structure

The general management of Bethany Manor is presided over by a sister Administrator with educational preparation and experience in nursing home administration; she is supported by the board of directors and the board of trustees. The Assistant Administrator, also a religious sister, specifically oversees the work of a number of the ancillary services (e.g., social service, maintenance, food service, and volunteers) and fills in for the Administrator when needed. A physician Medical Director and a Director of Nursing indirectly supervise all medical and nursing caregiving activities at the Manor, and a Director of Fiscal Services is responsible for the home's business office and purchasing department. Other key supervisory personnel at Bethany Manor include the Director of Social Services, the Director of Recreation, the head of maintenance, the nursing supervisors (days, evenings, and nights), and the head nurses for each resident unit. A detailed discussion of the home's administration and philosophy is presented in Chapter 7.

Admission Policies

Bethany Manor's brochure describing the home states that care is provided to "the infirm who require constant professional nursing care, and aging individuals seeking the independence and dignity of continued self-determination while having their daily needs met by someone who cares." The brochure adds that Bethany Manor is licensed by the state to provide "comprehensive nursing care for 230 residents" and that it is "approved by the Medicaid program."

The Manor maintains an active waiting list of persons wishing to be admitted, but administrative personnel do take into account emergency situations and individual needs in determining admissions priority. After first contact by a prospective resident or his or her family, a set of application forms must be filled out, including an application for admission, a social history, and a medical report. The application for admission form elicits basic demographic data about the prospective resident and his or her family as well as work history, means of support, insurance data, and plan for burial arrangements. The social history form solicits a description of the resident's activities of daily living and ability to care for self; physical and psychosocial impairments; present living arrangements; past life experiences; and hobbies and marital status. The medical report details physical or psychiatric deficits; it must be filled out by the prospective resident's personal physician. Also included in the preadmission mailing are an explanation of the admission procedure and a statement of the Manor's admission policies and procedures and services. On admission, a number of other forms are presented to the resident for reading or completion, including the home's Credo and the Resident's Bill of Rights, a financial statement, an admission record, a clothing list, the Manor's admission agreement statements, and a letter of welcome from the Administrator.

After the initial admission request, medical form, and social history have been completed and returned, Bethany Manor's admissions clerk schedules a preadmission interview with the resident. If the applicant is unable to come to the home for the interview, a social worker will visit or make some other arrangement to meet with relatives of the prospective resident. No applications are excluded on the basis of sex, race, religion, or socioeconomic status. Financial arrangements do vary, however, based upon the resident and/or the family's ability to pay for care personally. As already noted, the home is approved for Medicaid.

The Teaching Nursing Home Project

While the research was being conducted, Bethany Manor was also implementing a foundation grant-funded Teaching Nursing Home Project

(TNHP; Walsh and Small 1988, Burke and Donley 1987, Ciferri and Baker 1985, Knights 1984, Aronson 1984), through which a local university school of nursing joined forces with the home to provide certain educational and caregiving services and so enhance the quality of life and of care at the home. The project identified its primary purpose as twofold: to implement the concept of a teaching nursing home, and to develop a church-related affiliation model of care (the university was also a private Catholic institution with philosophies similar to those of the home in terms of God, man, and service). Primary goals of the project included (1) aiding the home in upgrading its standards of care and (2) helping the school to develop a gerontology nursing major. Specific areas that were addressed were the opening of a skilled care unit, correcting or alleviating staff shortfall and turnover, and overcoming general inadequacies in care.

In order to carry out the TNHP, five university faculty members were assigned either full- or part-time to Bethany Manor over a 5 1/2-year period. These included the project director, who assumed primary responsibility for initiating and evaluating the education, nursing services, and long-term care administration arenas, and who also administered the grant and coordinated the activities of the faculty-staff teams; several clinical nursing practitioners in gerontology; a staff education consultant; and a nurse researcher. All of the faculty's activities were directed toward achieving the overall aims of the TNHP.

A question might be raised as to the relationship between the TNHP and the research described here. First, it should be noted that no conflict existed between the research and the TNHP, as the study facility, Bethany Manor, had been identified early on as one of the TNHP sites *excluded* from the funding group's planned evaluative research activities. It was at this point that the idea of a case study of the home was conceived by the principal investigator, who also served as the TNHP nurse researcher. Although several exploratory investigations were already on-going at Bethany Manor, they involved smaller numbers of residents, and most were concluded within a few weeks. The TNHP was still in the relatively early stages of development and had not yet had a major impact on caregiving activities in the home. Thus, neither the research efforts begun earlier nor the TNHP itself appeared to pose a major contaminant to the case study.

Some positive benefits accrued to the research, however, from the presence of the TNHP staff at Bethany Manor. First, at least a beginning sense of rapport had been achieved between the university faculty and the nursing home staff; thus, the concept of the home being "studied" was less threatening to staff members than it might have been before the project. Also, the study's principal investigator was well accepted by both staff nurses and aides through her association with the TNHP, which had been discussed extensively at prior staff meetings. The case study plan benefited notably from the suggestions, advice, and assistance of other TNHP members who shared insights and observations related to their specific activities at Bethany Manor. A final aspect of the project that provided support for the research overall was the administrative linkage developed between the university and the home. Although implementation of the study protocol obviously depended on approval by the facility's Research and Education Committee, complete and unhindered access to residents, staff, nursing home meetings, records, and virtually all relevant data (excluding such materials as financial records or personnel files) was greatly facilitated by the trust established between the administration of Bethany Manor and that of the university school of nursing.

The Political Environment of the Nursing Home

Reimbursement: Medicare and Medicaid

The Health Care Financing Administration (HCFA) distinguishes between Medicare and Medicaid as follows: "Medicare is for everyone 65 or older regardless of income; Medicare also protects disabled people under 65 who have been entitled to social security disability payments for at least two years, and certain others with permanent kidney failure.... Medicaid is for certain groups of needy and low income people: the aged (65 or older), the blind, the disabled, members of families with dependent children, and some other children" (HCFA 1984, 6–7). It is noted that some individuals may benefit from both Medicare and Medicaid. Medicare has been called the "cornerstone of health protection for older Americans"; it not only "improved access to health care for the elderly, it reduced substantially the proportion of their income spent on health care" (Howard 1985, 4).

Medicaid, however, has been criticized as it applies to older persons as "a lopsided long-term care system favoring institutionalization while requiring impoverishment of participants" (Oriol 1985, 4). Recently the federal government has given state governments the power to "require that adult children of Medicaid recipients pay for part of the care delivered to their parents in nursing homes" (Buchanan 1984, 19). Presently Medicaid is the "primary purchaser" of care in nursing homes, "paying for roughly half the nursing home expenditures nationally" (Schlenker and Brunstein 1985, 275). Medicare covers only about 2% of the total expenditure for nursing home care (Schlenker and Brunstein 1985).

A report by the General Accounting Office to the House Subcommittee on Health and the Environment notes that indeed no overall national policy exists for providing our elderly population with long-term care services. The report reiterates: "Medicaid has become the primary single payer for the most expensive of these services, nursing home care. Medicare and private insurance support only a negligible proportion of nursing home services, and the catastrophic costs of long-term institutional care often exceed elderly persons' financial resources. Expenditures for nursing home care represent the largest single expenditure category in the Medicaid program" (General Accounting Office 1983). The report adds, "The Federal Government pays from 50-78% of the states' costs in providing medical care through Medicaid to eligible, low income individuals and families," and comments that currently the states are presently curtailing nursing home bed availability and/or reducing the amount of reimbursement in order to decrease spending for nursing home services (General Accounting Office 1983, i). Approximately 25% of Bethany Manor residents were Medicare or Medicaid recipients.

Federal and State Regulations

It has been suggested that a quality assurance program "is a basic essential part of a well organized nursing home" (Eliopoulos 1963, 177). Quality assurance means guaranteeing that a facility's problems will be identified and solutions sought (Trocchio 1984). There are three dimensions of government regulation for quality assurance in nursing homes: "(1) the criteria used to determine whether a nursing home is providing care of acceptable quality in a safe and clean environment; (2) the procedures used to determine the extent to which nursing homes comply with the criteria; (3) the procedures used to enforce compliance" (Institute of Medicine 1986, 69).

The Institute of Medicine study notes further that there are two sets of federal certification criteria, one for skilled care facilities and one for those providing intermediate care. The criteria for skilled care facilities consists of 18 "conditions of participation," which contain 90 standards of care. The intermediate care facility criteria have no conditions of participation but specify 18 standards of practice (Institute of Medicine 1986, 69-70). It is suggested that the distinction between the two types of facilities may be somewhat blurred, but in general skilled care facilities are more medically oriented, use the word "patient" throughout their regulations, and are required to provide more nursing staff on a consistent basis. Intermediate care facilities tend to refer to a recipient of services as a "resident" (Institute of Medicine 1986, 72).

Licensure

Licensing criteria may vary from state to state. States are "allowed under the Medicaid Law to set their own eligibility criteria for admission of residents for Skilled Nursing Facilities (SNF) and Intermediate Care Facilities (ICF)" (Institute of Medicine 1986, 72).

Bethany Manor had recently been licensed by the state as a skilled care facility. The home was evaluated at least yearly through visits from representatives of such federal and state agencies as Medicare/Medicaid and county and state health departments and welfare departments. The facility was also visited by external hospital cost analysts. Internal evaluation by the home administration was ongoing.

During the course of the research, Bethany Manor had several visits from the state and county inspectors. On the first day of an inspection, one investigator learned that the Manor had an in-house "code" communicated through the home's public address system ("Paging Dr. Barton") to let the staff know that the inspectors had arrived. A geriatric aide commented, "The inspectors are here. They'll have plenty to write about today. They always come when we are short of help." Another aide added, "I hate they're inspecting us when we're short staffed. They don't ever see the good days."

On the second morning of the inspection, a research team member wrote the following observational note: "Today is the second day of the state inspection for accreditation. The second floor looks great—corridors cleared of excess equipment, etc. The head nurse was busy checking charts and assignment records at the nurses' station. For the residents, it appears to be business as usual." The head nurse commented: "We're expecting them sometime this morning; things are going well." A staff nurse observed, "I'm not concerned about inspection. I've been through too many of them to worry about them. I know what I've done all along with the charts and so forth. They are up-to-date because we keep them up-to-date all the time. The nutrition inspector has been here already and things went well. I'm waiting for the nurse inspector to review charts. I'm confident things will go well."

Overall, this state inspection went very well indeed for Bethany Manor. The staff, however, were not happy with any criticisms that they perceived reflected inadequate or inappropriate patient care. The day after the inspection, a geriatric aide complained, "We were cited for using protective dressings to protect residents' skin. They've never worked in a nursing home. Would they rather see the residents have bruises? Then we'd get cited for patient abuse."

Overview

From the case study of Bethany Manor, new knowledge and understanding regarding behavior patterns in the adaptation and care of the institutionalized elderly have been derived. Residents, family members, and caregivers freely and generously shared their anxieties and their successes in the hope of helping others who might one day tread similar paths. In the pages that follow, these concerns and rewards are described in detail and, whenever possible, in the study respondents' own words. Through this manner of presentation it is hoped that the reader will be able to "walk," if only for a brief period, in the world of the nursing home—to share vicariously in the joys, the sorrows, the satisfactions, the hurts, and the myriad attitudinal and behavioral patterns that stress, support, and enhance the life career of the nursing home resident.

References

Abdellah, F. G., and E. Levine. 1979. *Better patient care through nursing research.* 2nd ed. New York: Macmillan.

Aronson, M. K. 1984. Implementing a teaching nursing home: Lessons for research and practice. *The Gerontologist* 24(5):451-454.

Buchanan, R. J. 1984. Medicaid: Family responsibility and long-term care. *The Journal of Long-Term Care Administration* 12(3):19-25.

Burke, M., and Sr. R. Donley. 1987. The educational experiment: A teaching nursing home. *Journal of Gerontological Nursing* 13(1):36-40.

Ciferri, W., and R. Baker. 1985. A nursing home/university exchange program: An alternative model for teaching nursing homes. *The Journal of Long-Term Care Administration* 13(1):27-30.

Eliopoulos, C. 1963. *Nursing administration of long term care.* Rockville, MD: Aspen Systems.

General Accounting Office. 1983. *Report to the Chairman of the Subcommittee on Health and the Environment, Committee on Energy and Commerce, House of Representatives.* Washington, DC: Government Printing Office.

Glaser, B. 1978. *Theoretical sensitivity: Advances in the methodology of grounded theory.* Mill Valley, CA: Sociology Press.

Glaser, B., and A. Strauss. 1967. *The discovery of grounded theory.* Chicago: Aldine.

Goeldner, L. M., R. L. Ludke, and J. M. Kuder. 1983. The impact of some proposed policy changes on the nursing home system. *The Journal of Long-Term Care Administration* 11(1):1-9.

Gubrium, J. E. 1975. *Living and dying at Murray Manor.* New York: St. Martins Press.

Health Care Financing Administration. 1984. *Medicaid/Medicare: Which is which?* (HCFA-02129-1984). Baltimore: Health Care Financing Administration.

Howard, E. 1985. Medicare cornerstone of health protection for older Americans. *Perspective on Aging* 14(3):4-6.

Institute of Medicine, Committee on Nursing Home Regulation. 1986. *Improving the quality of care in nursing homes.* Washington, DC: National Academy Press.

Kasl, S. V., A. M. Ostpe, G. M. Brody, et al. 1977. Effects of involuntary relocation on the health and behavior of the elderly. In *Second Conference on the Epidemiology of Aging,* 211-236. Washington, DC: Government Printing Office.

Kaufman, A. 1980. Social policy and long term care of the aged. *Social Work* 25(2):133-137.

Kayser-Jones, J. 1981. *Old, alone and neglected.* Berkeley, CA: University of California Press.

Knights, A. M. 1984. Teaching nursing homes. A project update. *Journal of Gerontological Nursing* 10(6):15-17.

Koff, T. H. 1982. *Long term care, an approach to serving the frail elderly.* Boston: Little, Brown.

Lanahan, M. B. 1982. Meeting the needs of elderly people. *Contemporary Administrator* 5(3):13-16.

Lewis, M. A., S. Cretin, and R. L. Kane. 1985. The natural history of nursing home patients. *The Gerontologist* 25(4):382-388.

Loomis, C. P. 1960. *Social systems.* New York: Van Nostrand.

McConnell, C. E. 1984. A note on the lifetime risk of nursing home residency. *The Gerontologist* 24(2):193-198.

Melemed, B. B. 1983. Formulating a public policy for long-term care: A different view. *Perspective on Aging* 12(3):4-5, 30.

Mendelson, M. A. 1974. *Tender loving greed.* New York: Alfred A. Knopf.

Oriol, W. 1985. Medicaid essential—provides critical protection for 23 million. *Perspective on Aging* 14(4): 4-8.

Schlenker, R., and C. Brunstein. 1985. Case mix and Medicaid payment. *Geriatric Nursing* 6(5):275-277.

Scott, D., M. T. Oberst, and M. J. Dropkin. 1980. A stress coping model. *Advances in Nursing Science* 3(1):9-23.

Siegel, J. S. 1977. Recent and prospective demographic trends for the elderly population and some implications for health care. In *Second Conference on the Epidemiology of Aging,* 289-315. Washington, DC: Government Printing Office.

Trocchio, J. 1984. Quest for quality: Forms and philosophy. *Contemporary Administrator* 7(3):44-47.

Vladeck, B. C. 1980. *The nursing home tragedy.* New York: Basic Books.

Walsh, M. B., and N. R. Small. 1988. *Teaching nursing homes: The nursing perspective.* Owings Mills, MD: National Health Publishing.

CHAPTER 2

The Residents

I am not mad, only old. I make this statement to give me
courage.

> Caro Spencer, protagonist, *As We are Now* (Sarton 1973)

The nursing home has been described as a place where one goes to die,
or at the very least as a place to wait until it is time to die. Residents of
nursing homes are usually thought of as "the frail elderly," no longer
competent either physically or cognitively (or perhaps both) to manage their
lives without assistance. Somehow with the wrinkling of the skin and the
graying of hair—that veritable metamorphosis that accompanies the aging
process—personal characteristics seem to blur.

A Bethany Manor resident, Catherine Duffy, had in her youth been
described as a "vibrant blue-eyed Irish girl with flaming red hair and a
temper to match." Now Catherine sits passively, a slight, silver-haired
elder, eyes hidden behind heavy lenses and spirit muted by the confusion of
senile dementia. Can our minds see beyond these external changes to that
beauty of spirit that informs Catherine's dignity as one who has long been
a contributing member of the human family? Can our hearts reach past the
halting speech and convoluted thinking to enable us to meet Catherine
Duffy and to try, just for a few moments, to cross over—to stand with her
in that place of illness where she is alone, and to try to understand? That is
the ultimate purpose of this in-depth case study of Bethany Manor Nursing
Home.

The Nursing Home Population:
A Demographic, Physical, and Psychosocial Profile

Demographics

Aside from Miss Duffy, then, who indeed are the residents of Bethany Manor? What are their ages, their sexes? Who are their families? What physical and cognitive abilities do they possess? In a sociodemographic profile of the 230 residents of the home at the time of the study, it was found that residents' ages ranged from 58 to 109 years, with the greatest number, 100 residents, falling in the 70- to 79-year group. The next most numerous group was the 80- to 89-year-olds, with 75 residents in this category. Only one resident was in the 50- to 59-year group, and one was over 100 years old.

One hundred and ninety-nine residents were Catholic; although the home does not discriminate as to religion, Bethany Manor has a strong Catholic image and philosophy. No Jewish patients resided at the Manor, perhaps because there are a number of excellent Jewish-affiliated nursing homes in the area. In terms of marital status, the largest group were widowed ($N = 142$), with the next largest being single women ($N = 58$). There were 192 women and 38 men, a proportion that appears to reflect the norm for most nursing homes. Two hundred and nineteen residents were White. Again, although the home has no policy (subtle or otherwise) of racial discrimination, the academic literature suggests that extended Black families tend to care for elderly relatives in their homes more often than do White kin groups. The home is Medicaid and Medicare certified, with 33 residents receiving such assistance, 23 receiving other financial relief, and 174 identified as private payers. One hundred and sixteen residents were able to ambulate on admission to the home, 63 came in wheelchairs, and 51 needed to be brought in by ambulance. Family members or persons identified formally as "significant others" for Bethany Manor residents included 15 spouses, 19 siblings, 108 children, 39 other kin (nieces, nephews, cousins), 5 grandchildren, 5 religious superiors, 18 friends, and 21 lawyers.

In terms of socioeconomic status, Bethany Manor residents appeared to fall somewhere in the lower-middle- to middle-class ranges according to their social history data, which will be discussed further on. Although reports of previous income were not available, combined measures of education and occupation document a profile of primarily unskilled or semiskilled workers, with the majority having a high school diploma as the highest educational level achieved (N = 127). However, 27 residents were identified as having baccalaureate degrees, 6 as being master's prepared, and 3 doctorally prepared. Forty-eight residents had only an eighth-grade education or less, and nine had left school after the tenth grade. These data are not surprising considering the mean age of the residents and the era in which they were educated.

The most frequently identified occupations were (in order of ranking) housewife, clerk, and secretary. Fourteen residents were identified as former teachers, at either the grade school, high school, or college level. Several were former career military officers, three were lawyers, five had been registered nurses, and three residents were Catholic priests. Other former careers listed included such titles as pathologist, administrator, bookkeeper, auditor, and dietitian. The most frequently identified former employers were the U.S. government and the telephone company. In controlling these socioeconomic status data by Bethany Manor floor, no notable differences appeared to emerge.

Health Status

A physical and psychosocial profile of the residents was prepared from the Bethany Manor assessment forms mandated by the state in which the home is located. This Assessment of Patient Progress form delineates the significant physical and psychosocial deficits and problems of each resident. Included in the assessment of patient problems are the following: health and functioning status, which includes such factors as illness conditions and physical deficits (hearing, vision, speech limitations, etc.), ambulation, muscle strength, transferring ability, personal grooming, dressing ability, toileting ability, oral status, and nutritional status; behavioral status which focuses on cognitive and emotional functioning; psychosocial status, including interactional and environment-related behaviors; recreational activities, both self-directed and participatory; and a discharge plan, if appropriate. These assessments are completed every month for all residents. The following profile was prepared at one point during the course of the research.

Data for the profile were coded with a score of one for each problem or deficit identified. Nursing problems reflecting the overall score for the Assessment of Patient Progress scale as well as for each of the subscales were totaled by the nursing home units in order to discriminate staffing problems and needs among individual resident care areas (Table 2-1).

Table 2-1 Staff-Identified Nursing Problems by Resident Care Area

Resident Problems	First Floor (Domiciliary Care)	Second Floor (Intermediate Care)	Third Floor (Cognitively Impaired)	Fourth Floor (Intermediate Care)	Fifth Floor (Skilled Care)
			Resident Group		
			Percent of possible total scale score		
Health and functioning (physical deficits)	32.3	41.8	35.7	29.3	44.0
Ambulation problems	17.3	57.6	41.3	41.6	50.0
Muscle strength deficits	33.3	64.9	45.3	69.6	75.5
Transfer ability problems	0.03	64.6	56.6	48.8	60.0
Personal grooming problems	24.3	84.0	92.0	71.2	70.0
Dress and undress problems	10.2	81.1	90.2	74.7	97.7
Toileting problems	0.09	47.5	34.1	27.6	65.1
Oral status deficits	24.6	35.3	28.8	37.2	30.6
Nutritional status deficits	15.3	25.8	25.5	17.8	27.7
Behavioral status deficits	11.9	42.8	36.8	16.6	34.8
Psychosocial status deficits	21.7	29.0	38.0	21.8	41.6
Physical, recreational, and social activities deficits	32.0	60.0	68.9	70.2	90.5
Total score	20.0	46.9	44.7	36.0	51.0

Note: Percentages (percent of total possible scale scores for the number of residents on a given floor) rather than numbers of resident problems are presented, as the care area populations varied in size from 13 to 72 at the time of data collection.

As expected, overall scale scores for the Assessment of Patient Progress by unit revealed the greatest number of problems and deficits, 51% of the possible total, for the skilled care patients on the fifth floor and the fewest for the domiciliary care group on the first floor. The second-, third-, and fourth-floor intermediate care areas were relatively similar overall; subscales, however, reflected some notable differences. Whereas data assessing fourth-floor residents demonstrated only 16.6% of the possible subscale total for behavioral status deficits, the problems of the second-floor resident group cumulated to a 42.8% deficit. Toileting problems on the second floor were also greater, at 47.5% of the possible total than those of either the third or the fourth floor, at 34.1% and 27.6%, respectively.

Across the five resident care areas, certain noteworthy differences include fewer behavioral status problems on the first and fourth floors, physical health deficits highest on the second and fifth floors, and muscle strength deficits notable on all floors but the first (domiciliary care unit). Data for all floors but the first also reflected important physical, social, and recreational activity deficits, with scores ranging from 60% to 90.5% of the subscale's possible total. Whereas the third-floor (cognitively impaired) group demonstrated the greatest number of personal grooming problems at 92% of the possible total, behavior status (36.8%) and psychosocial status (38%) were relatively comparable to those of residents on both the second and the fifth floor. One interpretation of these data might be that staff nurses accustomed to working with the cognitively impaired group employ a lower standard in identifying behavioral problems or deficits among them. In summary, data from the Assessment of Patient Progress instrument provide some insight for caregivers and administrators as to the degree and type of problems the residents are experiencing, which may be used as a jumping-off point for the planning of care.

Resident Case Mix

Bethany Manor residents, as can be seen from the above profile, have a variety of physical and psychosocial problems and deficits. The range is broad relative to the breadth of services provided at the Manor; these services range from domiciliary care for residents living on the first floor to skilled nursing care administered to fifth-floor occupants. The home's third floor is designated specifically for intermediate care of the cognitively impaired, whereas the other two resident care areas, the second and fourth floors, admit persons with a multiplicity of deficits and intermediate care needs.

A profile of resident diagnoses was developed to broadly demonstrate the case mix in the home. This profile must, however, be presented with caveats: First, elderly persons generally have accumulated a list—sometimes lengthy—of physical and/or cognitive deficits, one or several of which may or may not have been a precipitant of admission to the nursing home; second, labels of "early senile dementia" or "Alzheimer's-type syndrome" are sometimes applied to a resident while the specific neurological diagnoses remain unclear. A diagnostic profile of the more commonly identified illness conditions (those identified more than once) among Bethany Manor residents is as follows:

First-floor residents (domiciliary care; age range 68 to 96 years): (1) dementia, cerebral infarction; (2) nervous condition, confusion; (3) hip fracture; (4) left cerebral hemisphere infarction, expressive aphasia; (5) hypertension; (6) diabetes, cerebral vascular accident (CVA); (7) arteriosclerotic heart disease (ASHD), osteoporosis; (8) early Alzheimer's disease; (9) senility, hypertension, cataracts, degenerative joint disease, hepatomegaly, aortic stenosis, aortic regurgitation.

Second-floor residents (intermediate care; age range 61 to 95 years): (1) Alzheimer's disease; (2) senile dementia; (3) ASHD and arterial flutter; (4) organic brain syndrome (OBS), ASHD; (5) Parkinson's disease, hip fracture; (6) colon cancer, chronic obstructive pulmonary disease (COPD); (7) rheumatoid arthritis with deformities; (8) cerebellar dysfunction; (9) chronic brain syndrome secondary to arteriosclerosis.

Third-floor residents (intermediate care; cognitively impaired residents; age range 63 to 95 years): (1) dementia, ASHD, stroke, hip and wrist fractures; (2) Alzheimer's disease; (3) hiatal hernia, hypothyroidism, angina, ASHD; (4) cerebral arteriosclerosis; (5) senile dementia, depression; (6) chronic brain syndrome; (7) dementia, pernicious anemia; (8) OBS, cataracts, hip fracture; (9) breast cancer, anemia, arteriosclerotic cardiovascular disease (ASCVD).

Fourth-floor residents (intermediate care; age range 61 to 109 years): (1) ASCVD, peptic ulcer, ASHD; (2) glaucoma, arteriosclerosis; (3) Parkinson's disease; (4) diabetes, ASHD, blindness; (5) degenerative arthritis; (6) CVA, Parkinson's disease; (7) osteoarthritis; (8) partial deafness and blindness; (9) coronary artery disease; (10) urinary sepsis, arthritis; (11) Crohn's disease.

Fifth-floor residents (skilled nursing care; age range 58 to 97 years): (1) osteoarthritis, hip fracture; (2) CVA, blindness, severe diabetes; (3) Alzheimer's disease with hip fracture; (4) cholecystitis, hip fracture, hypertension, aphasia; (5) hypoxia, polymyoneuropathy, dysphagia, hip fracture; (6) thrombosis of right foot, hip fracture; (7) advanced COPD; (8) OBS, respiratory failure; (9) arteriosclerosis, Alzheimer's syndrome; (10) post-hip fracture, frailty.

As this profile demonstrates, multiple diagnostic labels for an individual were the norm rather than the exception.

Social Histories

On initiating the Bethany Manor study, the researchers found that some staff alternately referred to those living in the home as residents or as patients, the latter term being used especially in cases where physical and psychosocial deficits were severe. It was eventually learned, however, that the general norm was to refer to all individuals at the Manor as residents, with the possible exception of those receiving skilled nursing care on the fifth floor, who were frequently labeled as patients by both visitors and staff. To understand why and in what condition both the "residents," especially those on the domiciliary care unit, and the more seriously disabled fifth-floor "patients" were admitted to Bethany Manor, permission was requested to collect data from the social histories.

The social history form is a five-page form that the nursing home mails to potential residents and/or their families with the request that it be returned before admission. In many cases it appeared that a family member or friend completed the form for the resident.

After documenting the resident's name and how the resident wished to be addressed (e.g., Miss, Mrs., by first name—a very important item to many Bethany Manor residents), the social history form provides space for a detailed account of the individual's current physical and psychosocial situation and a brief social history of past life. The items describing the applicant's current situation include care of self (activities of daily living, bowel and bladder control); walking (need for assistance, wheelchair, cane, history of falls); eating (food preferences and allergies); sleeping (usual habits); physical and emotional impairments and problems (speech, vision, hearing, skin, medications, emotional state, temperament, satisfactions and frustrations with life, major illnesses, psychiatric history); reason for coming to the home (significant details and who made the final decision); present living arrangements (alone or with family, financial management); and miscellaneous current information (outlook for the future, goals or hopes, knowledge of the home, plan for possible discharge, special hobbies or interests). The past life history items include early family life (where born, native language, family members, childhood history); education; occupation; travels (history—where and when); retirement (work subsequent to retirement); and marriage (marital history).

The completed social history forms are ultimately placed in each new resident's chart to provide relevant information for the caregiving staff.

A descriptive analysis of Bethany Manor social history forms for the entire resident population (N = 230) was carried out over a four-week period; selected findings focusing on such variables as care of self, walking, eating, physical and psychological impairments, and reason for admission to the home are as follows (social history data, as diagnoses, were controlled for type of care required, i.e., the nursing home unit to which the resident was admitted):

First-floor residents (domiciliary care): Social histories for first-floor Bethany Manor residents demonstrate a pattern of need for minimal help with self-care in terms of activities of daily living. Some examples of responses are the following: "needs some help with hair and nails," "occasional leaking incontinence," "walks slowly with walker," "falls outdoors," "can't chew meat," "speech is slurred," and "has poor judgment and sometimes forgets where she is." Some reasons for admission included the following: "she can't manage in her home alone and resents having a companion," "she wants to be near her husband [in the home]," "there has been conflict between her and her daughter-in-law," "we [children] plan to leave the area," and "she made her own decision while still in good health." One comment made by a home social worker for a 78-year-old single woman read, "Miss Arness' health had deteriorated in recent months and she is not managing emotionally and physically in her present living situation alone in an apartment. Miss Arness has no close significant other, is depressed, and couldn't seem to organize her life after retirement. She has been work oriented all her life; she needs help planning her long-term care situation."

Of the 17 first-floor residents, 2 were admitted from another nursing home; 10 came from their own homes; 4 had been living with relatives; and one, a religious sister, came from a Catholic religious house.

Second-floor residents (semiskilled care): Second-floor resident social history data presented a profile of notably more serious physical and psychosocial deficits than that described for the self-care group. This pattern is exemplified by the following selected comments: "she needs help with all care—bathing, dressing, hair, nails," "totally incontinent," "walks slowly and is unsteady," "bedridden," "he has to be spoon-fed soft food," "sight and hearing are deteriorating fast," "he is very forgetful and confused and has not recovered from his wife's death." Reasons for admission included such comments as "his sister is 82 and can no longer take care of him [85-year-old patient]," and "she needs 24-hour supervision." A number of stated reasons for admission revolved around the religious orientation of the home. The daughter of a 95-year-old man diagnosed with senile dementia wrote, "He was admitted to Shady Ridge Nursing Home [a nearby home not affiliated with any religious denomination] until there was a place at Bethany Manor. He had difficulty getting transportation to church and the grocery store, and also had problems doing laundry and getting a balanced diet. He desperately wants to get into Bethany Manor so he will be near Mass and the sacraments."

Another daughter of an 86-year-old patient with a diagnosis of Alzheimer's-type brain disease asserted that her father "must have constant care" and added, "We believe people get better treatment in a place managed by the sisters."

Finally, a married couple wrote their own statement of reasons for admission to the home. Their joint decision to accept nursing home care was made "to continue attendance at daily Mass and to be assured of a place of safe refuge when we can no longer care for ourselves; to be assured that the survivor will be cared for when death us do part; and to avoid becoming an extra burden to our married children who are caring for their own families."

Twenty of the 53 second-floor residents were admitted from other nursing homes, 22 from their own homes, 7 from the hospital, and 3 from relatives' homes. One priest came to Bethany Manor from a religious house.

Third-floor residents (semiskilled care; cognitively impaired): Social history data highlighted cognitive deficits as well as a multiplicity of physical and psychosocial problems associated with the aging process. Some comments include "needs help with all her care," " dribbling incontinence controlled with pads," "confined to chair since he fell and broke his hip," and "her mind comes and goes; she has temper outbursts and cries easily." Some reasons for admission identified were "too forgetful to live alone and has outlived most of her friends," and "her daughter is unable to continue the strain of caring for a 94-year-old." The niece of an 84-year-old senile dementia patient wrote, "She can carry on a conversation but with increased anxiety she becomes less clear and details of life overwhelm her—then she becomes confused and disoriented." The daughter of another dementia patient, age 69, stated, "She needs the protection of a nursing home environment. She suffers from loss of memory and judgment but can care for her personal needs and grooming."

Two other families commented on the personal strain of caregiving in their homes. The son of an 84-year-old woman with a diagnosis of brain cancer, ASCVD, and dementia reported, "She does not do well if away from her room; she's forgetful—gets lost; her family needs a relief. My wife and I have looked after Mum for some 20 years. Now she is beginning to require 24-hour care and we cannot continue because of our own needs. She needs help taking medication and preparing food." The daughter of an 82-year-old, very confused dementia patient added, "My husband and I have full time jobs and with the children now gone to college there is no one to take care of her during the day or if I have to be away. Her condition is deteriorating. We can no longer keep up with her increasing need for care because of work demands and related problems." Of the 69 cognitively impaired residents on the third floor, 19 had been admitted from other nursing homes, 7 from the hospital, and 33 from their own homes. Nine residents had been living with relatives, and one was from a religious institution.

Fourth-floor residents (semiskilled care): Social history data on fourth-floor residents were relatively similar to those for Bethany Manor's second-floor group. Some physical and psychosocial problems included "needs help with bathing, hair and nails," "total incontinence," "walks very slowly with a cane," "doesn't hear very well," "is withdrawn and depressed a lot of the time."

Reasons for home admission included "lives alone and is afraid to go out since her sister died," and "can't manage living alone physically and emotionally." An 82-year-old wrote of herself, "At my age I can't get around and should be in a home for the aged," and a 73-year-old reported that she had fallen in the tub at home and couldn't get out for 24 hours. She said, "I knew it was time to come." The nephew of an 89-year-old confused patient wrote that home life for all family members had become increasingly strained because of the incompatibility between his aunt and his wife, which caused the wife anxiety and depression: "We [the nephew and his wife] have been advised by doctors, relatives and friends to find a home for my aunt. No other relative will take her." The daughter of an 88-year-old noted, "I'm going to be 63 years old soon. I do not know how much longer

I can keep taking care of my mother. She will be needing more care as she gets older and I'm getting older." Another daughter complained, "Mother needs to be with someone at all times, and she is much more cooperative with anyone other than her own children. She feels that her children should not boss her around. Secondly, I am still working and the only child that will buck her. It is not easy; I have taken care of my mother since my father's passing in 1958."

Nineteen of the 71 fourth-floor residents were admitted from other nursing homes, and 4 came from hospitals; 41 had been living in their own homes, and 7 lived with relatives.

Fifth-floor residents (skilled nursing care): An overview of the social history data for fifth-floor residents indicates a more significant level of physical impairment and need for nursing care than indicated on any of the other Bethany Manor wards. The response to "care of self" items was frequently "None"; many patients were described as "totally incontinent," "bedridden," "unable to eat," "unable to see or speak," "withdrawn." Families identified some reasons for admission as follows: "the family couldn't handle both her senility and a hip fracture" and "she has severe, uncontrolled diabetes and needs care." The family of an advanced Alzheimer's disease patient requested a period of "respite." An 80-year-old man with a fractured hip and mild confusion was described by his family as "never having recovered after being attacked by two men in his home." He was described as "confused and depressed since the attack" and unable to function alone. The family of a 74-year-old woman with advanced COPD wrote that a recent hospitalization "left her no longer able to care for herself and the family cannot carry that burden." She had become so dehydrated from lack of drinking that intravenous fluids were needed.

Almost half of the fifth-floor residents ($N = 9$) were admitted from their own homes, five had been living with family members, two were admitted from other floors at Bethany Manor, three came from other nursing homes, and one came directly from the hospital.

To summarize the social history data for all Bethany Manor residents, the majority required at least minimal assistance with activities of daily living and suffered from mild to severe physical and/or cognitive impairment. Reasons for admission to the home seemed to fall into two groups: (1) the residents' own need or desire and (2) the families' need or desire. Frequently the elders themselves expressed a desire or need for nursing home residency, often mentioning a desire for safety or protection from such things as falls, going outdoors (especially in winter), attackers in the home or on the street, and being alone if serious illness or accident occurred. The nursing home seemed to be envisioned by some residents as a "safe haven," where even if the environment contained undesirable stressors, someone was always there in case of need. Catalysts for a resident's felt need for nursing home care included such personal threats as falls, physical attacks, and hospitalization. Often families commented that a resident simply never recovered after one of these occurrences.

The second category of reasons for admission to Bethany Manor related to the needs or wishes of a resident's family. Such situations as the family moving to another city, serious illness of the primary caregiver, or even the aging process of adult children stimulated a family to consider the option of nursing home care. Sometimes the caregiver burden became too heavy for the family to bear either physically or emotionally or both, and the family physician would recommend institutional long-term care as the only viable choice. It appeared, however, that many families made this choice with great difficulty and after many years of personal sacrifice and caring.

The Study Sample

From a cursory assessment of the health status of Bethany Manor residents early on in the research, it was determined that approximately 70 to 80 of the 230 residents would be capable of participating in qualitative discussions lasting approximately 45 minutes to an hour. A significant number of residents were immediately excluded because of cognitive impairment; others were omitted because of serious physical deterioration, one notable problem being severe hearing deficit, which would prevent participation in face-to-face taped discussions. One of the study consultants advised that, if possible, an attempt be made to meet with all of those residents who were cognitively alert, physically capable, and agreeable to sharing their thoughts and feelings. This was done.

Only three individuals declined to be involved in the study, essentially giving as reasons a busy schedule and lack of interest. Most residents were gracious and enthusiastic about the meetings and openly shared their thoughts and feelings. Confidentiality was guaranteed. Several respondents requested that a tape recorder not be used, so handwritten notes were substituted. When conversations were taped, the residents were given the option of shutting off the recorder at any time during a discussion should they wish to do so.

In all, meetings were held with 71 cognitively alert Bethany Manor residents (62 women and 9 men). The discussions varied in length from 15 minutes to 1 1/2 hours, depending largely on the verbal abilities and pleasure of the resident. It was initially planned that although observation and informal conversations with all residents would be included in the research, only those individuals identified as cognitively aware and communicative would be involved in one-on-one meetings. However, as the study progressed, two gerontological consultants advised that if the researchers wished to present a complete picture or "anatomy" of home, cognitively impaired individuals must be formally included as study subjects. This unique dimension of the research and how it was carried out is discussed later in this chapter under the heading "The Cognitively Impaired Resident."

Relationships With Significant Others

Chapter 3 addresses the residents' significant other relationships from the perspective of the family member or surrogate. The import of relationships with loved ones from the residents' viewpoint is discussed here.

The majority of the cognitively aware residents of Bethany Manor spoke of their relationships with significant others, either family or friends or both, as very important to their lives in the nursing home. These family or surrogate family members provided the residents a link with both the present and the past. They were part of the resident's history, a dimension of life that becomes most important when the present and future begin to dim. Family and friends also provided a bridge to the larger community, to a world outside the nursing home. They shared news of the day, both familial and national, and helped keep the resident in touch with former social and professional activities. They also provided the resident with a feeling of advocacy and support—the knowledge that someone special was there to call on for needs that might not be met by the Manor community. Finally, family members provided the Bethany Manor residents with the special love, caring, and respect that supports the spirit when physical functions diminish and personal autonomy seems virtually lost.

One Bethany Manor resident, 91-year-old Mrs. Anna Gittings, described the caring and support that she had long received and was still receiving from her nephew and his family: "I lived with them for 13 years after mother died and they always treated me like part of the family. But then my nephew had to retire and that's one reason I didn't want to stay there and cause him any worry. He said he wanted the best home possible for me and this was it. I'm just as happy here and I don't want to put him to any trouble, that's the way I feel. He's done so much for me and his wife, she even wants to do my washing, do for me still, brings me things, so what more can I expect? In fact, I don't expect them to be bringing me things. I tell them that but they want to do it. They like me, I guess, as much as I like them."

A number of residents expressed more concern for their families' needs than for their own. Mrs. Ibach, a 97-year-old who had been at the home for four years, related her admonition to her daughter: "I told her, 'It is too bad for you to be saddled with me. I don't want you to sacrifice yourself. When you are invited to go places and do things, I want you to go, don't consider me.' I said, 'They will look after me.' She comes in always once a week, sometimes more often, and my grandson comes to see me when he has time. He has his wife and a little great-grandson. They all came yesterday afternoon. We spent the whole afternoon outside."

Mrs. Katherine Wassel, 88, described her need for support and enjoyment of family visits outside the home: "I like to put in a word of advice to every doctor and every social worker, to impress on people that if they have an elderly person in their family, to keep in touch with them. That is the most important thing." She added that on the coming Easter Sunday her family would visit: "They are coming here to take me to dinner with the family; that will be a great event in my life."

Overall, the majority of Bethany Manor residents spoke positively about their family support, often making excuses for family members who were "too busy" to visit more often. A few long-term residents did complain of neglect. This is discussed in Chapter 8.

Relationships With Caregivers

Bethany Manor residents had a great deal to say about relationships with their caregivers. Some of this is discussed also in Chapter 7, under the headings "Staff-Resident Interaction" and "Norms of Staff Behavior." However, because long-term caregivers often become significant others for nursing home residents, the topic of caregiver-resident relationships warrants attention from several perspectives. Whereas Chapter 7 examines these relationships primarily in terms of the social-interactional milieu of the home, the present comments focus more upon specific resident feelings: joys, satisfactions, fears, and anxieties related to the residents' relationships with Bethany Manor caregivers.

Mrs. Imelda Moreno, a fairly new fourth-floor resident, described the nursing staff in very positive terms: "Some of them are young girls, it's true, and they don't always have the skills with old people maybe they should but they really do try and they care about you. I can tell that and it helps make the life here more bearable. I praise them." Another resident on the same floor, Miss Gertrude Fraiser, also spoke about the staff's age: "I feel that young people, like a girl of 19, of course, they have to start and learn, but I don't think they are in sympathy with an old person. Anybody in their 80s to them is just senile." Miss Fraiser added, "They do work hard here, though, and some really treat you with kindness."

In distinction, Mrs. Nora Lucas, an 87-year-old fourth-floor resident, stated her bias: "The nurses are not the best because the best nurses don't work for nursing homes. They're not paid enough." Miss Martha Butler expressed ambivalence: "I'm always afraid who's going to wake me up in the morning and put me to bed at night. Some are nice and some are not so nice."

Finally, 94-year-old Miss Nora Holland, who described herself as a "feisty woman," reported that one day she got "mad" at an aide and told her, "Don't you dare come and look at me when I'm laid out in the coffin down there in the lobby, because if you do, I'll stick my tongue out at you." She confessed that she did like most of her caregivers, however: "They're good to an old lady." No reports of physical abuse were related in residents' accounts of staff interaction, but some anxiety about care and future care was detected.

Relationships With Other Nursing Home Residents

Personal friendships and even, for some, participation in small cliques were very important dimensions of Bethany Manor life for some of the more alert residents. One of the most active and involved members of the home group, Miss Martha Armstrong, a charming and very social 77-year-old resident of the domiciliary care unit, described it this way: "I really have a lot of jobs here to keep me busy. I check up on some of the older patients who can't get around, I'm active in two of the home's committees, I help get people to church and the dining room, and I have my group that I play cards with. I guess we're sort of a little clique, as you might say." Aside from Miss Armstrong, the card-playing clique consisted of three other ladies who had resided at Bethany Manor for some time: Miss Anna Neil, Miss Sally Barnes, and Miss Teresa Loughney. Although Miss Barnes' progressive arthritis necessitated her using a wheelchair most of the time, she was quite active and reported having a very busy schedule in the home. All of the clique members seemed to derive a great deal of satisfaction from participating in their group, and each spoke positively about the others. Miss Barnes commented, however, that it had been somewhat difficult to develop friendships at the home because, as she put it, some of "these people are really not with the program, if you know what I mean."

Many of the study respondents talked about one or two special friends at the Manor: "I made a close friend the day I came here and we've been close ever since"; "I've got a nice friend who's my special friend here. We visit and watch TV together"; "I have a friend who takes me down to Mass every day." Some residents, however, found friendships difficult to maintain partly because of their disabilities and because of the home schedule. Mrs. Grace Brener, 89, who had been at Bethany Manor for five years and was wheelchair bound and somewhat forgetful, explained, "I do have some friends on this floor and we get along, but sometimes it's hard to get together. They're here or there and I'm here or there. It gets a little lonesome at times." Finally a number of residents, in discussing nursing home friendships, echoed Mis Barnes' thought that not everyone at Bethany Manor was "with the program"; this posed some interactional difficulties for the cognitively alert group. Mrs. Anna Geyer commented, "Some of the people here, these poor dear things, they're in their own world. You try to talk to them but...my heart just goes out to them."

The Cognitively Impaired Resident

"Old age, they say, is a gradual giving up. But it is strange when it happens all at once. This is a real test of character, a kind of solitary confinement. Whatever I have now is in my own mind." So speaks the protagonist, Caro Spencer, in May Sarton's insightful and sensitive novel *As We Are Now* (1973, 3). The mind and its functioning were topics of great importance to Bethany Manor residents. Much anxiety revolved around the possibility of future cognitive impairment or becoming, in the words of some of the group, "a little squirrelly," " fuzzy-headed," "dizzy," or "not with it anymore." A transfer to the third floor, where confused residents were housed, was decidedly viewed as a fate worse than death. Perhaps because of this, residents employed a multiplicity of strategies to mask deficits such as confusion or memory loss; this sometimes caused notable problems for families and staff. Hladik (1982, 11) notes that "an impaired person's resistance to supervision and/or his denial of the condition presents specific problems" for caregivers, and Bartol (1983, 234) asserts, "Even the very oldest cling to the belief that they are persons, strong in their individuality, not part of this group, this world of confusion."

Dementia, often viewed as "one of the most feared diseases of old age" (Schwab et al. 1985, 8), accounts for the admission of "a large percentage of nursing home residents" (Mackey 1983, 5). Statistics suggest that upward of 50% of residents are "mentally or emotionally ill in the clinical sense" (Benedict 1983, 22; Lincoln 1984, 26). The true prevalence is probably much greater, however, as "many mental disorders in nursing homes are unrecognized or misinterpreted" (Lucas et al. 1986, 11). Cognitive impairments in the elderly are "commonly labelled senility, dementia, organicity, acute or chronic brain syndrome, or Alzheimer's disease" (Pavkov and Walsh 1985, 120). The label "confused' is "attached to individuals who demonstrate deficits in one or more of the following areas: memory, concentration, attention, orientation, comprehension, compliance, mood, and interpretation of the environment" (Nagley 1986, 27).

The elderly in nursing homes may also suffer from "chronic psychiatric diseases, including affective disorders and schizophrenia" (Salisbury and Goehner 1983, 231). Regardless of the specific diagnosis, psychological or psychiatric conditions that impair cognitive functioning frequently result in seriously disruptive behaviors, which pose significant problems in the high density setting of the nursing home. (Burgio et al. 1988, 31) define the term "behavior problems" as "a diverse array of patient responses which are considered noxious to staff, other patients or the patient himself." They describe three types of behavior problems: (1) acting-out behaviors ("directed at another person"), (2) aberrant behaviors ("considered noxious by staff or other patients"), and (3) excess disabilities (the patient's functional incapacity is "greater than warranted" by his or her physical incapacity). (Bernier and Small 1988, 12) identified those behavior problems that were perceived to be most disruptive to staff as troublemaking, verbal assault, physical assault, destructive behavior, and threatening behavior; residents identified another resident entering the wrong room as the most disruptive behavior for them.

There is a fair amount of literature on the topic of separation of confused from lucid residents (Salisbury and Goehner 1983, Lederer 1983). Opinions differ, with concern often centering more on the needs and security of the alert than on those of the confused resident. At Bethany Manor, mildly confused residents were integrated on all care areas; one unit, however, was designated specifically to house the more seriously cognitively impaired. The security measures and staff attitudes toward the residents on the third floor are discussed in Chapter 7.

To gain at least a minimal understanding of life for the cognitively impaired nursing home resident, a subsample of 30 moderately confused residents was chosen randomly from the third-floor group (details of sample selection and interviewing techniques are presented in the Appendix). On the advice of a nurse ethicist, third-party consent was sought to visit and converse with the cognitively impaired group. Details of this process are presented here rather than in the Appendix, as the response of the group's significant others displayed an important dimension of "family" support and concern for an institutionalized loved one experiencing symptoms of dementia.

Because the institutionalized cognitively impaired elderly were considered a captive, fragile population, significant others were identified and sent detailed letters describing the project. The letters identified the five specific discussion foci (phrased in the form of questions): (1) How are you? (2) What is it like living here? (3) What do you do during the day? (4) Whom do you talk to here? and (5) Is there anything you need? A signature was requested giving consent for their resident to be visited.

Letters were sent to 29 families. Within approximately two weeks, 27 family permissions had been received by mail. Some family members telephoned the study investigator to express their support for the effort and to offer any other assistance needed. Several respondents also included notes of gratitude for including their family member in the research, and one respondent typed two paragraphs of comments on the bottom of the consent form in order to provide added study data. The 27 "family member" respondents included 11 daughters, 3 sons, 3 sisters, 4 nephews, 2 nieces, 1 cousin, 1 friend, and 2 conservators. Selected family comments were as follows: (from a daughter) "It is very thoughtful of you to ask [permission]. I'd be interested in some of the answers to see if she's telling me the same answers. Thank you for your interest in our mother"; (from a son) "Please feel free to ask as many questions as you want, and to take any amount of time that is necessary; please feel free to call me if I can be of benefit"; (from a niece) "You certainly have undertaken a prodigious study—one that certainly needs to be done." Finally, one daughter wrote extensively; her letter is abstracted here: "I would be delighted to have you interview mother.

I would suggest talking to her in a quiet atmosphere in her room with the door shut because she is easily distracted by the noise and activity in the hall. She has a problem remembering names but is better at recognizing one's voice and touch. Many thanks for including her in your study."

The very positive responses to the study of these and a number of other family members reinforced the investigators' perception that it was important to attempt to understand the thoughts and desires of Bethany Manor's cognitively impaired residents.

Although consent had been received to meet with 27 cognitively impaired third-floor residents, only 24 individuals were finally included in the study, because by the time of data collection 3 of the 27 had become too ill to respond.

The data collector, a masters'-prepared psychiatric-mental health nurse experienced in working with the confused elderly, visited most of the study group before the actual data collection meetings to introduce herself and find out the resident's condition cognitively and emotionally. Some suggestions gleaned from observations and from her pilot work with third-floor residents were helpful in initiating the focused discussions: Touch the residents, allow them to touch you. Initiate some emotional contact. Make certain the resident can see your face. Kneel down if he or she is in a wheelchair. Use humor if possible. Lighten the mood of the discussion. Pick out something about the resident that looks nice (hair, clothing, etc.) and comment on it. Go for a walk if the resident is able, or take him or her outside or to a pleasant room. In carrying out the discussions: Speak about simple topics or ask uncomplicated questions (the residents may not be able to recall a question or retain it if long and complicated). Redirect conversation if necessary (attention span may be short and residents may digress). Go slowly, as discussions may take a long time. Observe nonverbal cues and communication. Other details regarding interviewing the cognitively impaired resident are presented in the Appendix.

The aim of interviewing this subgroup of cognitively impaired residents was descriptive: to document a profile of the thoughts and responses of the moderately confused nursing home resident to daily life and activities in the home. There was significant variance in the respondents' breadth of response, and thus in the richness of qualitative data generated, primarily because of mental confusion; in one or two cases the variance was related to hearing deficit. The researcher returned to visit several residents on more than on occasion to find an opportune time to talk. In presenting the discussion foci, the nurse researcher introduced herself as being from a local university and said that because we were writing a book about Bethany Manor, we would like to know what the people who lived there thought about life in the home. She then read the five discussion foci to the resident and asked the resident if he or she would be willing to help. No residents refused to participate in the study. Some, however, showed more interest than others, and several said they felt pleased or flattered to be asked to help. One respondent said she didn't know if she knew "the right answers," but after hearing the five discussion questions she "felt better."

One 85-year-old woman with severe short-term memory problems responded to the description of the study: "Why, that's very nice. I would be glad to tell you what I can." Another resident who described herself as "ornery" looked over the questions carefully and replied, "I think I will talk about these." Only three residents appeared to have virtually no understanding of what the study data were to be used for: two because of level of confusion and one because of a hearing deficit. A fourth resident seemed to understand the explanation and maintained eye contact but did not respond verbally. When asked if it was hard for her to talk, she replied, "Yes, we're not allowed to talk very much."

Of the 24 cognitively impaired study respondents, 7 gave only minimal or very brief responses to the discussion foci. Mrs. Whitlock, an 83-year-old woman with a diagnosis of organic brain syndrome, walked with the nurse researcher and talked, but her responses were not appropriate. Her mind seemed focused primarily upon her daughter and when she was coming to visit. Two other residents, Miss Green, a 78-year-old with chronic brain syndrome, and Miss Murdoch, an 84-year-old with senile dementia, gave only monosyllabic answers but seemed to enjoy the contact with the data collector and smiled at her during the visit. Mrs. Hardesty, an 80-year-old, tried to respond, but her mind kept wandering to concerns about whether "the children" were OK. Miss Pender and Mrs. Daniels focused primarily on their families as topics of conversation, and Mrs. Richards, a 90-year-old with a diagnosis of Alzheimer's disease, gave inappropriate responses to study foci but grabbed the interviewer's hand and continued to hold it while they talked. The nurse researcher wrote in her notes, "She continued to hold my hand very tightly and I think that touch is the best and most worthwhile communication at this time. I continue to hold her hand and stroke her arm. She seems to relax...after about ten minutes she falls asleep."

The remaining 17 residents in the cognitively impaired subsample did follow the focused discussion topics with occasional digressions. A descriptive content analysis of the data from these meetings reveals five dominant themes in the residents' attitudes and behaviors. These have been labeled "conformity," "privacy," "activity," "externality," and "reminiscence."

Conformity

Conformity relates to these residents' "desire to please," especially to please the nursing home staff. Conformity was evidenced also in the comment several residents made to the researcher: "I hope I can help you." Miss Mary Kidd, a 90-year-old with diagnoses of congestive heart failure and confusion, had been described on admission a year ago as "confused, sensitive, very forgetful and upset by changes. She knows that she needs nursing home care but hasn't yet accepted it." Miss Kidd's remarks reflected a definite desire for conformity at the home. She said, "I'm as good as can be expected. I try to fall in with what's expected of me or what they require me to do. It's as can be expected for my age." She added, "I've lived longer than any member of my family. I'm 90, I think. I hope that's the right answer." Several times during the interview she reiterated, "I hope I'm giving you the right answers." An 85-year-old resident with senile dementia, Mrs. Gallagher, asserted, "It's nice here [at Bethany Manor]. We go along with what they say to do," and a third respondent commented, "Everybody's very nice but I just hate to call the nurses unless I really have to, I just try to go along with everything."

Privacy

The concept of privacy for these Bethany Manor residents had to do with "minding one's business" and limiting the circle of friends even within the nursing home. Miss Anna Cowan, a 94-year-old with diagnoses of senility and depression, commented, "I don't go around too much. I like to keep to myself. Some people here are too much into everyone's business. I don't like that. I have my own 'family.' " An 84-year-old, Mrs. Smithfield, reported that she was "very quiet" and liked to talk to her niece, but added, "I don't want to know too many people here." Two other residents stated that although they like people around they didn't get too involved and didn't know people's names. One noted, "Sometimes I keep my distance because I can't visit with everyone."

Activity

Activity as a subject of interest for Bethany Manor's cognitively impaired group revolved around activities of daily living (getting bathed, dressed, eating), visiting with staff and other residents, and visiting with family. Some respondents reported "busy schedules" at the home. Miss Maria Gortner, an 89-year-old who had lived at the home for five years and was quite forgetful, commented on her days: "I don't live here [Bethany Manor], dear. I have a home to go to. I just come here during the day to see some people but I don't sleep here–no, dear, I have my own home." An 84-year-old resident with ASCVD and confusion described her life at home: "I can be busy and independent here. I can do what I want during the day. Like if I need to do something during the day, I can." A 73-year-old woman reported, "I don't do anything [all day]. I just like to have people around." She added, "I'm afraid I take too many naps." An 87-year-old resident stated, "I pray and thank God for a good life," a theme echoed by others.

Externality

Externality, a theme dominant in many discussions, related to the way in which some residents essentially "lived" in the worlds of others external to themselves: children, nieces and nephews, or other individuals residing outside of the nursing home. Sometimes a question such as "What do you do all day?" was responded to with an answer like, "I'm waiting for my niece. She is supposed to come and take me out today." Such responses were not always reality oriented. Some residents moved in and out of reality in the same response; for example, Mrs. Carpenter: "I feel good sometimes, sometimes bad. My babies are probably OK though, I don't know about the babies. I pray they are OK," or Miss Shultis: "I like my room here but I think I should get back to my own home [in another city] pretty soon." Mrs. Sheehan described her family: "My nephew has a home and would like to take me to live with him but I prefer to live here. I'm waiting for my nephew now. He's coming to get me. My nephew comes *every day* to take me out." Miss Mary Kidd spoke about a recent family visit: "They brought my baby to see me. The baby is named after me so it's 'my' baby, so to speak. It's special when a child is named after you. My niece comes to see me all the time." Mrs. Conklin talked about her daughter's life and family, concluding, "I love my daughter and I know she loves me. I would be better to live at home but...she couldn't take care of me any more and she comes all the time."

Reminiscence

A central focus of discussion with many Bethany Manor residents was on their earlier lives, often their childhood experiences with parents and siblings. Many cognitively impaired respondents spoke of events of several decades ago while discussing their present lives in the nursing home. Mrs. Paula Boyle, an 85-year-old resident with organic brain syndrome, said of life at the Manor: "You know I can't be doing the same things I did at home with my mother—in my family there were eight of us so there was always excitement." Mrs. Marie Douglas likened the grounds at Bethany Manor to her home city: "I lived there as a child and we used to take long walks with a regular group of friends."

Mrs. Stoner, an 88-year-old resident, fantasized that she was at home as a young adult: "I work every day except Saturday afternoon and Sunday. Then I go to church and go shopping," yet she also admitted, "I'm older, I'm slower. I don't go as much as you do." Finally, Mrs. Moreno, with organic brain syndrome, explained, "I don't [visit] too much here. There is only so much I can do because I'm busy with the kids and I have it very good. I clean house for my mother." She also added, "I'm getting old but I don't feel old."

Several other themes that arose in discussions with the cognitively impaired group included the following: relative deprivation ("many people here have worse problems than I do," "when you look at the handicaps all the people here have, I say God's been good to me"; illness perception ("I got sick when I got old; I lost interest in things," "I have to be very careful. I'm afraid I might fall and get hurt," "I'm sick now that I'm old," and socialization ("I can walk the halls and someone will say, 'Good morning to you, madam' and I love that. I'll call her 'madam' the same way and she'll say, 'Don't trip' and I'll say, 'I won't trip' and she'll say, 'You sweet girl'").

Several residents commented on their problem of short-term memory. Mrs. Frazier, an Alzheimer's patient said, "I remember the past with my husband and daughter but I can't remember yesterday!" Mrs. Boyle tried to remember her brothers and sisters who had visited recently. She mused, "Isn't that funny. I can't remember their names but I can see them in my mind as clear as anything." In sum, the majority of cognitively impaired residents who were visited seemed to enjoy their meetings, and many asked the nurse researcher to return. Miss Gertrude Hobbs had tears in her eyes when she said, "I have been waiting for you so long. Thank you for coming." (Note: Only one resident expressed some unhappiness living at Bethany Manor, but after her comment said, "Don't write that down." These specific data were therefore discarded.)

Visitors

The topic of visiting is addressed in Chapter 3 from the perspective of the significant other, and some "Tips for Visitors" are presented. The subject also warrants attention here as a notable dimension of social and in (some cases physical) activity for the Bethany Manor resident. For some, looking forward to and planning for a visit, the visit itself, and talking about the visit after it is over constitute important activities in the life of the home.

The importance of visitors to a nursing home resident is exemplified by the publication of an entire book entitled *The Nursing Home Visitor: A Handbook Written from the Inside* (Faunce 1969). In this small volume, the author, herself a nursing home resident, addresses such topics as who should visit, the loneliness of the residents, the need for attention and affection, and understanding life in the home. The import of visits and letters from friends and former colleagues and students is also eloquently addressed by Joyce Mary Horner, a former professor of English at Mount Holyoke College, in her chronicle of nursing home life *That Time of Year* (1982). Some of her journal notations include descriptions of visits from friends ("I felt really touched...by Nora's getting up at six to get me good roses and bringing them out, though it was her vacation" [p. 59]) and Christmas letters ("Just now I am full of family feeling as well as old student feeling, having had letters not only from Susan, Elsie, and Thomas, but Ted. I count my blessings, with a feeling I ought to throw salt over my shoulder or curtsy to the moon or something" [p. 185]). DePaul (1983, 30-31), in discussing the needs of the nursing home resident, quotes one elderly stateswoman who reports of her visitors, "I have a few friends who occasionally come to see me and say, 'I think of you so often' or 'I pray for you every night'...I think...if I only see you a couple of times a year, how can your thoughts help me unless you come and tell me about them?"

Visits for Bethany Manor residents took place both within and outside the home. On "special" days such as holidays—Christmas, Easter, the Fourth of July—families able to manage it both physically and emotionally made every effort to bring their relatives home for a visit, a trip usually looked forward to eagerly by the resident. Of course, there were exceptions. One Thanksgiving morning early in the research, a wheelchair- and walker-bound 84-year-old fourth-floor resident told the study's principal investigator that her daughter-in-law had "really wanted to take me home for dinner" but that she had refused. The resident said, "It's not fair to her. Her husband had a stroke last year, and she has to half-lift me into the car; she has her own family to worry about. My life is here now and I'm at peace with it."

Bethany Manor visits also took place inside the home, either in the residents' rooms, or sun porches, in the home lobby, or, in nice weather, on the front porch or surrounding grounds. Many residents liked to get out and walk with their visitors, weather and their physical condition permitting.

Mrs. Mary Nettles liked to walk outside with her family on nice days. She said, "I just don't go outside on my own. I think, 'Well, I know what's out there,' but it's good to do it with people you care about. They give me a reason to go."

A Bethany Manor social worker summed up the concept of family visiting at the home: "It varies. Some people are very conscientious about coming to see relatives. Others, let's face it, they don't come in. We always feel badly about the resident who is in that position. It's only factual to say it does happen. It's a shame, but it occurs. Families don't see the relatives that often in some cases."

Overall, most Manor residents considered visits, either within or outside the home or even through letters or telephone calls, to constitute one of the most important and satisfying dimensions of their lives.

Activities of Daily Living

The topic of activities of daily living (ADL) is central to the world of the nursing home resident. ADL are addressed briefly in Chapter 7 within a discussion of the "work" of the resident, and in Chapter 4 in the context of accommodation to nursing home life. The term "activities of daily living" is generally understood to mean those physical behaviors necessary to maintain and sustain the continuation of life in its most basic form. For the severely cognitively impaired Alzheimer's patient, the maintaining of ADL may involve having the activities of bathing, feeding, toileting, and dressing carried out by a caregiver with little or no response from the resident. For the cognitively alert resident, however, the maintaining of ADL may have important symbolic significance in terms of self-concept, self-esteem, and perception of personal autonomy. Moderately deteriorating Bethany Manor residents were observed to retain control over personal ADL as long as possible, attempting to comb their hair, even if no longer able to wash it; wash hands and face, although a shower or bath might require assistance; and to feed themselves, even though fixing a meal would never again be a viable option. For residents who were up and about and still able to maintain their usual ADL, it was learned that time became a significant factor, related to both the cognitive and the physical deterioration associated with the aging process. One reason why nursing home residents frequently seem to have busy schedules is that they need a great deal of time to personally carry out their ADL.

Levels and types of activity varied greatly at Bethany Manor, from the most basic ADL to the more meaningful and satisfying types of hobbies or involvement with others. Mr. Ted Merrick, a first-floor (domiciliary care) resident, reported, "They have activity programs here, which are for the people who don't have initiative of their own. I don't need that at all because I will be busy every time I am able to with something of my own. They'll have a program downstairs—maybe some of the women are making a little fancy work and something like that, but I don't need that."

Eighty-five-year-old Mrs. Eileen Cavanaugh identified bingo as her primary social activity: "Some of my family used to say, 'Oh, that nasty old bingo is a waste of time.' It is not a waste of time; it is a social hour. So now it has gone into the same 10 or 12 people, we play at big round tables, and that's the time I see my close friends."

Mrs. Julia Crowley, 83, described a very busy schedule beginning each day with seven o'clock rising, dressing, and breakfast in time to be down in the chapel for 9:30 Mass. After that she suggested, "Well, you can do a lot of things. You can pick up your newspaper and come up here and sit in the sun and read your paper, or you can write a letter, or you might have a date with the hairdresser, or you might have a date with the dentist or the podiatrist. You see, that is all here, all those wonderful things, we don't have to go out of the building."

Some residents' activities were carried our primarily in isolation, although their schedules were described as busy nonetheless. Miss Lucille Pittman, a wheelchair-bound resident, stated, "Really praying and reading are my main hobbies now. There is nothing like getting newsy letters from home. Since I had these cataracts on my eyes, when I get my reading done for prayers and Mass, that's as much as I feel I can read. I have to rest my eyes. Maybe sometimes I'll take a little nap. The day goes too fast, to tell you the truth."

Eighty-nine-year-old Mrs. Grace Locke, who was fairly independent yet needed the assistance provided on an intermediate care floor, described her average day at the Manor:

"I usually get up around six o'clock in the morning because it takes me so long to do everything and I don't want to hurry, so 'til I get myself washed a little bit and 'til I get dressed and poke around a little bit and then I go down to eat. Sometimes I have to wait for the elevator and then they start serving at eight. Mostly always around nine I come up and you know the morning's pretty well gone. I rest a while and sit with my feet up, get started my reading. From nine o'clock until time to go down to eat, it doesn't seem any time, and the same way in the afternoon 'til time to go eat again. I can't imagine it's three o'clock already. At five-twenty we eat. That's the time they have the evening meal. I'm down there a long time because by the time you get served, it takes a while, and then we sit at the table and talk a while. The day goes fast. If I don't get any worse I'll be happy."

Finally, several other residents echoed the sentiment that the day went by too quickly. One of these was 83-year-old Miss Claire O'Rourke, who commented, "There are people here that say to me, 'Oh, the days are so long.' I say I wish they could be longer. I can't do all I want to do in a day. I stay up sometimes until eleven o'clock, eleven-thirty. It's quiet in here. I read and I enjoy it. Of course, I do have to go to bed sometime, so it's very near midnight many a night."

Quality of Life

In the contemporary gerontological literature one finds a number of articles, portions of articles, and books dealing with the issue of quality of life. One chapter of the National Association of Social Workers (NASW) presents on the cover of its brochure the statement: "To Enhance the Quality of Life—Social Work in the Nursing Home" (NASW, undated). Several nurse researchers studying nursing's impact on nursing home life found that "nurses had an effect on residents' life satisfaction when they were in the role of confidant" (Huss et al. 1988, 35). Rainwater and Christiansen (1984, 17) report that a wellness or quality-of-life program in a long-term care facility resulted in "positive attitudinal changes by a majority of program participants."

What exactly is quality of life, and how is it defined for the nursing home resident? Aristotle noted that positive quality of life related to "the life that is good to live," and as commonly used, the term seems to refer to that degree of positivity or negativity, in terms of physical, psychosocial, and spiritual variables that supports or intrudes upon an individual's continual productive existence. Quality of life is decidedly subjective, and perceptions of positivity and negativity of certain factors may vary notably, as can be seen from the comments of individual Bethany Manor residents.

Miss Claire O'Rourke compared her quality of life at Bethany Manor to that of the more seriously disabled residents: "You feel sorry for them. Of course, you say to yourself, 'There but for the grace of God, go I.' My doctor told me only last week, 'You can be thankful for many things, that you have your mind and are pretty well physically.' He is satisfied for a person of 83. He says, 'So many younger than you are not able to do what you are doing.' " Miss O'Rourke added, "I wake up in the morning and say, 'Thank God, I've got another day.' I mean it."

Eighty-eight-year-old Mrs. Hobbs, however, confessed that she didn't want to do much of anything now: "I made up my mind I am at the end of my rope. You do sort of get that notion. I have felt I really don't have any incentive to live." Eighty-seven-year-old Miss Gould expressed ambivalence about her life and future at the Manor: "It seems to me anybody in their eighties could know they don't have much longer to live. You don't have any future, and I think about the past most of the time. I told somebody that I don't want to continue to live, and yet I don't want to die either."

Davis and Plage (1981, 18) assert that "making the life of the resident as meaningful as possible is a primary purpose of the long term care facility." They suggest some appropriate methods for accomplishing this, including activities programs, resident councils, work incentive programs, and family interaction. Dychtwald (1983, 18) comments that elderly persons are much less vital than they could be, that geriatric health care must become "future minded," and more competent and caring aides and more frequent physician visits are needed nursing home improvements to benefit quality of life (Perspectives on Aging 1982).

Uncertainty About the Future

Although uncertainty about the future might be a cause of some anxiety for everyone, it becomes a most immediate problem for the elderly nursing home resident, who is faced daily with both seeing and sometimes interacting with persons whom they may soon become: the cognitively impaired and the physically disabled. In analyzing data from residents' social histories prepared before their nursing home admission, one finds that the most frequent worries about the future include financial worries ("running out of money") and self-care concerns ("getting sick and not being able to take care of myself"). In postadmission interviews and discussion, however, although a few residents focused upon finances and autonomy in terms of personal care, the majority directed their future worries toward such issues as cognitive impairment—"I really don't want to lose my faculties like some of the old ones around here"—or loneliness—"So many of my family and friends are gone. I'm afraid I'll be all alone at the end, the last one. Nobody wants to be the last."

It is suggested that older age and retirement are welcomed by some and feared by others (Sinick 1984). Bethany Manor residents exemplify both attitudes. Miss Helena Burns, 77, who had been admitted to the Manor because of physical and emotional disabilities that prevented her from continuing to manage life alone in her apartment, was disillusioned and bitter. She complained, "All your life you work hard to get nice things and keep up your way of life, and now it comes to this. I'm all alone and I don't know what I'll do when my money runs out. I'm so upset. I don't know what the future will bring." In contrast, Mrs. Marrow, 83, described her life as very satisfactory, with no anxieties for the future: "I have nowhere else to go, but I'm at peace and I hope to die here," and Mrs. Merrick commented, "I have reached a good age. The things that could make me wonder about things, worry me, are lost. I don't care. Death doesn't frighten me."

Discharge or Death

Neuman (1982, 21), herself a senior citizen, comments on death in relation to the fear of cognitive impairment: "Most of us do not fear death. The far greater concern is to what degree will our capacities decrease and how will that be met when it afflicts us?"

Discharge was something rarely encountered during the Bethany Manor study, as most residents were admitted to the home with a plan—either their families, or their own—to reside there until death. Death, as a developmental and social phenomenon, and funerals are discussed in more depth in Chapter 7. The present purpose is to describe the variations in attitude toward and immediacy of desire for death manifested among certain of the study respondents.

Although a few Bethany Manor residents actively desired death, most were prepared to accept what was given. Miss Amy Pierce was an 85-year-old early Alzheimer's patient whose memory was described as "remarkable" despite her tentative diagnosis. She was very decided in her attitude toward the future: "I want to be in my room, and be in bed. I do not want food. Why don't you let me just die? Because I just want to die. I am suffering."

Eighty-three-year-old Mrs. Owens echoed her thought to a degree: "I'm ready for God to take me now. I'm tired of this life. I don't see why He's waiting so long." Mrs. Merrick did not desire death but reported, "I have no fear of death. I know I'm going to die one of these days soon," and Miss Franklin asserted, "I'm not quite ready to go yet, but if it's the Lord's will, I'll accept."

Several residents also spoke about deaths or potential deaths of friends at the home. Mrs. Cavanaugh spoke about a friend who was dying: "Well, there is one friend of mine who is very near death right now, and it's a little bit of a shock, but we have to look forward to that. We don't pine over death all the time. That's God's will. The older we get, the more we have to deal with that." Mrs. Locke commented: "I feel when your time comes, God takes you. He appoints your time and when you go you have to go."

Religion and Spirituality

To appropriately address the issues of religion and spirituality as they affect the elderly nursing home resident, these terms must be defined both conceptually and operationally. The term "spirituality" can be assigned various meanings and definitions, but essentially it is that dimension of a person concerned with ultimate ends and values. It may or may not be associated with the participation in and practice of an organized religion. In this discussion, spirituality will be considered in a broad context as "relating to the non-material forces or elements within man. Spirituality is that which inspires in one the desire to transcend the realm of the material" (O'Brien 1982, 88). Organized religion or a religious institution is "considered to consist of a set of values, beliefs and norms concerned with the ultimate meaning and purpose which govern man's day-to-day activities and which, within a system of roles, provide for him an organized framework upon which his life may be grounded" (O'Brien 1982, 89-90). Religious belief generally is undergirded conceptually by a strong faith in a deity or God who is ultimately responsible for the existence and continued support of the individual believer. Thus, a person may have either spiritual or religious needs, or both, and sometimes the two overlap.

Sr. Mary Byrne (1985, 30, 32) asserts that for some elderly clients, "spiritual support is their greatest need." She adds that "emotional support alone will not suffice if the person's problem is spiritual in nature." Forbis (1988, 158), in discussing the spiritual problems of the elderly, notes that spiritual needs may revolve around the concepts of love, hope, and finding meaning in "life, sickness and death" and suggest that meeting elders' spiritual needs may well help them become more satisfied with their lives. Several studies of aging and religion or religious participation support the importance of organized religions in the lives of the elderly. Ainlay and Smith (1984, 362) found that "religious activities of individuals do not cease with advancing age." Markides (1983) reported that church attendance and practice of private prayer remained stable and self-rated religiosity increased with aging. Hunsberger (1985, 617) concluded that elderly individuals' retrospective accounts "indicated a tendency to become more religious over time." One reason for this may be the fact, as posited by Boettcher (1985, 29), that as the older individual's physical world begins to shrink, "an inner expansion of awareness and spirit can develop."

Many of the Manor residents discussed their religious beliefs. Miss Teresa Kearney, 90, spoke about the importance of religion and spirituality in her life now and commented, "My belief [in God] means everything to me. It is so lovely to have the chapel in this building. We don't have to go outside in any weather. We have Mass in the chapel. During Lent now we have the Rosary and then we have Benediction. So the day goes along very well. I have an awful lot to be thankful for." Another long-term resident, Mrs. Riddley, observed, "The hereafter is pleasant to think about. I have been brought up a Christian, and my belief is a great support to me now." Mrs. Cavanaugh asserted that her practice of religion was a great comfort now, noting, "I don't like to sound preachy, but the ability to have that chapel and to go to daily Mass after you have worked in the world for 70 years like I did, or 50 years—yes, I worked 52 years and didn't have time, except to rush to Mass on Sunday, then you appreciate that chapel."

In summary, the residents of Bethany Manor Nursing Home represent a multiplicity of educational and occupational backgrounds, a great diversity in age, myriad physical diagnoses, and diverse abilities and deficits, both cognitive and physiological. Domiciled members of the Manor population and those residing on the intermediate care units are generally referred to as residents; those residing on the home's fifth floor, the skilled care unit, are sometimes labeled patients. Residents are admitted to the home because of either their own needs or those of their families, and sometimes both. Ongoing relationships with families provide much support and satisfaction to residents, as do positive relationships with caregivers and with other residents. Quality of life varies both for cognitively aware and cognitively impaired residents. Overall, however, many unique and creative patterns of attitude and behavior are operationalized by Bethany Manor residents in coping with the multiple demands and stresses of nursing home life.

References

Ainlay, S.C., and D.R. Smith. 1984. Aging and religious participation. *Journal of Gerontology* 39(3):357-363.

Bartol, M.A. 1983. Reaching the patient. *Geriatric Nursing* 4(4): 234-236.

Benedict, S.P. 1983. The decision to establish a closed psychiatric unit: some ethical and administrative considerations. *The Journal of Long-Term Care Administration* 11(4):22-26.

Bernier, S.L., and N.R. Small. 1988. Disruptive behaviors. *Journal of Gerontological Nursing* 14(2):8-13.

Boettcher, E. 1985. Linking the aged to support systems. *Journal of Gerontological Nursing* 11(3):27-33.

Burgio, L.D., L.T. Jones, F. Butler, and B.T. Engel. 1988. Behavior problems in an urban nursing home. *Journal of Gerontological Nursing* 14(1):31-34.

Byrne, Sr. M. 1985. A zest for life! *Journal of Gerontological Nursing* 11(4):30-33.

Davis, J., and C. Plage. 1981. A better life for residents. *Contemporary Administrator* 4(8):18-20.

DePaul, A.V. 1983. Aunt Ellen and the nursing home. *Journal of Gerontological Nursing.* 9(1):29–31.

Dychtwald, K. 1983. Older Americans less vital, active than they could be. *Perspective on Aging* 12(3):16-18.

Faunce, F.A. 1969. *The nursing home visitor. A handbook written from the inside.* New York: Abington Press.

Forbis, P.A. 1988. Meeting patients' spiritual needs. *Geriatric Nursing* 9(3):158-159.

Hladik, p. 1982. *Once I have had my tea: A guide to understanding and caring for the memory-impaired elderly.* Syracuse, NY: Hladik.

Horner, J.M. 1982. *That time of year.* Amherst, MA: University of Massachusetts Press.

Hunsberger, B. 1985. Religion, age, life satisfaction, and perceived sources of religiousness: A study of older persons. *Journal of Gerontology* 40(5):615-620.

Huss, M.J., K.C. Buckwalter, and J. Stolley. 1988. Nursing's impact on life satisfaction. *Journal of Gerontological Nursing* 14(5):31-36.

Lincoln, R. 1984. What do nurses know about confusion in the aged? *Journal of Gerontological Nursing* 10(8):26-32.

Lederer, A. 1983. Confusion: Recognition and remedy. Notes on a nursing home. *Geriatric Nursing* 4(4):223-227.

Lucas, M.J., C. Steele, and A. Bognanni. 1986. Recognition of psychiatric symptoms in dementia. *Journal of Gerontological Nursing* 12(1):11-15.

Mackey, A.M. 1983. OBS and nursing care. *Journal of Gerontological Nursing* 9(2):74-85.

Markides, K.S. 1983. Aging, religiosity, and adjustment: A longitudinal analysis. *Journal of Gerontology* 38(5):621-625.

Nagley, S.J. 1986. Predicting and preventing confusion in your patients. *Journal of Gerontological Nursing* 12(3):27-31.

National Association of Social Workers. *To enhance the quality of life—Social work in the nursing home* (pamphlet). Baltimore: National Association of Social Workers.

Neuman, J. 1982. Old age: It's not funny. *Perspective on Aging* 11(6):20-21.

O'Brien, M.E. 1982. The need for spiritual integrity. In *Human needs and the nursing process,* edited by H. Yura and M.B. Walsh, 85-115. Norwalk, CT: Appleton-Century-Crofts.

Pavkov, J.R., and J. Walsh. 1985. Mental impairment of the elderly: Three perspectives. *The Journal of Long-Term Care Administration* 13(4):120-126.

Perspectives on Aging. 1982. Many improvements needed in nursing homes, long-term visitor says. *Perspectives on Aging* 11(4):12.

Rainwater, A., and K. Christiansen. 1984. Wellness/quality of life program in a long-term care facility. *The Journal of Long-Term Care Administration* 12(4):13-18.

Salisbury, S., and P. Goehner. 1983. Separation of the confused or integration with the lucid? *Geriatric Nursing* 4(4):231-236.

Sarton, M. 1973. *As we are now.* New York: Norton.

Schwab, S.M., J. Rader, and J. Doan. 1985. Relieving the anxiety and fear in dementia. *Journal of Gerontological Nursing* 11(5):8-15.

Sinick, D. 1984. Retirement is welcome to some, dreaded by others. *Perspective on Aging* 13(3):9-11.

CHAPTER 3

The Families

We are made by relationships with other people.

Carlo Carretto, *Summoned by Love*

Traditionally within American society, the "family" has meant those significant persons who provide love, care, support, and companionship for (and receive them from) an individual. Generally, the word "family" evokes first the "nuclear" or "conjugal" family with or without offspring; beyond that there is the consanguine or extended family, that association derived through "the blood relationship of a large number of kinspersons" (Horton and Hunt 1968). In contemporary society, however, "family" may also describe a variety of nonkinship or legally sanctioned relationships. For the single person, a partner or housemate or close cadre of friends, church members, or even co-workers may be labeled "family." In cases of elderly single individuals with a lifelong history of such relationships, friends or colleagues who are elderly themselves may become too ill or incapacitated to provide care and support any longer. In such cases, the lawyer or conservator is sometimes the only "family" that can be identified.

Thus, for this study, "family members" were considered those persons identified by the Bethany Manor records as significant others or as legal guardians. As not all family members could practically be included in the study, a subgroup of 32 significant others were contacted and queried in reference to their perceptions and attitudes about their relative's life and needs in long-term care, as well as about the impact on the family of nursing home admission of a relative. (See the Appendix for study tools, including a Family Discussion Guide and a Family Observation Guide.) An attempt was made to identify a broad range of types of family members in order to gather a variety of opinions on the type of support provided by and needed for family members of persons experiencing long-term care. The study "family" group consisted of 12 daughters of residents, 5 sons, 7 nieces, 1 nephew, 3 sisters, 1 brother, 2 wives, and 1 friend (a Catholic religious). The residents of these family members were predominantly female, with 28 women to 4 men. This picture, however, is not atypical of most nursing home resident profiles.

The "Older" Family

It is not only the single elderly person who may find himself or herself lacking an active and viable support system. Because of increasingly long life spans in our society, many adult children of persons needing long-term care are themselves rapidly moving past middle age into the older age category. One is struck by the frequency with which graying hair is encountered in meetings with the children of Bethany Manor residents. Frequently these "older children" have their own burdensome nuclear family responsibilities with which to cope, and the added support or care of an elderly parent can become overwhelming. What often results is a state of severe ambivalence, with resentment and guilt pitted against love and loyalty toward the elderly person in need. The adult offspring's loyalties may be divided. One may find oneself forced to choose between caring for one's parent and responding to the demands of one's own spouse and children. In this situation, Feigen (1983, 4) suggests that, "A nursing home can become the best solution."

Nursing home placement may also become a necessity if problems result when the adult offspring's developing career precludes physical proximity to the parent. Hays (1984, 149) comments that, "Although both psychological support and financial support can be provided by kin living too far distant for frequent face-to-face interaction, the provision of such direct support services . . . personal care by kin, important in maintaining independence and preventing institutionalization, is only possible when children or siblings reside near enough to the older relative for daily or weekly contact to occur."

Another problem noted among middle-aged and older children is difficulty in allowing the parent to withdraw from life—the "no code" phenomenon. One reason for this reluctance may be the deep attachment that develops when two persons not only have experienced the parent-child relationship but also have grown to know each other as adults and friends with a significant history of shared experiences. As one daughter commented on her inability to say the words "no code" at her mother's final illness, "I realized that my grief was not for this fragile, suffering woman. My grief related to that mother who took me to see Santa at Christmas, shared my joys and sorrows of adolescence, let go so gracefully when I married and who traveled across the continent to be present for the birth of my children" (Ivey 1984, 18).

Much has been written about the "multigenerational family." Cohler (1983, 34) asserts that "studies of older persons and their relatives have shown that participation in family life may be less satisfying for family members after middle age." He adds, "Continued family responsibility among older persons may be associated with lower morale and increased psychological distress." This may vary, however, depending on the location or type of multigenerational family, for example, urban, upper-middle-class family versus a rural, lower-socioeconomic status family. Frequently, the latter possesses characteristics that support the older family member as the clan pater- or materfamilias, who maintains a role of wise counsel to the younger family members. In terms of economic support, it is reported that "Non-white families and those residing in rural areas tend to rely on intra-household forms of aid" (Moon 1983, 50).

Adult Children

Brody et al. (1984, 736) surveyed three generations of women ($N = 403$) in order to determine their opinions on the appropriate role responsibility of a daughter toward elderly parents. Their findings supported such behaviors as "adjustment of family schedules and help with the costs of professional health care"; "adjustment of work schedules and sharing of households" were not seen as necessary or appropriate. The authors concluded that "for themselves the women preferred adult children as providers of emotional support and financial management but not of income." They did not want to be a burden on their families. This idea is reflected in the words of a Bethany Manor resident, Mrs. Gallagher, who reported that although her children did invite her to live with them, "They have their own needs financially . . . they have their young ones to think about. It was just not right for me to do that to them."

Family relationships for Bethany Manor residents were also seen to vary with the geographical location of the family in relation to the home. Although mail and telephone calls were always welcomed by residents, family distances of more than 100 to 150 miles from the Manor seemed to significantly weaken the resident's own perception of family care and support. As one long-term Bethany Manor resident observed, "I hear from my family especially at the holidays—they write cards and letters and the children do, too, but it's not quite the same as a visit. I sometimes forget who everybody is and what they look like. I know they care about me but I wish they lived here [in the local area]." These comments are supported by reports in the literature that geographic distance does indeed affect the quality of relationships between elderly parents and their children. Moss et al. (1985, 138), after reviewing research in the area, conclude that "the frequency of interaction tends to decrease with distance," and functional assistance is impeded. They note that although such factors as affectional exchange and value consensus may not be disturbed by distance, needs may be harder to identify when family members are geographically separated.

A Bethany Manor social worker commented on the residents' adult children: "Our residents now are coming in a lot older and a lot sicker. They are in their late 80s or their 90s, so the children are in their 60s and they are dealing with their own impending aging process and the fact that 'When am I going to be at this point?' " The 65-year-old daughter of Mrs. Elsie Decker, an 89-year old third-floor Manor resident suffering from senility and depression, reported, "When she was with me it was like a senior citizen taking care of a senior citizen." In a very similar vein, the son of 94-year-old Mrs. Helen Englejohn described his situation and feelings: "She is occasionally forgetful, requires assistance with bathing and dressing, and uses a wheelchair. There is also a history of falls, some resulting in fractures. Nursing home admission was very difficult because she had been independent for so many years. I feel guilty about putting mother in a nursing home because I should be taking care of her myself, but we're in our sixties and it would be like the old taking care of the old."

The Family Member as Primary Caregiver

Many family members of Bethany Manor residents had assumed the role of primary caregiver before their loved one's admission to the home. Occasionally it was the breakdown of the caregiver's health, rather than that of the resident, that necessitated the nursing home admission. Mrs. Hanna Bernhardt's daughter reported, "Mother broke her hip and we had to put her in the hospital. Then just when she was ready to come home, I had a heart attack and the doctor said we had to put her in a nursing home."

Caregiver burden has recently become a subject of interest in the gerontological literature. Poulshock and Deimling (1984, 230) suggest "a multidimensional perspective in which burden is viewed as a mediating force between the elder's impairments and the impact that caregiving has on the lives of caregivers and their families." Findings from their study of 614 families, in which impaired elderly persons received care assistance from relatives in the home, revealed that caregivers do indeed perceive a burden and that these feelings are related both to the impairment (e.g. in activities of daily living, cognitive incapacity, or disruptive or antisocial behavior) and to objective changes in conditions within the family.

Variables such as age, sex, and kin relationship of the primary caregiver may also influence the degree and type of caregiver burden. Among the reasons for nursing home admission cited in the literature, and among those focal in the Bethany Manor study as well, caregiver age was significant. Frequently, the primary caregiver's advancing age was associated with first, an extended length of time over which the burden of care had been borne, leading to a kind of burnout phenomenon for the caregiver, and second, a multiplicity of physical problems experienced by the caregiver related to the stress of his or her role over time. In a gender-controlled study of 131 adult caregivers to an elderly parent, Horowitz (1985, 612) found that, "sons tend to become caregivers only in the absence of available female siblings; are more likely to rely on the support of their spouses; provide less overall assistance to their parents, especially 'hands-on' services; and tend to have less stressful caregiving experiences independent of their involvement." The study findings indicated that, overall, the caregiving role was assigned primarily to daughters or daughters-in-law, who felt the much greater burden and who were ultimately at greater risk of stress reactions.

Such stress was reported by a Bethany Manor niece, the former primary caregiver of an 89-year-old aunt: "She was very negative toward me. If I'd say it was white, she'd say it was black. She was hard of hearing—it just got to me. Everything I would do was wrong. She would accuse me of stealing. I had a family of my own. We had her about 13 years. She would pick on one family member—the kids would back away. Nobody came in her room.

She was getting confused. We do worry about her. I go over, wash her hair, I cut her nails. My husband and I try to go. There are a lot of times we can't go. There was a sense of relief when we put her in."

Kin relationship of the primary caregiver was generally observed to be related to the degree of commitment and support provided for an elderly Bethany Manor resident, with children and spouses appearing more centrally involved, and siblings, nieces, and nephews more peripherally associated with the resident's life. There was, however, an occasional exception to this pattern; for example, Miss Dolan was an 87-year-old former elementary school teacher whose married niece Ellen had for some years provided love and care in her home and became a faithful and constant visitor after Miss Dolan's serious physical decline necessitated nursing home care.

The Bethany Manor findings are supported by the work of Kivett (1985, 228), who examined the relationship between levels of kin relationship and help received among old rural adults. In a study of 321 older adults, it was learned that kin more distant than the child or child-in-law provided little functional assistance in the older adult's helping network. The findings of the study, in part supported "the kin-selection theory in that helping behaviors were usually based upon degree of consanguinity (and associated marriage tie) and extend of dependency of older adults as measured by their health status or age."

Life satisfaction of primary caregivers has been studied in a variety of settings, particularly that of the multigenerational household. In one such effort, the three factors determined to be of influence included (1) primary caregiver characteristics such as marital status, socioeconomic status, race, and consanguinity; (2) elderly relative dependency characteristics such as age, impairment, activity level, and number of roles; and (3) ecological characteristics associated with inconveniences in living arrangements (Mindel and Wright 1982, 489). As predicted, Mindel and Wright's study determined that "the more dependent elderly, as measured by age, impairment, activity and role behavior, produced lower satisfaction" [in the caregiver]; that "greater inconvenience in daily living produced lower satisfaction" [in the caregiver]; and finally, that "certain characteristics of the primary caregiver that might be expected to provide rewards (such as race and martial status) for the most part, did so" (490).

A number of Bethany Manor family members described their experience of caregiver burden prior to their relative's admission to the home. Mrs.

Marie Buell spoke of her 72-year-old mother's living with the family: "She lived with us for three years after having lived alone for many years. She was very set in her ways and hard to get along with. She is a hypo-chondriac who thinks everything is wrong with her. It was just too much to handle day-in and day-out." The niece of 87-year-old Mrs. Bertha Fitzpatrick described her burden: "I have an elderly mother at home who also requires supervision. I am the only relative who can care for them both, and I just couldn't manage them both. The load was too heavy." Finally, the sister of a confused 83-year-old resident reported, "I couldn't cope with her at home. She would wander out and get lost. I'm the main support of the family. I'm 76 years old and it got harder over time. All the stresses just pile up."

In summary, one almost universal finding relative to perceptions of caregiver burden was the significance of the relationship of burden to performance of personal care tasks; (the more personal care tasks required, the greater the perception of burden); this was identified by, among others, Hooyman et al. (1985, 144). Following their research with 80 family member caregivers of elderly persons, Hooyman et al. suggested that a reason for their finding of a strong association between perception of caregiver burden and performance of personal care tasks may be related in part to the family's expectations about the appropriate family-caregiver role: "Assisting an older relative with intimate bodily tasks may violate family norms about appropriate familial roles and interactions and may create feelings of role reversal."

Role Reversal

Role reversal is not an infrequent or unexpected phenomenon in cases of chronic or serious illness. In situations where personal and/or family responsibilities and decision-making were managed in the past primarily by a now-debilitated individual, such activity may be thrust upon a less well prepared family member, resulting in significant stress for that individual. Role reversal is particularly difficult when it involves parent and child, as it may appear to present a serious violation of learned norms of behavior on the part of both. Role reversal was reported to be a unique element of caregiver burden for certain of the Bethany Manor families. One daughter of a relatively new resident described it this way: "It's been a definite role reversal between us. I used to go to her for guidelines. Now I have to make the decisions." Another daughter also described the kind of modified role reversal that she accepted in order to maintain her mother's dignity: "I have to take charge of some things like her money because of her illness, but she is German and she is still very much in charge. I am still her daughter. I can't treat her like a child because she won't take it."

Burnout: The Breaking Point

Frequently the critical incident leading to a nursing home resident's admission was the primary caregiver reaching a point of "burnout" or general inability to carry on with the day-to-day demands of long-term geriatric care in the home. This burnout may be of an emotional or psychological nature as well as being related to physical fatigue. Role reversal may itself be exhausting for a family member, especially a son or daughter who is forced to observe a loved and respected parent's progressive deterioration into a childlike state of dependency. Often the family caregiver must walk a very fine line between relegating an elderly parent to a primarily dependent role with minimal autonomy, and allowing the elder to try and maintain control over his or her life, with the risk of failure and even, perhaps, disaster, always looming on the horizon.

As one daughter noted of her still quite active 80-year-old mother: "I kept wondering when was the time to tell her that she couldn't go out alone any more. I knew she wasn't ready to hear it, but every time she did I was afraid we were risking a broken hip. Then one day it happened!" This daughter commented that one of the greatest stressors in her role as primary caregiver was worry—worry when she left the house, worry when she went to sleep, and worry about her mother's own perception of her deteriorating mental and physical health. The daughter reported that the direct physical care needs were not really burdensome at all, but the "mental needs" were "horrendous."

The wife of a Manor resident described her "breaking point" in her husband's battle with Alzheimer's disease: "He was in the hospital for three months, then I brought him home for nine months, but one night I had to get up 19 times to change him. My husband was a large man. I am small [less than five feet]; he's six feet, heavy. He became incontinent and there was no way I could reason with him; I fell and broke two ribs." A daughter spoke of her stresses related to her mother's increasing confusion: "For about a year she was getting really confused. Even if she just went down for the mail, she would get lost. She loved to sew but she began just cutting up her clothes. It did cause some stress on the family, but the stress was on me in particular. I had to carry the burden. They could get upset sometimes, but I was the one who would break. I had to get away to retain my sanity. I had to get away for a weekend every fifth week. I could handle it for four weeks but at that fifth week, I would just start crying." She added a comment about her mother's nursing home admission: "It's hard, but it's a relief, too. It's like a cross has been lifted. The heaviness at home is relieved. It's hard to see her in the home, though."

The Family's Role in the Admission Decision

As noted in Chapter 2, social history forms are filled out by a family member (generally) or by a social worker for all Bethany Manor residents before admission. From an examination of social history data describing family problems that had served as catalysts for the decision in favor of nursing home admission, five family caregiver-related themes emerged: (1) nuclear family needs of the primary caregiver, (2) illness or physical limitation of the primary caregiver, (3) increasing age of the primary caregiver, (4) work needs of the primary caregiver, and (5) travel needs of the primary caregiver. Examples of these themes follow.

Nuclear Family Needs

Mrs. Pearl Fisher, 95 years, diagnosis of hypertension, confusion, fractured hip: "her daughter can no longer care for her at home as she is also caring for a 9-year-old daughter who has brain damage and needs constant watching"; Mrs. Gwen Jacobs, 81 years, arteriosclerosis: "She has been living with her daughter whose own six children now demand their mother's time and attention."

Illness and Physical Limitations

Mrs. Claudia Morgan, 80 years, diagnosis of breast cancer, confusion: "She will soon be needing 24-hour care and we [daughter and son-in-law] do not have the physical strength to do it"; Mrs. Sylvia Bennet, 94 years, diagnosis of fractured hip, senile dementia: "I am the only relative available and illness has made me unable to continue the strain of caring for an elderly senile mother."

Increasing Age

Mr. Marcus Budd, 85 years, diagnosis of Parkinson's disease, hip fracture: "His 82-year-old sister can no longer care for him"; Mrs. Mae Lambert, 88 years, diagnosis of arteriosclerotic heart disease: "I [daughter] am going to be 63 years old soon. I do not know how much longer I can keep taking care of my mother. She will be needing more care as she gets older and as I get older."

Work Needs

Mrs. Millie McCray, 91 years, diagnosis of arteriosclerotic cardiovascular disease, peptic ulcer: "Everyone in the family works and she is alone in the house with no companionship. If she would collapse again (as she did recently only we were home), there might not be anyone to help her"; Mrs. Mary Carlucci, 83 years, diagnosis of organic brain syndrome: "Her daughter needs to work full time and is no longer able to care for her."

Travel Needs

Mrs. Cornelia Brunner, 75 years, diagnosis of Parkinson's disease: "We feel she shouldn't be by herself. We [sons and daughters] travel a significant amount of time and it puts our minds at rest to know that she would be in good hands"; Mrs. Rita Shultis, 81 years, diagnosis of Alzheimer's syndrome, peptic ulcer: "She needs 24-hour supervision. Her roommate travels a great deal and cannot leave her alone."

Residents' responses to their families' decision about their admission to the Manor varied; overall, however, residents seemed happier and better adjusted to the home if the decision was their own, or if they participated to some degree. Unfortunately, this was not always possible, as in the case of Miss Ruth Edison. Her situation was described by her niece:

"She had been going downhill for about three to four years but what really started her on the road to decline: I had invited her for lunch to see a Christmas display. She had on floppy old galoshes and she was having some trouble walking. I took her on the subway. I shouldn't have left her, but I did—she wanted to get some cards. I don't know what happened, but she did fall and a nice Navy captain helped her up. I couldn't find her that evening; she still had not arrived home. We went to the police and they called the hospitals. Finally, we reached her at home about 10 p.m. She was OK but indignant that we had called the police.

"After that she quit going to church every morning and began to use it as an excuse not to do lots of things. We tried to get her out, but she continued to stay in and the apartment was a mess; we saw that she was also letting her clothing go. She couldn't get to the tub and she wasn't eating properly. She couldn't coordinate her clothes and dressing. She fell beside the bed but, stubborn as a mule, didn't want to get out of her apartment. She began to talk in nonsequences.

"I began taking her to her doctor and he said she shouldn't be living in the apartment alone. It became a heavy burden on the family because we had to do all her shopping, and everything, and I didn't have time to go running over there. The doctor said we should make application to the home. She wouldn't consent but then she began to get very confused. She burned her pots and pans. Just before Christmas she got worse. She began to lose track of time—didn't know what day it was. She dressed up at night, went to the wrong apartment. The doctor came and said she was dehydrated and had heart problems, so we admitted her."

Guilt

Guilt is a central concern verbalized by family members when discussing even the possibility of institutionalizing an elderly family member. Although the large extended family is no longer considered viable for many, there remains in many individuals a strong sense of family responsibility or the need to care for and support all family members, especially those who are elderly. Admittedly the contemporary nursing home has had, and in many instances still does have, a very bad reputation. It is sometimes considered as a socially acceptable "dumping ground" for aging parents who begin to drain family resources both physically and financially. Thus, it is not unusual to find defensiveness as a first characteristic of a family member's comments about institutionalization of a relative.

A study report of familial guilt feelings surrounding nursing home care, entitled "We Had No Choice," asserts that "transfer of an older adult to a nursing home frequently engenders feelings of anxiety and guilt among the individual's family members" (Johnson and Werner 1982, 641). The authors add, however, that in nursing home placement "the more people who are involved in the decision...the less prevalent the guilt feelings," and, "if the patient him/herself agrees that it is the correct decision," the family experiences less guilt. In discussing the elderly psychiatric patient, Stotsky (1970, 228) suggests that guilt over institutionalization may result in the family's visiting the patient frequently at first but then less and less, especially if the resident voices complaints that make the family member feel "remiss in both attention and concern." Overall, however, it is pointed out that "contrary to popular opinion, families continue to support their institutionalized members" for whom they may have for many years been providing care in the community (Hirst and Metcalf 1986, 24).

Bethany Manor families often expressed the concept of guilt in describing their feelings about a resident's admission to the home. Two Manor social workers reported that family members frequently either directly spoke about or in some way gave evidence of guilt feelings before or during the admission process. One commented on the admission plan: "The family, it's almost like they are going through the same processes that they would if somebody died because, in a sense, they're dealing with their own guilt, a tremendous amount of guilt. Even though they know it's best for everybody concerned, they still always wonder whether it's the right thing. They were always brought up that your parents raised you and then you turn around and help them, and it's really difficult for them."

Another social worker gave her perception of why guilt became a family problem after a nursing home admission: "Some have a real hard time dealing with it. There's a lot of guilt over putting mom or dad or whoever in a nursing home. Families can keep going while they are taking care of somebody at home, and then after they put them in the nursing home and get rid of the physical burden, the family member might then become ill or depressed, then they [the family] have time to sit back and think about everything and then the guilt comes."

One of the home's head nurses commented on families and guilt feelings: "If they can see that their family is well cared for—and you know that doesn't always happen—that's why there is a lot of guilt that lingers. If they really saw the quality of care that they thought they were paying for, entitled to, or would want their parent to have, I think they would feel less guilty."

Family members of Bethany Manor residents shared their feelings about guilt. The daughter of a 77-year-old confused resident admitted, "I feel wretched because I told my mother a white lie that she was going back into the hospital to get better instead of going to the nursing home. I feel guilty because when I was young we didn't believe in putting old folks in nursing homes. The hardest thing about having her in a home is knowing she's older and there is not much time left." Another daughter reported, "My mother lived with me for 26 years. Sometimes she's happy, sometimes she's unhappy [in the nursing home]. I feel guilty from this. It was like having a child. I miss her." A third daughter spoke about visiting and guilt: "It's difficult for families to have a member in a nursing home. My oldest daughter can't handle it. She went home and cried and cried. I try to get there [the nursing home] every other weekend. I can go only on Sundays. Every time it gets worse, especially the last couple of months. I get the impression that she is not happy so I try to put it off, but I feel guilty if I don't go."

Impact of Admission on the Family

The impact of a loved one's nursing home admission on the family varies with such factors as whether the elderly person was a central figure in the family's interactional pattern (this often relates to whether the individual was cognitively alert or not); whether and for how long the older family member had been living with the nuclear family group; the family's cultural and religious beliefs about care of the elderly in general and, especially, how the potential resident feels about admission to a nursing home—specifically, whose choice the admission was. At Bethany Manor, admissions observed by the researchers clearly demonstrated the importance of this last point. In one case, Mrs. McGuire, a charming, gracious 78-year-old who came to the home surrounded by her family, had indeed first initiated the decision for admission to the Manor. She was beginning to have difficulty ambulating outdoors (she always worried about getting to Mass), her hearing was deteriorating, and she was beginning to feel that she might become a burden on the family she loved. Mrs. McGuire had visited friends at Bethany Manor, liked the Catholic character of the home, and decided it was, as she put it, the place to spend her last days. Also, since it was local, her family could visit frequently.

Mrs. McGuire's daughter, a social worker, seemed to have some hesitation on the day of admission but stated that she accepted her mother's decision. She commented that Mrs. McGuire was very pleasant and uncomplaining and, she felt, would get along well with others in the home. Although Mrs. McGuire's family seemed somewhat apprehensive when it came time to leave, they stated that they were relatively comfortable with the admission to the home as they knew Bethany Manor had a good reputation and they planned to visit often. Mrs. McGuire's family did not appear to feel nor did they verbalize any feelings of guilt.

Quite a different scenario, however, presented itself on the admission of Miss Lancaster. Miss Annie Lancaster was brought—indeed sadly almost pushed—into the home's front entrance by her very fragile appearing and tearful sister Mrs. Holley. Miss Lancaster is an 83-year-old single former secretary who is moderately cognitively impaired. Although she does sometimes respond appropriately to time, place, and person, she also at times believes that she is in another city and needs to go to her job.

Miss Lancaster was silent and obviously angry during the admission process. When asked how she felt, she said her sister was forcing her to come to Bethany Manor and that all she wanted was to go home. She refused to look at or speak to Mrs. Holley, who dissolved in tears and said she didn't know what to do. Mrs. Holley explained that Miss Lancaster could not live alone or with her because of her "wandering" and intermittent confusion, and that she had been at another, less structured home, which refused to keep her for the same reasons she could not be kept at home. At Bethany Manor, Miss Lancaster could be admitted to the third floor with its special provisions for cognitively impaired residents. Mrs. Holley tearfully commented that she felt "bad" about having to institutionalize her sister, was not sleeping well, and was constantly worried. She felt that the nursing home admission was negatively affecting her life but she didn't know what else to do.

In discussing the family impact of long-term care, Del Sordo (1982) comments that it sometimes appears that "the patient is doing well but the family just is not going to make it." Trying to assess the primary cause of family problems, Del Sordo suggests that key factors are "all based upon the family feelings of guilt in placing a relative in a nursing home." Reasons for this guilt, according to Del Sordo, include the general view of nursing homes as dumping grounds, media accounts of nursing home atrocities, perceived responsibility to care for a person who had cared for others, the taking away of control over decisions from an elder, and fear of not being able to visit regularly.

The myth that the nursing home is a "dumping ground where middle-aged children can place their relatives" and its impact upon families are addressed by Sands and Bjorklund (1982, 29). In reviewing research in the area, the authors conclude that "families do support their elderly constituents, and this support continues in spite of the fact that it has ceased to be enjoyable—that is, after confusion and disorientation begin to be apparent" (Sands and Bjorklund 1982, 33). Suggestions for support of these families include provision of services such as classes on aging, counseling, and advice on visiting; dissemination of public information about the supportive roles that family members may play in nursing homes; and provision of therapy programs such as reality orientation, music therapy, and behavior modification to alleviate symptoms of dementia (Sands and Bjorklund 1982, 33-34).

Bethany Manor family members spoke of the impact of a loved one's nursing home admission on their lives. Mrs. Sarah St. Dennis described her feelings about her husband, an Alzheimer's patient, becoming a Manor resident: "He has been in two homes. I was so unhappy with the situation. I go every other day and it's very difficult. I'm under such stress that I left my keys in the car and left the motor going. It is so hard to go and see him and go home. There's a terrible desire for him to communicate. I see it in his eyes. People don't understand Alzheimer's disease. I can tell he's just lying there and wants to say something. I see his lips move. It's harder for the family than for the patient."

The daughter of 83-year-old Mrs. Guzzetta reported that she visited every other day: "While I am here, I do the things for her that they would ordinarily do, like make her bed and straighten her clothes. Then I think on the days I am not here they will do it. The hardest part for me is to have to leave her. She knows I'll be home, but I wonder when I'm home if she is going to be all right, if somebody is going to take good care of her. It's not ever off my mind."

It should be emphasized that frequently the anxieties, cares, or feelings of guilt rest notably on the shoulders of the former primary caregiver who is usually a woman. The report of the Secretary's Task Force on Alzheimer's Disease (Department of Health and Human Services 1984, 49) asserts that, while most patients are cared for initially by relatives in the community, "often the bulk of the burden falls on women." Their report adds however, that "radical shifts in sex roles in general and the rapidly increasing labor force participation of young and middle-age women are likely to influence this pattern in the future." In the Bethany Manor study, although there were exceptions, in the main, woman presently provided and had previously provided the most significant degree of support for the elderly resident.

Family Involvement With the Nursing Home

Because many Bethany Manor residents and their families were from communities in the immediate geographical region, a number of family members did become involved in the home's activities. Families also tended to establish personal relationships with staff members, especially the charge nurses, on the units where their resident was placed. As one of the Manor charge nurses said of the family members, "They like to get to know you so that then they call up and ask how their resident is doing and know who they're talking to. It's real important to them, and some, they know when you have your days off and so forth or if you're sick they miss you." Families were also observed to know many of the Bethany Manor aides by name and could comment on who gave the best care and who was "lazy." Elliott (1985, 119) advises family members that the "nurses aides will be the ones responsible for dressing, bathing and feeding," and she notes that family members often report that keeping a high profile seems to improve the care.

During the course of the Bethany Manor study, the home initiated, under the guidance of a part-time patient care nurse clinician, the opening of unit patient care conferences to interested family members. That is, when a particular patient was scheduled for assessment and discussion by the caregivers, the family member or members were invited to attend and ask questions or supply information as desired. Because these conferences were usually held on weekday mornings, attendance was difficult for working family members; however, those who did attend reported that the experience was very beneficial. Hearing and participating in the staff discussions supported their conviction that their relative was receiving appropriate care and attention. (Patient care conferences are discussed in more depth in Chapter 5.)

Gross (1985) admits that involving the family in long-term care may be a risky business because of possible threats to administrative control, unrealistic family expectations, and strong empathetic reactions by staff. He suggests that a dilemma arises as to whether the institution or the family is the primary caregiver and advises, as a resolution, the recognition that "both the institution and the family have an essential role to play in providing care." This appeared to be well recognized by the Bethany Manor administration and was reflected in the initiation of a monthly "Family

Circle" organized by the home's Social Service Department. The purpose of the Family Circle, which generally began with a lecture and discussion on a topic pertinent to the needs of the elderly, was to bring together families and staff to discuss patient problems and needs. Ceronsky (1983, 51) found in working with long-term care patients that family-staff interaction indeed opened the lines of communication and resolved problems.

Among the topics at the Bethany Manor Family Circle lectures were "Medicare/Medicaid Reimbursement for the Elderly," "Coping with Alzheimer's Disease," "Visiting," and "The Teaching Nursing Home Project." Following the formal lecture and discussion, a social hour was held during which family members could mingle and talk with staff and with each other about resident problems. Family Circle attendance varied depending on the topic and/or the time of year. The sessions were generally held on Sunday afternoons or evenings for the convenience of working family members.

Manor residents' family members shared their observations about the caregiving staff quite freely. The wife of a 93-year-old severely debilitated resident reported that, although she visited the home every other day in good weather, the wintertime was difficult for her: "I call in the winter and talk to the head nurses; they do tell me everything. The aides are pretty nice to me. I have a neighbor who calls all the time to fuss but you get a lot more with honey than with vinegar." She added, "I bend over backwards to be nice to them [the staff]. I give them little things to try. I just want them to take good care of my husband." A daughter repeated her advice to some of the aides: "I have said to one or two of them who are very sharp with some of the patients, 'Just be wary of the fact that you might yourself be one day disabled and need somebody to take care of you.' You see, most of the people who take care of these people are not nurses. You get some who are really dedicated, but to others it's just a job—it's not a nice job."

Another daughter of a confused resident commented that in her opinion the label "nursing home" was a euphemism: "I think the transition for the resident is very difficult because it's an entirely different way of living." She reported that she visited the home to intercede with the staff because her mother was withdrawn and did not ask for things: "She doesn't speak up for herself." The daughter also observed that, although her mother was generally well cared for, sometimes she was addressed as a child. She noted, "Residents should not be treated as children. You can show admiration and respect without using the word, 'honey.' "

Visiting

Interestingly, although it seemed a common and generally understood topic to the researchers, "visiting" in the nursing home was discovered to be a subject that was fairly frequently explored through either lecture, discussion, or written commentary. One of the Bethany Manor social workers observed that family members often did not "know how" to visit an elderly relative in the home. She explained that, especially if the resident was cognitively impaired, the family may be left feeling totally helpless about what to say or do in the resident's presence. Thus, family members sometimes traveled fairly long distances only to end up terminating a visit after a brief period because of their discomfort with the reaction, or more often lack of reaction, of their loved one.

Kayser-Jones (1981, 35), in her comparative study of two nursing homes, found that in the United States home (Pacific Manor), "visitors rushed in, stayed briefly and were gone." She also observed that "children were never among the visitors." One of the Manor's social workers commented that she liked to bring her little daughter to visit her grandmother, but feared that some Manor relatives felt uncomfortable in having their children see the confused or infirm elderly whom they might encounter.

A helpful brochure published by the American Health Care Association (undated) presents some tips on visiting residents of a nursing home: (1) when to visit—it is suggested that it might be useful to phone the resident to set a time or schedule the next visit during a prior meeting (a resident may feel better or have more energy at a particular time of day); (2) who should visit—anyone supportive to the resident; (3) preparing for the visit—plan ahead, according to the physical and mental status of the resident, what you will talk about and do; (4) the visit—request entrance, greet the resident, and touch appropriately.

Bethany Manor one month devoted approximately three-fourths of a page in one issue of its newsletter to "Visitors Tips," which are reprinted here with the nursing home's permission:

VISITOR TIPS

What does one do on a visit to a friend or relative in a nursing home? People sometimes run out of ideas, so we compiled a list of suggestions for our readers. Anyone with a little imagination should be able to take this list and turn his or her visits into stimulating and enjoyable occasions.

1. Discuss today's newspaper stories.

2. Play a musical instrument.

3. Admire a hairdo, dress, shirt or sweater.

4. Try simple chair exercises together.

5. Bring in small pets.

6. Take the resident out for a walk or a wheelchair ride up and down the halls or outside on the porch.

7. Make transparencies to hang in or on a window.

8. Share your vacation pictures; bring in family photo albums.

9. Reminisce about the "good old days."

10. Share a hobby, teach or ask to learn a craft.

11. Fix resident's hair, do grooming, makeup and manicuring.

12. Play a record or tape.

13. Attend a recreation activity together.

14. Ask these questions: What is the best present you ever received? What is the best place you ever lived? Do you remember the first time you fell in love? What was your first job? What is your favorite vacation? What were your parents like?

15. With a disoriented resident try to stimulate the senses with an "awareness bag" full of smells to identify (perfume, onion, cinnamon, baby powder), textures (silk, sandpaper, wool, a feather), sights (photographs, magazines), sounds (taped music of animal noises, classical music, oldies), and tastes (hard candies, favorite snack).

The wife of an 83-year-old, severely debilitated Alzheimer's patient described her ambivalence about visiting: "If he dies, I hope that really I'm with him. I don't want him to die alone. But it's so hard when I go—when I'm there and when I come home. If I go around noon, it breaks up the whole day. It's taken over my life. If I don't go, I feel so guilty, but you know, I just don't want to go over there any more. Now isn't that terrible, to go for a visit of two to four hours and just sit there? I'm 15 miles away and my car is wearing out fast. I'm going to be 67 soon and I worry about myself too."

Coping with Death

Aspects of death in the nursing home are also discussed in Chapters 2, 5, and 7. In these discussions, death in a long-term care facility, from the perspective of both the resident and the staff member, often seems to become routine. Tisdale, in her contemporary portrait of a nursing home (1987, 138) reported that death at the home became "so much a part of the daily routine" that one staff member commented that she took no note of one long-term patient's passing because "she died on my day off." Although most Bethany Manor caregivers appeared more affected by residents' death than is expressed in that comment, they did admit that death was an expected part of care in a nursing home. As one aide put it, "The folks here know it's their time to go, and if they accept it, why can't we?"

However, the death of a resident, even though expected, was not so easily or calmly accepted by members of the family. Sometimes there was ambivalence. As the daughter of a long-time resident, 90-year-old Mrs. Courtney, commented, "I know it's a blessing and I thank God for taking her easily but there's still an emptiness that she's gone. I got used to worrying and now there's a space there that has to be filled with something else. She was my mother and somehow I just knew she was here if I needed her." Another daughter, in thinking about her mother's future death, said, "My only real worry, the thought that I have most—I hope she goes before I do." She added that although she did not want to lose her mother, she had real fears about her outliving her immediate family because no other relatives lived in the area.

Staff members at Bethany Manor reported that, surprisingly, family members were sometimes uncomfortable with requests for a DNR (do not resuscitate) order or with deciding not to use extraordinary means to prolong life. It was observed that this might be somehow associated with unrealistic feelings of guilt for having placed a resident in the home or be related to religious or morale concerns about "pulling the plug." Some family members, however, looked forward to the death of a loved one as a "gift from God." Mrs. Hartnett spoke about the future death of her 70-year-old husband who was suffering from both Parkinson's and Alzheimer's diseases. She mused, "I wonder how I'm going to feel if I'm still living when he dies. Will I feel grief? My friend [whose husband died of Alzheimer's at the home] said, 'You've already grieved; you'll feel relief.' I don't know. It's an awful load. You know you've done this [institutionalization] to somebody who's taken care of you all your life. My son can't go [to visit]. He says, 'My father died.' I don't feel like that's my husband. That's why I feel guilt. He won't even look at me anymore. My husband was a very handsome man and athletic and now he weights 138 pounds. I feel guilty but I don't want to see him. It will be a blessing when he goes."

Family Support

Overall, family members of Bethany Manor residents generally gave much, worried a great deal, and, to a degree, felt a sense of relief, both for themselves and for their loved ones, at the time of the resident's death. From family observation and discussion data collected during the Manor study, four themes related to family support emerged. These might be labeled in terms of family types: the "involved" family, the "marginal" family, the "disenchanted" family, and the "distanced" family.

The "Involved" Family

"Involved" families were available and accessible to their residents and to nursing home staff. They visited or called the home frequently, assumed responsibility for any of their resident's material needs not covered by the home, and generally provided continued psychosocial (and sometimes spiritual) support to their loved one at Bethany Manor.

The "Marginal" Family

"Marginal" family members (who were often not members of the resident's nuclear family) generally tried to provide a moderate degree of psychosocial support for their resident, visiting periodically to check on needs and caregiving, partially assisting with material needs if their resources allowed, and providing caring and emotional support to the degree possible without major interference in their own family or career activities.

The "Disenchanted" Family

"Disenchanted" family members (either nuclear or nonnuclear) are those who have been worn down, sometimes over a period of years, by an elder's physical and/or psychosocial needs, either at home or in the nursing home. Often these family members have given extensively of their financial and emotional resources and are disheartened at the downward spiral in their loved one's physical and cognitive abilities. Disenchanted family members provided only minimal or socially acceptable support to their resident, visiting briefly on major holidays or anniversaries and seriously limiting their emotional investment in the resident's day-to-day life at the home.

The "Distanced" Family

The fourth type, the "distanced" family (which may also consist of members and nonmembers of the resident's nuclear family) consisted of significant others who provided virtually no ongoing support, either material or psychosocial, to their nursing home residents. In some cases these families were geographically distant; in others the distancing was of an emotional nature. In either case, their interaction with residents and staff was virtually nonexistent.

Finally, for some Manor residents the only "family" member formally identified was a conservator or lawyer designated as legal guardian. For these individuals the home staff and other residents became family. It was they who cared for and supported the resident, and it was they who attended funerals and grieved their loss at the time of death. In summary, the "family" provided by the Bethany Manor environment might be said to reflect the comment of Howard (1978, 26), who noted, echoing Robert Frost, that families provide a place where "when you go there, they have to let you in, and where at the very least you can waken without surprise."

References

American Health Care Association. *Here's help! Tips on visiting for friends and relatives* (pamphlet). Washington, DC: American Health Care Association.

Brody, E.M., P.T. Johnsen, and M.C. Fulcomer. 1984. What should adult children do for elderly parents? Opinions and preferences of three generations of women. *Journal of Gerontology* 39(6): 736-746.

Ceronsky, C. 1983. Family/staff conferences open communication, resolve problems. *Hospital Progress* 64(8):51-52.

Cohler, B.J. 1983. Autonomy and interdependence in the family of adulthood: A psychological perspective. *The Gerontologist* 23: 33-39.

Del Sordo, K.A. 1982. Group family counseling: An aid to long-term care. *The Journal of Long-Term Care Administration* 10(1):37-42.

Department of Health and Human Services. 1984. *Alzheimer's Disease. Report of the Secretary's Task Force on Alzheimer's Disease.* Washington, DC: Government Printing Office.

Elliott, L. 1985. What about Mom and Dad? *The Washingtonian* (March): 104-128.

Feigen, J. 1983. Divided loyalties. *Geriatric Nursing* (September/ October):4-5.

Gross, J. 1985, update: Family involvement in long-term care. *The Journal of Long-Term Care Administration* 13(2):41-43

Hays, J.A. 1984. Aging and family resources: Availability and proximity of kin. *The Gerontologist* 24:149-153.

Hirst, S.P., and B.J. Metcalf. 1986. Learning needs of caregivers. *Journal of Gerontological Nursing* 12(4):24-28.

Hooyman, N., J. Bonyea, and R. Montgomery. 1985. The impact of in-home services termination on family caregivers. *The Gerontologist* 25:141-145.

Horowitz, A. 1985. Sons and daughters as caregivers to older parents: Differences in role performance and consequences. *The Gerontologist* 25:6.

Horton, P.G., and C.L. Hunt. 1968. *Sociology.* New York: McGraw-Hill, 215.

Howard, J. 1978. *Families.* New York: Simon & Schuster.

Ivey, J.M. 1984. "No code—why won't middle-aged children consent? *Journal of Gerontological Nursing* 10(5):17-20.

Johnson, M.A., and C. Werner. 1982. "We had no choice." A study in familial guilt feelings surrounding nursing home care. *Journal of Gerontological Nursing* 8(11):641-654.

Kayser-Jones, J.S. 1981. *Old, alone, and neglected.* Berkeley, CA: University of California Press.

Kivett, V.R. 1985. Consanguinity and kin level: Their relative importance to the helping network of older adults. *Journal of Gerontology* 40(2):228-234.

Mindel, C. H., and R. Wright. 1982. Satisfaction in multigenerational households. *Journal of Gerontology* 37(4):483-489.

Moon, M. 1983. The role of the family in the economic well being of the elderly. *The Gerontologist* 23(1):45-50.

Moss, M., S. Moss and E. Moles. 1985. The quality of relationships between elderly parents and their out-of-town children. *The Gerontologist* 25(2):134-140.

Poulshock, S. W., and G.T. Deimling. 1984. Families caring for elders in residence: Issues in the measurement of burden. *Journal of Gerontology* 39(2):230-239.

Sands, D. and L. Bjorklund. 1982. Fighting a myth: Families in need of support. *The Journal of Long-Term Care Administration* 10(1):29-35.

Stotsky, B.A. 1970. *The nursing home and the aged psychiatric patient.* New York: Meredith.

Tisdale, S. 1987. *Harvest Moon, portrait of a nursing home.* New York: Henry Holt and Co.

CHAPTER 4

Early Adaptation
to Nursing Home Life

Do not go gentle into that good night; Rage, rage against the
dying of the light.

Dylan Thomas

For some, facing the continuance of life and of the aging process in an
institutional setting such as a nursing home presents a notable test of faith,
courage and forbearance. As the Bethany Manor social history data in
Chapter 2 demonstrate, elderly individuals come to a nursing home for a
variety of reasons, physical, social, and familial. In a study of Canadian
elderly, Beland (1984, 184) found that elderly persons' decisions to leave
their homes were significantly associated with the variables of social
isolation (living alone), frequent interaction with professional health caregivers (because of sickness), and housing and economic problems. General "physical and mental impairments and functional capacities" were not
related to "wishes to leave home." However, Christ, Visscher, and Bates
(1988, 236), in a study examining the factors influencing admission to adult
congregate living facilities, found that "ability to function" was indeed a
major factor in deciding to give up one's home. The functional variables
assessed included such concepts as communication, level of consciousness,
motor skills, coordination, gait, sensory perception, and muscle strength.
The authors added that "finances, social support, environmental fears,
loneliness and inability to meet transportation needs" were also frequently
cited reasons for wishes to move to congregate living facilities. Whatever

the reason, however, once the decision to leave home and abandon one's former life-style has been made, the potential nursing home resident is faced with a new anxiety, that of learning to cope with and adapt to the congregate living experience operant in institutional long-term care. This new life-style experience begins with the home's established admission process.

The Admission Experience

The admission experience at Bethany Manor begins with the completion of the preadmission assessment or social history, as described in Chapter 2. In describing the admission process at their facility, Vivens and Woolfork (1983, 362) report that preadmission nursing assessment of physical and cognitive deficits and needs was very helpful in making decisions about future care. Following submission of the Bethany Manor physical and social history forms, potential residents were interviewed by the home's admissions clerk and/or a nursing home social worker, at the Manor if possible, or in their homes. Whenever the potential resident and the family were able, a brief preadmission tour of the nursing home was also provided.

Tracy Warner, one of the admissions clerks at Bethany Manor, described her role: "I am the admissions coordinator. I handle all inquiries that come in over the phone. I also handle walk-ins if I have time. I respond by sending out information, [an] application packet that includes medical update and social histories. I coordinate interviews with nursing staff and the social workers. I take people on tours. When the interview is done and all the information is in, I compile it all and write out a little synopsis of diagnosis, medication, age and present it in front of the Admissions Committee. The Admissions Committee members are the ones who decide which floor would best meet the needs of the resident."

The Manor Admissions Committee consists of the Director of Social Services, the Director of Nursing Services, the Medical Director, and the Administrator when available. An example of a potential resident reviewed at an Admissions Committee meeting during the study was Victoria King, an 85-year-old single woman whose only family consisted of several nephews. She was presently living in a local senior citizens' residence. Miss King had been on the Bethany Manor waiting list for some time. She was described as alert but very forgetful, with increasing confusion and need for assistance in some activities of daily living such as bathing. She had fallen twice in the past six months. It was reported that Miss King was aware of her own mental and physical deterioration and wanted to come to the home. It was also noted that the domiciliary facility where she lived "wanted her out." It was agreed that Miss King would be admitted to the Manor but "not on the first floor."

A closely related committee is the Utilization Review Committee, which consists of the Administrator, the Director of Nursing, the Director of Social Services, the Medical Director, the physical therapist, and other nursing representatives. This committee evaluates the appropriateness of use of the home's care services. Some topics discussed at one of the Utilization Review Committee meetings included whether a certain fifth-floor resident needed to continue receiving skilled care, whether a second-floor poststroke resident might be a candidate for speech therapy, and whether a seriously ill resident's family had accepted the fact that the resident's condition was progressively deteriorating.

One of the Manor's social workers described the personal interview dimension of the admission process: "Prior to admission we generally interview the family, and then we request that the prospective resident come in for an interview if they can. We like to see the prospective resident prior to admission so that when we place them we are placing them in an appropriate setting and we have a good picture of what kind of person they are now and what kind of person they were previously." She added, "As far as race or religion, that never is a consideration. Financial is sometimes. Obviously we like to take care of everybody, but sometimes financial consideration is given. However, we do not limit our applications for admissions to just private pay. A good portion of our admissions are Medicaid, and it's not profitable to take a Medicaid patient. You lose money on it, but we don't screen out. There are other, more important factors than financial. We look at the resident and the immediate need—are they in crisis in the community, or are they really at risk in the community? If a person really wants to come in, I don't think we've ever refused admission. Usually when they are ready to come in they need to be here in some form."

Tracy Warner, the admissions clerk, spoke also of the admission and preadmission difficulties she observed the potential residents' families experiencing: "In terms of a family member's illness, the families, the relatives, cannot deal with it. They don't feel they can provide adequate care; emotionally it is too much of a drain on them. Physically sometimes they are just not capable of doing it. A lot of these people are coming in at

85 and 90 years old and their daughters are 60 and 65. Quite a few [family members] will start talking about how guilty they feel about placing their parents here. Sometimes it's resentment toward that parent for being incontinent or elderly or not ambulatory or not coherent. The roles have changed. Now the children are the parents and the parents are the children."

Despite the family members' anxiety and guilt, however, Tracy reported that she tried to be honest and "realistic" with family members in describing the care that Bethany Manor could provide:

"I say to them, 'We do our best, but this isn't home.' You try to warn them that there are times when you come in that you might observe one of the support staff talking or handling your parent or relative in a manner that you are not too comfortable with, maybe a little harsher than you would like. Maybe they are not giving them the totally undivided attention that you would; maybe they are being a little more firm with them. You have to warn them [the families]. I certainly don't want to dissuade them, and nine times out of ten the people need the care we offer them and I think it is a good home. But I will say, there is no place like home, according to the meals, according to the caregiver. It's a whole new world here."

Although all of the preadmission processes were reported to be anxiety provoking for potential residents and their families, perhaps the most difficult stressors occurred at the time of actual admission to the nursing home. To better understand the impact of the admission experience on residents and their families, the study's principal investigator sought and received permission from the home's admissions office and from the residents and families involved to observe and collect data about three Bethany Manor admissions that occurred during the course of the research. The researcher met the potential residents and their families at the home's front door and accompanied them through the admissions office greetings and paperwork, the introduction to the unit nursing staff, the process of getting the residents settled in their rooms, and the family's leave taking. The case studies that follow are the result of the investigator's observations, questions, and chart data collection for the three admission experiences.

Case 1

Mrs. Mary Duvall, a charming, white-haired, 88-year-old widow, was admitted to the home from her own residence. She arrived dressed fashionably in an attractive outfit appropriate to her age and gave the appearance of having been supported by a comfortable and caring family. Mrs. Duvall's accompanying family members—a daughter, a son, and a younger sister—appeared solicitous and somewhat anxious about the admission. A review of Mrs. Duvall's social history revealed her to be mentally alert, sociable, cheerful, and cooperative. She prefers groups to being alone, is slightly forgetful and a worrier, but has a complacent temperament and accepts reality. She had been staying off and on with her son or daughter but wanted to come to Bethany Manor to be near other older people and to be near medical care if needed.

Mrs. Duvall is quite hard of hearing and has occasional dizziness and fainting spells. She is, however, capable of caring for herself in all activities of daily living, and bowel and bladder control are normal. Her gait is steadied by the use of a cane.

Mrs. Duvall sleeps well, enjoys reading and visiting, and has no undue financial worries. Her reaction to coming to the home was positive; special goals identified were "safety and security." Mrs. Duvall has excellent relationships with her children and her sister.

On arrival at the Manor, Mrs. Duvall seemed a bit shy and nervous. She and her family arrived 30 to 40 minutes later than expected but reported that they had had some difficulty with directions. After being brought into the admissions office and welcomed to Bethany Manor, explanations were provided by the admissions clerk about such topics as the nursing home contract, the laundry system, the call bell, housekeeping, the dining room, and religious services. After signing the contract, Mrs. Duvall confessed, "My hearing is worse if I'm a little nervous." She added, "I like the word 'resident.'" After being given her copy of the nursing home credo and an explanation of the complaint system to be used if needed, she observed, "Well, we're not perfect—none of us are." Her comment upon signing a Medicaid form (just in case it was ever needed) was, "They won't put me out in the rain."

Mrs. Duvall was told, "We want you to feel that you're part of the nursing home community, but we realize that some people aren't 'joiners' and we respect that." She was also told that her doctor would make a routine visit within 48 hours after admission. Mrs. Duvall seemed most pleased to learn about the Catholic religious services. (Mass, Confession, and Benediction). When the "Christian Affirmation of Life" (the statement that no extraordinary means shall be used to prolong life; see Chapter 7) was explained, however, she asserted, "I don't have to do that now." Mrs. Duvall was very gracious and interacted well with the home staff, but several times she admitted that she was "a little bit nervous."

Mrs. Duvall was assigned to a private room on the Manor's domiciliary care floor. On first appraisal, the room looked rather barren and institutional, but as small personal items, a television, and family pictures were assembled, it took on a more homey atmosphere. Mrs. Duvall's family were very supportive during the process and also somewhat anxious. A great deal of effort was expended on fixing "mother's new TV" so that the picture, the color, and so on would be just right for her. It seemed that the family felt a need to do something to alleviate the strain of having to surrender their loved one into the care of strangers. Mrs. Duvall's daughter, herself a health care professional, confessed that, although she had checked out the home's reputation carefully, this was not an "easy" day.

In sum, Mrs. Duvall arrived at Bethany Manor reconciled to the move and with strong family support. Plans were already formulated for a visit out in a couple of weeks to spend the Christmas holiday at her daughter's home. Overall, her reason for choosing nursing home care was to have companionship in her later years and to be assured of the security she desires if medical care is needed. On several follow-up visits approximately two, four, and six weeks postadmission, Mrs. Duvall appeared well adjusted to Bethany Manor.

Case 2

Mrs. Angela DeStefano, a 77-year-old widow, was admitted to Bethany Manor from a local retirement center, which could no longer provide the care she needed. Mrs. DeStefano has multiple diagnoses including Parkinson's disease, hypertension, hypothyroidism, decreased mobility, and occasional depression. Her social history revealed that although she can carry out some activities of daily living independently, she does need help with such activities as bathing and hair care. She suffers from occasional incontinence, and her gait was quite unsteady, requiring the use of either a walker or a wheelchair. She has fallen multiple times but to date has sustained no fractures.

Mrs. DeStefano has some slurring of speech and occasional temper outbursts. She occasionally suffers from depression and prefers to be alone. She is mentally alert and desires independence. She had been quite resistant to the idea of a nursing home but was convinced of the need by her brother and a social worker. It was explained to her that she needed to be in a 24-hour supervised environment because of her frequent falls due to unknown cause.

Mrs. DeStefano was also late in arriving, alone, at the home, and her first statement was, "I'm tired of living. I didn't want to come here today." She seemed slightly confused and her responses were garbled. A significant anxiety revolved around finances. When told that a telephone could be put in her room, she complained, "Will I have to pay them to move it?" She was also anxious about how she would use her walker to get down to Mass. Mrs. DeStefano seemed overwhelmed with the admission paperwork and sighed, "Is that all?" After signing her last form, she settled into her room on the fourth floor rather quickly and commented that she "needed to rest." On a follow-up visit two weeks later, Mrs. DeStefano still had a number of worries and complaints, especially about mobility.

Case 3

Miss Annie Lancaster, a seriously confused 83-year-old, was scheduled to be admitted to the home's cognitively impaired care area on the third floor. She was being admitted from another nursing home where there were not adequate services to monitor her disabilities resulting from confusion. On arrival at Bethany Manor's front door, Miss Lancaster, accompanied only by her 70-year-old sister, appeared angry and was crying and refused to enter the home. She also refused to speak to her sister, Mrs. Holley, who was herself on the verge of tears and very anxious and embarrassed by Miss Lancaster's behavior. With the intervention of the sister Administrator, a social worker, and the admissions clerk, Miss Lancaster was finally convinced to come in. She did so reluctantly.

Miss Lancaster's social history documented that she was very confused, forgetful, and suspicious of strangers; she had not willingly agreed to come to Bethany Manor. She needs direction carrying out the activities of daily living and is occasionally incontinent, but she can be sociable and cheerful at times. Her wish, however, is to live in her sister's home, and this has resulted in her wandering away from her previous nursing home. Mrs. Holley had indeed tried to care for her sister but was unable to cope with her cognitive impairment. She admitted feeling "very guilty" about putting Miss Lancaster in Bethany Manor and dissolved in tears, sobbing, "What else can I do?"

The admissions clerk and the third-floor head nurse got Miss Lancaster settled in her room as quickly as possible. She was docile but still refused to look at or respond to Mrs. Holley, who finally left in tears, after Miss Lancaster said, "If you want to get rid of me I'll stay here, but don't ever come back to see me. I don't ever want to see you again as long as I live." The staff suggested that Mrs. Holley give her sister a few days to settle in before visiting. A follow-up visit by the investigator about a week after admission found Miss Lancaster calm and relatively satisfied with the home. She participated in singing and dancing the following week at the Bethany Manor Christmas party. Mrs. Holley reported that, at her first visit to her sister, Miss Lancaster had again accused her sister of wanting to "put me away here." Mrs. Holley said she would visit again when her own "nerves settled down a bit."

For a number of the residents of Bethany Manor the primary rationale for nursing home admission related not to their own needs but to concern for their loved ones. Mrs. Julia Crowley described her feelings: "Well, both of my daughters invited me [to live with them], but I know that young people nowadays have a great many interests and a great many friends that they go around with socially. They do things for the church, they have their own little occupations, they have their young people to think about. It was just not right for me." She added, "I don't think it's right for the girls' husbands. 'What are we going to do with Mother tonight?' 'Will Mother come or won't she come?' I don't want that burden for them."

Prior to admission, according to their social histories, 52 (22.6%) of the Manor residents were living with immediate families (children or siblings), and 20 (12.6%) were living with other relatives (nieces, nephews, or cousins). In 66 (28.6%) cases, nursing home admission was brought about through family influence, and for 32 (13.9%) residents a physician advised nursing home care.

Experiences similar to those of Miss Annie Lancaster are found frequently in nursing home admissions. Chenitz (1983, 92), following a grounded theory study of the nursing home admission process, asserted, "When new patients come in here they often feel abandoned by their families. They don't understand why they have to be here."

Overall, it was reported at Bethany Manor that although the admission experience itself was often traumatic for residents and their families, adaptation to the regimen of Manor life generally followed rather quickly.

Accommodation to Nursing Home Life

One of the most difficult aspects of nursing home life for some new residents is coping with time-constrained activities such as bedtime, morning rising, mealtimes, and specific recreational activities, described by one resident as "programmed fun." For those whose previous life-styles lacked the structured consistency of that of Bethany Manor, the schedule could indeed be trying. Many residents, however, related their acceptance of the constraints of nursing home life to their real need for care and support.

Mr. Michael Fisher, an 82-year-old fourth-floor resident, commented that he did not like all the "rules and regulations" that went with nursing home life but admitted that he "needed to be here." He described why: "I had a good friend and he used to take me to the seven-thirty Mass. One morning he called up and got no answer from me on the telephone. I was flat on the floor. I couldn't get up. He decided there was something wrong and came and got the manager to open up and found me there. So I decided then I had better come to this place."

Mrs. Annie Scott, an 88-year-old also on the fourth floor, observed, "It's nice here but you have to live here to know what it's really like. I don't like being told what to do but I had to come in and I accept it." Her critical incident leading to admission was 22 hours spent unable to get out of the bathtub: "I'm in the tub and can't get out. My neighbor who called every night got suspicious and called the resident manager and the rescue squad who broke in the door to my apartment. I could have died there, so I came here."

Mrs. Julia Crowley described her period of early adaptation to Bethany Manor: "I couldn't judge what happened when I first came in because everything was new to me. I just walked around, did what I was told and found out things, a lot of them on my own. I had to make an adjustment." She explained a bit further, "Before I came in, one of my daughters asked if she could bring me over here. They took you from room to room, showed you the dining room. I looked at everything and I just wasn't impressed at all. I just wasn't ready for any of that institution business. I just wasn't ready for that. I just didn't want it. So it took me a long time to adjust."

Dietary Adaptation

Dietary inadequacy is a serious health hazard of the elderly adult, and sometimes newly admitted nursing home residents demonstrate the symptoms of months or even years of poor nutrition. Even persons who had previously lived with family sometimes received inadequate nutrition because of refusal to eat, or refusal to admit inability to eat certain foods such as fruit, vegetables, or meat that require adequate masticatory power.

Fluid depletion is found fairly frequently among the more aged new residents. Salerno (1985, 132) asserts that dietary changes may begin with retirement: "Alterations in dietary patterns may be the result of changes in role, activity, daily routine and financial income." She adds that income may also be a factor in inadequate nutritional status among the elderly: "For the great majority of persons, retirement income is significantly reduced."

The data from the Bethany Manor social history forms spoke to the residents' preadmission eating behaviors. Frequently families reported such behaviors as "no appetite," "eats very poorly," "can't chew meat," "has difficulty swallowing," and "must be spoonfed." Home staff, nurses, and aides frequently commented that the older and more infirm residents would eat desserts such as Jello, pudding, ice cream, or strained fruit but might often leave the more nutritious meat and vegetables, even if soft of pureed. "Sweet things" and foods with a strong taste seemed most palatable to the more frail and older residents. Some residents complained about Bethany Manor food. Mr. Fisher described it as "too much, too often," Mrs. Moreno called her pureed dishes "that awful baby food," and Miss Donley said it was "institutional fare, pure and simple." Others, however, such as Mrs. Mary Sheehan, described the meals as "nice and tasty," adding, "On the holidays they do a special treat and it's presented so nicely. They do try to do the best for us."

Bethany Manor social history data revealed that 52 (22.6%) of the residents were reported to have "poor appetites" before admission to the home, 34 (14.7%) required special diets (such as diabetics), and 22 (9%) were identified as unable to chew regular food. (Mealtime as a social concept is addressed in Chapter 7, and residents' special nutritional needs are examined from the dietitian's perspective in Chapter 6.)

Medications

Considerable concern about the importance of medications for the elderly nursing home resident is reflected in the gerontological literature. Wallace (1982, 34) asserts that, although general principles of therapeutic drug administration apply in whatever setting an older person received medication, "there are differences in managing medications in a long-term care facility." Certain specific medication-related problems cited include the fact that "a few elderly residents exaggerate the slightest ache or pain to get attention," that "some residents are not sufficiently aware to report unusual drug effects," and finally, "that many residents deny symptoms or try to disguise them because they fear hospitalization."

Another medication-related problem generally recognized among the elderly is the significant number of adverse side effects of administered drugs. The elderly individual with decreased metabolism and sometimes diminished renal clearance often cannot tolerate dosages of prescribed medication that would not cause problems for a younger adult. Berlinger and Spector (1984, 45) note that "numerous studies suggest that adverse drug reactions are more common in elderly (past 60) than young patients," and they add that drug-induced illness is a significant cause of hospitalization among the elderly.

The administration of PRN (as needed) medications in the nursing home is a subject of special concern to the nursing staff. Miller (1982, 37) reported that "managing 'as needed' drugs wisely is a demanding task" in the nursing home. She commented, "A responsible decision for each PRN drug administration is based on thoughtful consideration of the drug action, its possible adverse side effects and the nursing goals for the patient."

At Bethany Manor drugs and drug administration were indeed topics of concern to residents, staff, and families, as was exemplified by the existence of a nursing home Pharmacy Committee composed, among others, of the home's Medical Director, Administrator, Director of Nursing Services, and consultant pharmacists. The committee meets monthly. (Bethany Manor's pharmacy services and the Pharmacy Committee are described in Chapter 6).

Some Manor residents discussed their concern about receiving prescribed medication when they should. Mr. Ted Merrick, a fourth-floor resident, focused on his pain medication: "The doctor's orders were that I could have the pain pills when I asked for them. I would turn on my door light maybe at nine o'clock. I waited an hour and nobody even answered the light. I had to get up. Finally, I went out and one of the sisters was there and she got the nurse for me. The nurse has to bring you the pain pills." However, another fourth-floor resident, Miss Cairns, commented, "I don't pay much attention to my medications. I don't know what it is. I just take it."

Early Socialization

Nursing home friendships are an important part of life for the resident who has been totally transplanted from his or her former social interactional group. Admittedly, significant barriers to the development of friendships in a long-term care facility exist, especially for those who are severely impaired either cognitively or physically. Friendships do develop among some residents, nevertheless, as demonstrated by the research of Retsinas and Garrity (1985, 380), who found that "the key determinants of sociability were the resident's lucidity, speech and vision." Such friendships provide the elderly with "acceptance, support and companionship that are vital to a sense of personal worth and fulfillment in later life" (Roberto and Scott 1986, 241). Larson et al. (1985) found in a study of 92 retired adults that spending time alone was not a wholly negative experience for those who had regular companionship. Friendships among Bethany Manor residents have been discussed in Chapter 2.

Initiating new friendships at the home, however, was not always easy as the residents themselves related. Miss Anna Gittings reported that when she first came to the Manor she would get "so tired" that all she wanted to do was "sit and doze." She added, "I made some friends but not of a real close nature. Especially when you're new and you don't know your way around, it's hard to do." Mrs. Julia Crowley also described her early socialization efforts at Bethany Manor as limited: "I was just in a daze. I mostly tried to find my way to go back to my room. I wasn't too interested in friends at that time though I do have several now." Finally, Miss Martha Butler explained her perception of the dilemma of early socialization in the home: "We all, when we first come here, find it a bit trying, so to speak, to adapt to different types of personalities. We have had our own little ways and little rules for a long time, and it's sort of hard to look at others which are different. So, as a result, you sort of stay inside yourself where it's safe."

Distancing From Previous Life-Style

"Letting Go of People"

Bethany Manor residents spoke of the difficulty of "letting go" in the sense of accepting separation from loved ones, family, and friends, on their admission to the home. Although many ties indeed remained through visits, phone calls, mail, and even memories, the physical distance from significant others was painful. In the words of one newly admitted resident, "I just had to make up my mind when I came here that I can't do the things I used to do and have all my friends around or my husband. I really miss him. I was so lucky. He always considered me first." Mrs. Julia Crowley also described the difficulty of leaving her friends: "My daughter said to me, 'Come down and visit us. I know of a very good nursing home.' So I came over here and, of course, I didn't like it at all. I dreaded the change. I dreaded giving up my things and my friends. But I just had to face it; I had to do it. So that's what happened, that's how I came. I just gave in."

"Letting Go of Things"

Being forced to give up precious and treasured possessions was frequently mentioned by new Bethany Manor residents. Miss Marguerita Simpson, a newly admitted 83-year-old with multiple physical deficits but an alert and interested mind, spoke of the difficulty of letting go of her possessions: "I brought a few things from home. It's difficult. The sisters wanted me just to give things away, but they represent a lifetime of work— ten, twelve thousand dollars. It's hard to give up those things. You form an attachment to them. They do mean something to you. Sometimes you don't touch some of these things for a long time—like my books. I can't read anymore, but you know that they're there. You can see them and touch them. That's the hardest thing about coming to the nursing home. It's giving up your things. Some people have family, and then they can give them their things and know that they're being taken care of, but if you're alone like me, it's so hard. You just have to let somebody sell them."

Mrs. Cavanaugh also admitted that letting go of things was very hard: "Of course you miss your own home, but once you make up your mind, you just have to go through with it. It isn't easy giving all my possessions away. It was awfully difficult." But she added, "First, I put everything aside that I wanted, then I asked all my family to come in and take their choice of what they wanted, from vacuums down to jewelry." Residents such as Mrs. Cavanaugh who had families, in contrast to single residents such as Miss Simpson, often found great satisfaction and pleasure in distributing their treasured items to loved ones before coming to the nursing home.

Mrs. Crowley is a case in point. She described the distribution of her possessions: "My house was full of antiques. My daughters got to like antiques and they divided the whole lot, tables, chairs, a cherry table, my grandmother's corner cupboard, that you can't even find in an antique show now, my silver, my crystal, all those things. They divided peacefully among each other. And they have daughters who will see these things as they are growing up and take care of them." Mrs. Crowley added with delight, "They are so appreciative of what I had, and when I go there they use my dinner plates, things like that, little touches. 'Mother, have this nice drink out of one of your own crystal glasses.' The whole thing is so lovely. When my grandson got married, I had an old dresser belonging to my grandparents, and he just loved that for his room. The whole thing is very pleasant."

Despite such generosity as Mrs. Crowley exemplified, one is nevertheless struck by the radical adaptation that must occur for residents who were possessed of a multiplicity of material items such as clothing and furniture. The Admissions Clothing List (which lists all personal articles brought to the Manor) for Miss Eleanor Jacoby, an 85-year-old former secretary who had recently been admitted from her own home, documents the limited number of possessions to which many residents have been reduced:

> 2 coats; 8 dresses; 6 slips; 2 pair stockings; 1 bed jacket; 3 afghans; 1 camisole; 1 pair socks; 3 pair underwear; 3 nightgowns; 2 pillows; 6 pillowcases; 1 cosmetic bag; 1 handbag; 3 clutch purses; 3 cake tins; 6 pictures; 1 cookie tin; 1 partial plate; 1 clock; 1 radio; pair glasses; 3 medals; 1 TV set and stand.

Another dimension of letting go of things relates to coping with the knowledge that theft is a significant problem in most homes. Taylor (1984, 12) asserts that "the disappearance of residents' personal property is a frequent and chronic problem even in good facilities" and adds that since, by law, nursing home residents' rooms cannot be locked, "the maintenance of strict security of property is exceedingly difficult." Major thefts of residents' property (items such as chairs or lamps) were not observed to be a problem at Bethany Manor, but some residents did suggest (whether accurately or not) that small things left in their rooms sometimes disappeared (e.g., change left in one's purse, candy, new items of makeup, or toilet articles).

Dependence and Control

Being placed in a dependent position and losing control over certain dimensions of life is difficult for anyone, not least for the elderly nursing home resident who may have spent many years being "in control" and having others depend on him or her. It sometimes appears that society envisions the elderly individual as less than really human, as someone who expects not to be taken seriously, because certain "human" functions have begun to diminish. This is not so. Surely it is not so in the minds of the elderly. Indeed, being respected as persons and being allowed at least some small measure of control over life are among the most significant desires of the majority of the elderly.

In speaking with Bethany Manor residents, the researchers learned that in most cases individuals recognized and generally accepted their physical and even their cognitive deficits ("my old brain just doesn't work like it used to"). They understood their dependency upon the home for physical security and care, yet at the same time they desperately clung to the wish for as much personal autonomy as possible given the circumstances of their condition.

Mrs. Annamae Jenkins, 87, who had been confined to her wheelchair in the home for several years, complained, "I feel so helpless now and so dependent. Everybody else is in control. That makes me like a lost soul. I don't have any relatives and very few friends, and I don't have a home or any possessions whatever and that makes you feel kind of lost." Mr. Merrick also commented on loss of control and independence in his life: "Well, every rule takes away some of your independence; every law takes away some of your freedom."

Some other residents, however, while aware of the limitations the nursing home structure placed on their lives, tried to see the positive aspects of their situation. Miss Rebecca Phillips reported, "I keep telling myself I am lucky that I was able to come here and I ought to stop griping about a few little things that don't suit me." Mrs. Eileen Cavanaugh laughingly asserted, "I try to enjoy every minute of my life and say, 'Remember, old gal, you're not as young as you used to be.' '

Communication Deficits

Inadequate communication, or the lack of meaningful interaction, is a notable problem among the elderly. Although some lack of communication may result from emotional factors (depression, anxiety, or apathy), physiological deficits associated with the aging process, such as hearing and vision loss and slurred speech, play a significant role. Examination of the Bethany Manor social history data revealed that a large percentage of residents (between 50% and 75%) came to the home already possessed of hearing and vision deficits significant enough to interfere with such activities as carrying on conversations in a normal tone of voice or reading usual-size print. A small percentage of newly admitted residents also had speech problems; for some these were related to hearing difficulties, for others the result of stroke or some other cerebral dysfunction.

The causes of problems in communication may be summarized in six categories: brain damage ("aphasia" or a defect in or loss of the power of speech), physical problems ("dysarthria" or difficulty using speech muscles due to injury or disease), hearing difficulties, psychological factors, senility, and language (e.g., a foreign-speaking individual's inability to understand the language spoken; Hoffman-LaRoche 1973). For the confused individual, communication may be particularly difficult (Richardson 1983); it may be facilitated, however, by using both verbal and nonverbal forms of interaction (Hollinger 1986, 9).

It is generally accepted that acuity of both hearing and vision decreases with age. Calvani (1985, 16) suggests that hearing loss has two components: "decrease in hearing sensitivity which is measurable, and the handicap imposed by this hearing loss which encompasses the range of psychosocial/ situational elements which are difficult to evaluate." Vision loss may begin early in life or may not be significant until the "golden years." Eye diseases also increase in prevalence with age. Sullivan (1983, 228) suggests that "some elderly people assume that their failing eyesight is normal and that nothing can be done to help," and in others "the rate of decline in function is so gradual that the individual is unaware of the magnitude of the loss."

Social history data for Bethany Manor residents revealed that on admission to the home approximately 31% of the group had previously identified serious hearing loss, 43.9% had vision loss, and 10.4% had speech difficulties. The reported number of residents identified as having hearing deficits on admission to the home ($N = 72$) was somewhat less than anticipated. This may be related to the fact that a minor hearing deficit or one compensated with a hearing aid might not be noted by residents or their families on the preapplication forms.

Incontinence

Incontinence of body wastes is a personal and sensitive topic. Some literature on the nursing home has left the impression that incontinence totally dominates the lives and care of the majority of residents. This is not so. Surely incontinence, which often accompanies severe physical and cognitive disabilities, is a problem of concern in the nursing home. It is embarrassing to the resident, unpleasant for the caregiver, and painful for a family member or visitor to observe. It is clearly another symbol of loss of personal autonomy and control so important to the maintenance of self-esteem and a positive self-image. The topic must be dealt with in any realistic study of long-term care. It should not, however, so contaminate the profile of nursing home life—the love, the caring, the joys, the sorrows, and the minute-by-minute struggle for survival, for dignity, for respect—as to denigrate the role of either resident or caregiver, who interact as best they can to manage this stressful physical deficit.

Long (1985, 30) reports that surveys in the United States have determined that "50-60% of elderly in nursing homes suffer from urinary incontinence" and adds, "caregivers who accept the elders' episodes of urinary incontinence passively and give way to apparent feelings of hopelessness, contribute to that elder's feeling of low self worth, dependence and social isolation." The effect of incontinence on self-confidence and self-esteem is examined by Simons (1985, 37), who points out that some clients do not wish to reveal the condition. The result may be social isolation and restricted social activity. Simons also notes that "urinary incontinence is not only a problem for the elderly but also for their families and friends." Finally, physical problems are related to urinary incontinence in the nursing home, including "decubitus ulcers and urinary tract infections" (Burgio et al. 1988, 40).

Bethany Manor social history data on incontinence revealed that 44 (19.1%) of the residents were experiencing total incontinence before admission, and 73 (31.7%) were described as having partial or occasional incontinence. Several residents were admitted to the Manor largely because of inability to manage their incontinence.

One such individual was 94-year-old Miss Mamie Flanagan, a fourth-floor resident whose identified primary diagnosis was constant incontinence of urine. Miss Flanagan was described as slightly confused and depressed, a chronic worrier who had been living alone in an apartment. Her vision and hearing were poor, and her mobility was limited to the use of a wheelchair or walker. She had fallen several times. Miss Flanagan was very distressed by her incontinence. She described her experiences and feelings: "I am incontinent. I am just running all the time. I feel dirty and I like being clean. As long as I could bathe myself, I bathed myself every time, but since I have not been able to bathe myself. . . It's not all the time but it's very constant. It's miserable, very miserable. I need to go so much and I haven't gone away from this place because somebody would have to be changing me, and you can't expect to go visit your friends and have them change you. So I never go and visit like I used to. I am so limited from what I used to be, it's pathetic."

One of the Manor head nurses spoke about incontinence: "It's a real problem for these residents to deal with. It's embarrassing for them. A lot of them are alert enough and they know it's happening. Those are the ones it's toughest on because they don't want anyone else to know." She added, "It's really hard on their families, too, because nobody wants to see their mother going through something like that. So we try to use protection pads especially for the 'up walking around' ones. We try to keep it at least as unpleasant as possible."

At Bethany Manor incontinence also constituted a significant physical problem for bedridden or wheelchair-bound residents in the form of skin breakdown. Caregivers were continually trying new and creative strategies to keep residents comfortable and prevent decubitus ulcers while avoiding the long-term use of catheters or other intrusive procedures.

Anxiety and Depression

Anxiety and depression are conditions also identified as related to incontinence in the nursing home (Burgio et al., 1988). Anxiety in general is particularly common (and even expected) among new nursing home residents. The physical relocation process, emotional distancing from friends and relatives, and accommodation to the nursing home schedule are significant stressors leading to anxiety and resultant depression during the early months of nursing home life. Depression among the elderly is not well understood, as it is sometimes masked by the aging process and interpreted as a state of mind reflecting the onset of senile dementia. Depression does exist as a specific emotional manifestation in the elderly, however. Newman and Gaudiano (1983, 137), studying the relationship between subjective time (an awareness of events in one's life) and depression, found that depression was significantly related to decreased subjective time.

Bethany Manor social history forms filled out by family members identified a significant proportion of the nursing home population as having experienced either anxiety or depression or both prior to admission. Often these conditions were related to the elder's initial awareness that either physical or cognitive functional deficits associated with older age were beginning to occur.

Both anxiety (many individuals were described as "chronic worriers") and depression were identified as preadmission problems for 63 (27.3%) and 53 (23%) of the residents, respectively. Families wrote such comments as "She worries constantly about taking care of the house and the yard and gets herself and us into a terrible state," and "For the last year she has been very depressed and withdrawn saying that she doesn't want to live to go into a nursing home." Some other psychological concerns identified in residents' social histories included forgetfulness (N = 165, 71.7%), withdrawn state (N = 42, 18.2%), alienation (N = 19, 8%), reserved state (N = 29, 12.6%), aggressive or angry behavior (N = 15, 6%), poor judgment (N = 17, 7%), and extreme sensitivity (N = 16, 6%). Most frequently commented on by significant others was forgetfulness, affecting more than two-thirds of the home population. Forgetfulness was sometimes cited as a primary reason for nursing home admission. Descriptions were common of elders who would forget how to get home if away, forget to take care of themselves or of their households, or even forget their own names or the names of relatives.

Security

Among residents who themselves made the decision for admission to Bethany Manor, perhaps the one personal reason articulated most frequently, either directly or indirectly, was the need for security or protection. Three security-related themes appeared to emerge from the data: (1) physical security, or physical safety—that is, protection from falls outdoors, from bodily attack by perpetrators of crime, and from becoming ill when alone with no one to help; (2) emotional security, or protection against isolation from the love, support, and caring of other persons; and (3) spiritual security, or protection against being unable to attend church, receive the sacraments or go to confession (for Catholics), and the assurance that a priest or minister would visit in time of need or physical suffering and at the time of impending death.

Mrs. Julia Crowley spoke about physical security at Bethany Manor: "I love to visit my daughter, but I don't stay overnight there. I think I have more security here, personal security, than I even have at her house, because all night long there is somebody out there, if I should have an accident. There's a light on all night if I want to go to the bathroom. It's quiet here at night, people are put to bed early. I read or I write letters or I look at good programs." She added, "Oh, each day I am thankful because I couldn't go back to a house and worry about who's going to rake the leaves and a leak in the roof, and this and that. Somebody knocking on your door late at night.

I don't want any of those worries. So I am very thankful to be here." Miss Amy Pierce described her perception of emotional security: "It's just lovely, dear, because you're never alone here. There are lots of activities and people around and always someone to visit with. I would never have tried to live all alone in an apartment. Here I don't have to be alone or lonely."

Finally, Miss Catherine Jenkins commented, as did many other residents, on the joy of the spiritual support and security provided at Bethany Manor: "It's so wonderful to have the chapel and Mass and the Rosary. And you don't even have to go outside. If it rains or it snows, you don't have to think, 'How will I get there?' or 'How will I get home?' Or if you get really sick, the priest will bring communion to your room. When you get to my age, these things are really important to you."

Satisfactions

Bethany Manor residents experienced a great variety of cognitive deficits in terms of both type and degree. An immediately noticeable problem to the researchers was that of short-term memory. Sometimes during a study discussion a resident would gently ask, "Now tell me, dear, what are these questions for again?" Data collectors were therefore instructed to explain the purpose of the project, the use of the study data, and its confidential nature not only at the beginning of a meeting but also at least once during the course of the discussion and again when the interaction was terminated. Memory for things that happened earlier in the day was sometimes lost, as well as memory of family names, although incidents happening years earlier could be described in detail. It was observed that residents seemed to find great satisfaction in being able to relate to contemporary issues or activities, especially to things going on in the "outside world." Study respondents often shared points of view about world news and were very pleased to discuss these with the researchers. If the data collector brought up a contemporary domestic or political topic, residents responded with enthusiasm, if able. This was interpreted as personal satisfaction in being able to make the connection with the active world outside of the home.

"Covering" was a term used for residents' careful attempts to disguise lapses in memory. One of the nursing home's regular attending physicians reported that sometimes, right before he visited, a patient would ask someone the date, time, and place, and the U.S. president's name, as these were questions that they knew he might ask in assessing their cognitive orientation. Some residents also responded with illogical remarks to questions for which they did not know the answer. The perception seemed to be that some answer was better than none.

Allied to the concept of covering was that of conformity, or the attempt to fit within the perceived norms for a Bethany Manor resident. Many of the resident's comments reflected a desire not to violate nursing home rules or standards of behavior. For some this desire for conformity was related to a rather tolerant attitude of "keeping the peace"; for others it almost seemed related to a fear of being asked to leave the home. Remarks such as "This is the only place I've got" or "I don't have anyone to take care of me" sometimes followed statements about behavioral conformity. Mrs. Eileen Cavanaugh asserted, "I just do what I am told. I asked to come here and I accept anything they tell me to do. I have relatives, but I can't be dependent upon them. They all have their own families and their own problems and their own happiness. And they are all scattered."

Mr. Frederick Bradley described his feelings: "I just do everything they tell me to do. Suppose I did leave and then could not care for myself and I needed to come back. Perhaps they'd tell me they were full or I could not come back. Then what would I do? I just don't trust myself or my judgment."

Finally, Mr. McClaren commented, "I expect to live and die here. If I behave myself, they will let me stay."

Fear of Dying

As is discussed in more depth in Chapter 7, fear of dying was not found to be a significant problem for Bethany Manor residents. Death in the nursing home is anticipated, expected, and in some cases anxiously awaited. Death may be a release and a relief from a life that has become too painful to continue. Although there were a few exceptions, little fear of death itself was found among Manor residents. What was feared was the way in which one might die or the circumstances leading up to death.

Mrs. Nell Poole expressed ambivalence about dying: "Well, as I say, I'm 'tired of living and feared of dying,' just like the man in 'Old Man River.' I guess as you get along naturally, like the doctor said, 'We are all dying from the very day we are born.'" But Mrs. Harrison described herself as "more than ready" to go: "I feel I am overlong, like somebody has taken me out in the field and left me." Mrs. Mamie Flanagan related her age (94 years) to her readiness for death: "When you get to this point we are all waiting to die. Some are cheerful about it and some are not. I am one of the cheerful ones, but it's kind of hard to stay that way, because I am not afraid to die. In fact, I am ready to die. I want to die, the sooner the better, because I can't help myself, I can't help anybody else. I am nothing but existing, not living. No good to anybody or myself. It's a miserable feeling." Finally, 77-year-old Miss Gert Speckman described her fear of experiencing painful physical disabilities during the process of dying: "I see these people who are lying in bed crying and in a lot of pain. I hope that I won't live to be that way. I would be better off dead than lying around like that."

Fear of Not Dying

Most frightening to a number of Bethany Manor residents was the thought of surviving with a lingering cognitive deficit, which would result in significant emotional pain for both the resident and his or her family. One of Bethany Manor's social workers spoke about the residents' fear of "going to the third floor," where cognitively impaired residents are housed: "The third floor is definitely stigmatized. I can understand the residents' side, [they think] 'That's where those people are crazy' and 'I don't want to lose my mind.' That's the biggest fear. By not identifying, by not going to visit somebody there, by not interacting with them, is their defense against the reality that 'This might happen to me.' " She added, "I think residents are much more afraid of their minds going than of dying."

Miss Emily Hobbs, a 78-year-old, commented, "I said to myself, 'You ought to be thankful you have got your brain.' Anybody that is nuts, they don't realize it, they don't know they are crazy. Maybe they are happier than I am but I don't ever want to be that way. I'd rather be dead."

In discussing the residents' fear of cognitive impairment, one of the Recreation Department staff members commented that "It happens to more of them than you think. Someone just estimated that out of 230 [Bethany Manor residents], 169 are somewhat confused."

Settling in for the Long Run

The comments shared in this chapter were made by Bethany Manor residents who were relatively new to the home or who were reflecting back upon their early days. Many residents admitted that adaptation to nursing home life was indeed more difficult during the first six months to a year. After that, as one 93-year-old put it, "You just kind of 'settle in' to the place as if you'd always been here. It's our home, you know. At my age, you can put up with a lot because you've lived your life." This "settling in" was frequently observed during the course of the study, especially for the three residents who were observed and interviewed during their admission experience. Early adaptation to nursing home life poses unique problems and stresses, and there are special needs associated with long-term adaptation (discussed in Chapter 8). Overall, however, most residents seem to cope amazingly well with a style of living that for many is radically different from that which they have pursued for a lifetime.

References

Beland, F. 1984. The decision of elderly persons to leave their homes. *The Gerontologist* 24(2):179-185.

Berlinger, W.G., and R. Spector. 1984. Adverse drug reactions in the elderly. *Geriatrics* 39(5):46-58.

Burgio, L.D., L.T. Jones, and B.T. Engel. 1988. Studying incontinence in an urban nursing home. *Journal of Gerontological Nursing* 14(4):40-45.

Calvani, D. 1985. How well do your clients cope with hearing loss? *Journal of Gerontological Nursing* 11(7):16-20.

Chenitz, W.C. 1983. Entry into a nursing home as status passage: A theory to guide nursing practice. *Geriatric Nursing* 4(2):92-97.

Christ, M.A., E.M. Visscher, and D. Bates. 1988. Adult congregate living facilities: Factors influencing admission. *Geriatric Nursing* 9(4):234-236.

Hoffman-La Roche, Inc. 1973. *Problems in communicating. Workbook No. 8 in a series on rehabilitation in the nursing home.* Nutley, NJ: Hoffman-La Roche.

Hollinger, L.M. 1986. Communicating with the elderly. *Journal of Gerontological Nursing* 12(3):9-13.

Larson, R., J. Zuzanek, and R. Mannell. 1985. Being alone versus being with people: Disengagement in the daily experience of older adults. *Journal of Gerontology* 40(3):375-381.

Long, M.L. 1985. Incontinence. *Journal of Gerontological Nursing* 11(1):30-35.

Miller, C.A. 1982. PRN drugs...to give or not to give? *Geriatric Nursing* 3:37-38.

Newman, M.A., and J.K. Gaudiano. 1984. Depression as an explanation for decreased subjective time in the elderly. *Nursing Research* 33(3):137-139.

Retsinas, J., and P. Garrity. 1985. Nursing home friendships. *The Gerontologist* 25(4):376-381.

Richardson, K. 1983. Assessing communication. *Geriatric Nursing* 4(4):237-238.

Roberto, K.A., and J.P. Scott. 1986. Equity considerations in the friendships of older adults. *Journal of Gerontology* 41(2):241-247.

Salerno, Sr. M. 1985. Nutrition for the older adult: Diet needn't be hazardous to health. *Occupational Health Nursing* 33(3):132-152.

Simons, J. 1985. Does incontinence affect your client's self-concept? *Journal of Gerontological Nursing* 11(6):37-42.

Sullivan, N. 1983. Vision in the elderly. *Journal of Gerontological Nursing* 9(4):228-235.

Taylor, E.A. 1984. A consumer's guide to nursing homes. *Perspectives on Aging* 13:12-13.

Vivens, S., and C. Woolfork. 1983. Nursing home admissions made more rational. *Geriatric Nursing* 4(6):361-364.

Wallace, C. 1982. Special considerations for the nursing home resident. *Geriatric Nursing* 3(1):34-37.

CHAPTER 5

The Medical and Nursing Caregivers

The healer has to keep striving for...the space...in which healer
and patient can reach out to each other as travelers sharing the
same broken human condition.

Henri Nouwen, *Reaching Out*

Who are the medical and nursing care providers—the physicians, the
nurses, the aides—who choose to spend their days, and in some cases their
evenings or nights, devoted to the support and life maintenance of the
elderly nursing home resident? Why do these individuals choose to work in
a medical and nursing care setting that may well be less than the ideal,
because of lack of funds or inadequate staffing, and in which they may even
suffer the disdain of professional colleagues?

The area of gerontological medicine and nursing is coming to be
recognized as important in the professional community. This was not
always so. In the past, the bright, creative, outstanding physician and
nursing students frequently opted for a career in an exciting field such as
critical care, emergency, or pediatric medicine or nursing; few directed their
energies toward the medical and nursing needs of the older individual.
Professional identity and status aside, however, one might still ask, What
stimulates medical and nursing caregivers to pour out their hearts and their
minds in the support of persons who often have intractable medical
problems, knowing that, in all probability, the patient-caregiver relationships upon which they embark will be cast in the context of "til death do us

99

part?" A related question is, How do medical and nursing staff cope with the myriad personal and professional problems frequently associated with long-term caregiving, such as dealing with the confused resident, high staff turnover, inadequate supplies, excessive paperwork, "bad press," and personal burnout?

These questions directed that part of the Bethany Manor case study that focused upon the medical and nursing care providing staff. During the course of the research, many informal observations were made and conversations held with the care providers in an effort to understand their roles. Also included were formal meetings with a selected group of Bethany Manor medical and nursing care providers: four attending physicians, three Directors of Nursing, a nursing supervisor, all four unit (caregiving area) head nurses, a patient care clinician, three staff nurses (days, evenings, and nights), eight nurse aides, and three nurse faculty members of the Teaching Nursing Home Project. The study's principal investigator made rounds with three of the home's visiting physicians, attended patient care conferences, sat in on head nurse and staff nurse meetings, and observed nursing care at the bedsides. Other research team members attended shift-change reports (at 7 a.m., 3 p.m., and 11 p.m.), accompanied staff transporting residents to treatment or recreational activities, and interacted informally with nursing caregivers on all three shifts both during and after their caregiving activities.

The Role of the Physicians

Although, in the past, care of the elderly has not been a priority among a large number of physicians, this situation is changing, in part because of the increasing numbers of older persons living in our society and the federal government's interest in the care and support of the elderly. Mezey (1983, 243) reported that "in 1982, the National Institute on Aging awarded two Teaching Nursing Home Grants totalling $7.43 million, to support research on health problems of the aged, such as Alzheimer's disease, sleep apnea and osteoarthritis." Five principles suggested as considerations in the physician's approach to caring for the institutionalized elderly are the following: (1) Cognitive dysfunction sometimes accompanies acute illness; (2) an elderly patient may not demonstrate classic symptoms of a disease; (3) many elderly have a multiplicity of chronic illnesses; (4) care of the elderly must address not only physical problems but also functional and psychosocial problems that coexist with them; and (5) the older patient reacts more severely to stress and tends to respond to intervention more slowly (Pomerantz 1982, 311). It is also advised that "the elderly person needs not only a physician but a health advocate in the present complex health care system" (*Contemporary Administrator* 1982, 19). Managing physician services in a long-term care facility has historically been difficult, but because "the emphasis placed on geriatric medicine is growing rapidly," Black (1984, 39) asserts that indeed "more physicians will want to treat nursing home residents" in the future.

Even though the nursing home physician does not represent a continuous caregiving presence at Bethany Manor, the role has important implications in terms of the overall direction of patient care activities. Physician services at the Manor are organized to support the needs of residents and previous physician-patient relationships that the residents established. Although there is one identified physician Medical Director for the home— a department chairman at a nearby hospital—all residents are free to call in their own personal physicians. The home is therefore visited by a variety of physicians; however, three or four local internists appeared to consistently carry the largest caseloads of Bethany Manor patients. Two of these physicians had been serving Manor residents for 10 to 15 years.

Dr. Parsons, a senior attending physician, spoke of his role and his history with the nursing home:

"A major difference between nursing home care and practice in the acute care setting for the physician is *intensity*. In the hospital you see the patients daily, in the nursing home perhaps every 30 or 60 days. Patients in the nursing home tend to get forgotten by the physician. I think that the type and degree of attention which is given to residents depends a lot on the physician's previous relationship to the resident and the family. If this is a patient and family that I've been taking care of for 30 years, I'll know what they want. I'll know what extraordinary measures they may want. And they know me and they trust me. 'Well, if that's what Dr. P. says, that's what's best; we'll do it.' But if I have to make decisions regarding a resident I just met in the last month or two, it's much more difficult." He added, "Sometimes you have to make tough decisions for these residents. This gets into the ethical decisions. You give it your best shot and then walk away. You have to forget it or you won't be able to give your next patient your best shot. This is what we're trained to do as physicians. This comes with American-trained physicians—not that they don't have feelings but they have to be able to put that distance. I think the best word to describe it is 'objectivity.' "

Dr. Parsons also spoke to caregiving in the home: "We can be critical of the personnel, but these people [the residents] can be difficult to deal with also. Old folks are a little bit different. They tend to be a little demanding, a little more critical. You have to meet them halfway. I always smile when I walk in, especially in the summer, and there are the two rows [of residents] out in the front. They watch who comes and goes with a pretty critical eye. This is their home." Finally, Dr. Parsons commented on the changes in Bethany Manor as they affect the physician: "This place has changed 180 degrees in the last 20 years. Back then we had one floor to take care of the 'sick' residents, and the rest of the home was residential—a retirement home. They came in to the residential floors and later, if they needed it, moved to the care unit. Now there's only one residential floor and we admit intermediate and skilled care to the other floors. Some reasons for this are that age and disability are increasing when people are admitted; families can't cope; sometimes both adult children need to work."

To supplement an understanding of the physician-gerontologist's role at Bethany Manor, permission was requested to accompany the three physicians with the largest patient caseloads on their rounds at the home. One of the physicians, Dr. John McCorkle, was himself a senior citizen with many years of practice in internal medicine and gerontology. The other two, Dr. Reimer and Dr. Davis, were younger and associates in partnership practices. All of the physicians seemed to enjoy gerontological medicine and enthusiastically responded to the investigator's request to accompany them and conduct informal discussions during their resident rounds.

Making physician rounds at Bethany Manor serendipitously provided an "exercise" experience for the investigator, especially when accompanying Dr. McCorkle. Although he was one of the most senior of the attending physicians, he seemed to make a habit of taking the stairs between all five floors two or three at a leap and traversed the Manor's hallways in double-time in search of his patients. Despite Dr. McCorkle's marathon mobility, however, he did not rush residents during his visits and responded graciously and with concern to staff questions and needs. Some of the resident problems observed and addressed during Dr. McCorkle's rounds were pain control for Mrs. Courtney, an 87-year-old with metastatic breast cancer; request for a diuretic to alleviate Mrs. Hinshaw's leg edema; the need for a stool softener to ease Mrs. Delodder's constipation; and the signs of a beginning urinary tract infection necessitating drug therapy for Mr. Pickens.

In commenting on his Bethany Manor practice, Dr. McCorkle reported that usually residents are admitted when some specific physical problem requires intermediate care. He observed that in caring for the older patient several things that a physician must bear in mind are the fact that the patient usually has not one disease but a complex of symptoms and illnesses; that elderly patients are more sensitive to medications and dosages must be titrated accordingly; and that life prognosis modifies the plan for treatment and care. For example, Mrs. Clark, a 96-year-old with a rectal mass, will not be scheduled for radical surgery.

Rounds with Dr. Reimer revealed comparable patient problems: a decubitus ulcer, persistent weight loss, coughing. Dr. Reimer encouraged all of his ambulatory patients to walk but received excuses from several: "I have no need to walk," "Why should I?" "I have no will." Some patients choose immobility. Another elder-specific problem for physicians surfaced when Dr. Reimer asked Mrs. Sheehan if she had been having much angina lately. She replied, "I don't know—if I did, I've forgotten." Mrs. Sheehan also could not remember if she had taken her nitroglycerin tablet.

Dr. Reimer described some differences in the medical care of older and younger persons: "When you see a younger person with a multiplicity of symptoms—joint pains, vision problems, shortness of breath, hypertension—you immediately try to find the one underlying syndrome [or]disease which will tie together all or most of the presenting symptoms—one illness that puts everything together. With elders, multiple symptoms and multiple illness conditions are the rule. You may have a long list of unrelated problems. In the older person, you look less for one underlying disease." He added, "Examining the elder, one looks especially for evidence of heart failure—pain, edema; lung conditions—pneumonia, bronchitis; cognitive impairments—you check for orientation: time, place, person."

Dr. Davis clearly enjoyed interacting with and gently teasing his patients on rounds. When he greeted 90-year-old Mrs. Bloch with the label "my favorite patient," she replied, "All you have to do around here is have a slight heart attack and you get lots of attention." Dr. Davis commented that with an elderly patient population, one should "treat what's treatable but don't go overboard." He asserted that "side effects might outweigh the positive benefits of treatment" and cited 94-year-old Mrs. Larson's lung crackles and mild chest pain: "You don't treat this. You don't learn that in a residency. You learn these things as you go along."

With few exceptions the Manor physicians were well-liked by residents and nursing staff, and interactions were positive and supportive. Bethany Manor records showed that although indeed all physicians were contracted privately by the residents, a Manor-contracted dentist visited the home one to six hours per week, as needed, to see residents unable to leave. A podiatrist had also been visiting the Manor two to eight hours a week for the past six years.

The Role of the Nursing Staff

The role fo the gerontological nurse or the nurse in long-term care has received much attention in the literature of the past decade. Although gerontological nursing is generally described as having the potential for profound challenges and rewards, Jordan (1983, 171) notes that the profession is still fraught with misconceptions: "Nurses who are dedicated to practice in long-term care settings are often judged by unknowing colleagues as not practicing in a 'real nursing position.' " A distinguished nursing leader, Ida Martinson (1984, 11), asserted, "Nursing has a paucity of nurses—educators, practitioners and researchers—with specialized knowledge and clinical practice in gerontological nursing."

The Bethany Manor nursing staff presents a diverse profile. The following staff profile includes all levels of nursing caregivers, including geriatric aides. Of the Manor's 20 RNs, 3 had master's degrees, 3 had baccalaureate degrees, 6 had associate degrees, and 8 were diploma graduates. Eighteen nursing care providers were LPNs, and 106 (74% of the staff) were geriatric nursing aides. The caregivers' ages ranged from 22 to 64 years, with the highest numbers, 42 and 37, falling into the 20-to-29-year and 30-to-39-year categories, respectively. As expected considering the heavy work of gerontological nursing, both physical and emotional, 77% of the staff were under the age of 49. Two aides were male, 121 (85%) were black, and 69 (48%) were single. Twenty-five percent of the staff members had been with the home longer than five years, and 66% less than three years. Fifty-five Bethany Manor staff members had prior work experience in another nursing home, and 36 had greater than five years of geriatric experience before coming to the home.

The Director of Nursing

Four different Directors of Nursing were in office during the course of the study: Three were members of the Catholic religious community that ran the home, and one was a laywoman. The high turnover among Directors of

Nursing was due both to routine changes of assignment for the sisters and, in one case, to illness. One of the directors described her role as consisting of the following activities: "Dealing with finances, the budget; staffing; Medicare and Medicaid standards; determining with the staff what supplies are needed for the home and meeting with salesmen; making daily rounds on the resident care areas; meeting with head nurses and supervisors; and sitting on all of the home's major committees—pharmacy, admissions, etc." The director also described what she labeled her "mediator" role in problem solving, and she noted that, although it was not a formal part of her role, staff with problems sometimes came directly to her office for support or guidance. She commented, however, that staff were encouraged to work out difficulties or grievances with their immediate supervisor. The Director of Nursing was also responsible for acting as informal liaison with a number of visitors to the home such as physicians and nursing students.

Basically this director admitted that her role was primarily at the policy level and that an assistant dealt more directly with practice issues—a necessary division of labor due to the continually increasing complexity of nursing home administration. In concluding the discussion of her role, however, this director commented: "There are good days and bad days. On bad days I go up to one of the units and take care of a patient. They are really what I'm supposed to be here for. They are such neat people. It always makes me feel better."

Another Director of Nursing discussed some of the resident problems her office encountered. She told of an incident in which a staff member had called very upset because a long-term resident, Miss Pritchard, had suddenly refused to get up one Saturday morning to go to breakfast. When the director went in to see the resident, the resident explained, "I'm taking the day *off*. I'm sick and tired of getting up at the same time every day, seeing the same faces. I need a break, so I just decided to take a day off." The resident was given a tray and allowed her day off.

Special permission was obtained for one of the researchers to attend a staff nurse meeting consisting of the director, the nursing supervisor, and head nurses and staff nurses from all units. An LPN commented, "If you really want to know how we feel on some issues, you should attend this meeting." The director, Sister Judith, opened the meeting with the statement that she wanted to learn about the nursing care problems being experienced on the units: "I want to get in touch with problems at all levels of nursing management from director to GAs [geriatric aides]. I want you to be aware that the problems going on have been here for a few years and we can't solve them overnight. I don't have all the answers—this is a meeting to list problems. I will then meet with NAs [nursing aides], head nurses, and medication nurses separately. I need help and ideas from you." Several specific caregiving-related problems were identified by the staff. One of these was staff shortages on the weekends, which occurred frequently because of "call-in" absences (a head nurse commented, "All during the week we have to play catch-up.") Another problem discussed was linen delivery: A staff nurse reported that too much linen arrives on the floor for the staff to put away at one time, and she complained, "If it's not put away then the residents have no clothes to put on. The clothes will end up in someone else's closet." A shortage of geriatric aides at mealtime was yet another problem; six aides are not enough to feed 50 to 60 people. Finally, the need for larger supplies of disinfectant and insect spray on the units was discussed. Two final concerns related to the caregivers' roles. An LPN observed, "I think we need to know from maintenance and housekeeping whose job is whose. We need to know what nursing is expected to do." A head nurse reported that "The aides are feeling that they are not recognized by nursing administration."

Sister Judith responded to the staff's concerns with potential solutions or plans to alleviate the problems in the future. The meeting concluded with Sister Judith issuing a challenge to the group: "How much are people willing to give in order to get this house back on its feet?" An LPN responded, "We have done it in the past; we've worked hard. It's important to be recognized for that by the administration. The importance will be how the need is communicated. How nursing supervisors communicate and ask for our support sets the tone for cooperation."

The Nursing Supervisors

The nursing supervisor's role is to oversee nursing activities in an on-site capacity, making periodic rounds of all of the home's resident care units to observe, advise, and support the staff in their caregiving activities.

The Manor has three primary nursing supervisors, one each for the day, evening, and night shifts. One of the day nursing supervisors working at Bethany Manor during the study, Margaret Bentz, described how her staff's activities differed from those of hospital caregivers: "You do bios [biographical sketches], you do blood pressures, we have tube feedings here, we have catheters here. What we don't have is patients going to surgery, patients going to x-ray, and that type of thing, but we have physical therapy. They do the same thing in the hospitals, except patients are here for a much longer period of time. That's the main thing; it's the long term and you really get to know them a lot better than somebody that's here for five days. You don't have quite the amount of paperwork for admissions and discharges as you do in regular care hospitals, but you do have Medicare/Medicaid documentation. You have some of the same conditions as hospitals, like congestive heart failure, also strokes, but with the added imposition of the fact that they are geriatrics."

Ms. Bentz spoke very positively of the staff, especially the geriatric aides, whom she worked hard to support: "I personally think I have a good relationship with all of the aides, but I have had to work at it very hard—get acquainted with them on a personal level, talk to them, communicate with them, put my arm around them, let them know they've done a good job when they have."

The Patient Care Nurse Clinicians

During and immediately following the study, Bethany Manor employed several RNs to work part-time in the role of patient care clinician (or clinical coordinator). The duties of this role varied with the incumbent but generally involved such activities as staff development, patient care consultation, and policy review and revision. One nurse clinician, Kathy Miller, described her primary responsibility as coordination of the residents' care. Her activities consisted of record review (resident charts), planning of patient care conferences, and procedure manual revision. Another dimension of Kathy's role related more directly to employment of her own caregiving skills. She elaborated, "The second part of my job is to perform in a practitioner role, to use my health assessment skills to identify health problems in the patients, to review their therapies, treatment plans, and so forth and to collaborate with the various disciplines on that kind of thing, and to be a resource person for the nurse on the unit if she wants an assessment about some problem."

The Head Nurses

Bethany Manor has four head nurses, one each for the third, fourth, and fifth floors, and one whose office is located on the second floor but who also directs care activities and responds to patient needs on the first floor, the domiciliary or self-care area. The role of the head nurses consists primarily of such activities as constructing floor staffing patterns; assigning staff patient care activities; assessing overall physical and psychosocial deficits and needs for residents under their charge; ensuring that physicians' orders are properly carried out; maintaining communication with all of the home's ancillary care systems such as pharmacy, social service, physical therapy, and recreational therapy; and generally overseeing all patient care-related activities occurring on her floor.

Formal discussions involving role perceptions and activities were held with all of the Manor head nurses. The group was comprised of four very diverse individuals. One head nurse was an LPN currently working on an associate degree, and another was an RN with a master's degree in gerontology; the remaining two were a diploma-prepared RN and an RN with an associate degree who was working on a baccalaureate degree. Three were laywomen, two married and one single, and the fourth was a member of a religious community. (To preserve anonymity, all will be referred to using lay pseudonyms.) All had similar role responsibilities, but their view points differed on some dimensions of role behavior. Ms. Walters viewed her role as primarily administrative: "It's not that much of a hands-on because you don't really have that much time unless you have a resident who is getting into some type of trouble or is acutely ill. Usually, it is from a psychological point of view or you are observing the resident and making decisions; it's more of that. And of course, that paperwork goes on forever and ever."

Another head nurse, Ms. Snyder, took a slightly different view: "My feeling is that the head nurse should have some hands-on, because if I do not see what is going on, I cannot in any way assess a patient, and it has to be continual assessment. It can't just be one time when they come in and that's it, so I think the best way to assess a patient is to go in and really have hands-on with the resident and have communication."

Ms. Stevens saw herself primarily as a coordinator and teacher: "The aides do the ADL [activities of daily living]. I see my job as teaching them the mental and social ways of the residents. I also see my job as finding out needs from the families and as a PR person with the institution, family, and aides for the residents' best care. I think that a lot of what we do is just commonsense knowledge, the kinds of things you would do if you had an elderly ill person in your home."

Ms. Powell described her head nurse role as consisting of a combination of direct, hands-on care slightly outweighed by administrative chores: "I would say it goes back and forth, but I guess about 70% of the time it's managerial."

The head nurses also expressed their attitudes about care of the elderly. Ms. Walters commented, "There really has to be a lot of patience and understanding. As these residents stay here they get older and it takes longer to take care of them. Some of the residents have been here longer than I have been, and I can see how they are really going downhill. I wonder just what's wrong with such and such a patient today. I think, 'He's really not himself.' Then I remember, this man is 80 or 90 years old. You forget and it's usually that the patient is just tired."

Ms. Snyder's remarks reflected a similar theme: "I think that probably empathy would be the greatest quality needed in working with the elderly. You have to understand that some of their problems and needs come simply from the fatigue of old age."

All of Bethany Manor's head nurses spoke in support of the staff, nurses and aides alike, awarding them accolades for their commitment and care in a difficult nursing situation. All also admitted that there were staff problems at times, related to such areas as resident-staff conflict, staff-staff conflict, and staff turnover, but generally they felt such occurrences were to be expected in the long-term care setting.

The Staff Nurses

Staff nurses at Bethany Manor, both RNs and LPNs, appeared to have similar roles and responsibilities. Generally they carried charge nurse responsibilities, either relieving a head nurse on the day shift or being in charge of the unit nursing activities on evenings or nights.

A staff RN, Jean Donnelly, described her work with nursing home residents as "more physical, actual hands-on direct care" than she had experienced working in a hospital. She commented, "I work on the third floor with a lot of patients with Alzheimer's, so you have a lot of patience. They don't understand you and one has a tendency, while I am trying to do the dressing, to go over it with her hand. We have to have a lot of patience, a lot of empathy, a lot of understanding. We have to talk to people, listen to them." Jean went on to relate, however, that her friends, "a lot of nonnurse people," weren't interested in hearing about her work at Bethany Manor. She said, "They think it's boring. In fact, they tell me I am a young nurse, I shouldn't be working here, why don't I work in a hospital."

Another staff nurse, Peg Briscoe, described her role activities: "I do medications; I am charge nurse on the floor a lot of the time when the head nurse is off, to fill in, treatments, overall staffing, taking charge of the nurses' aides, making sure the patients are cared for, monitoring the dining room. A licensed nurse has to be down there. Just about a Jack-of-all-trades on the floor." Peg also described a "power" issue that had been a problem for her early in her employment at the home: "When I first came here I came from a head nurse position, and I am used to being in authority and having people answer to me. It was an adjustment for me at this facility because I was a staff nurse. There was a problem here, and one day we just confronted each other, myself and the aides, and I just told them what my title was if they weren't sure what I was, that I was not a medicine aide, that I was a licensed nurse, and I could handle any responsibilities that the head nurse could handle, and that I would relay any problems to her. The head nurse agreed with me. She reinforced what I told them, so from that day it went a little smoother."

Finally, a staff nurse commented on the teamwork spirit on her floor: "The only time that they expect the licensed nurse to get out on the unit and help is when they are short, and quite naturally we do. We don't expect the aides to do everything when we don't have enough staff. We do patient care. I am out there whenever I see there is a need. There is no problem with us on this floor assisting with patient care. We don't have time to really do it but sometimes we just have to make time. We try to work together as a team."

The Nurses' Aides

Despite the complex and debilitating physical and cognitive deficits experienced by most nursing home residents, "it is the nurses' aides, largely untrained, who give the majority of nursing care" (Fisk 1984, 119). In discussing the contemporary nurses' aide's role in long-term care, Barney (1983, 45), a master's-prepared social worker who herself assumed the aide role in order to observe, reported, "Residents appeared very old. Many were almost or entirely helpless. Many required feeding or help with eating. Many residents were hard to communicate with; either they couldn't see or hear or speak or be understood. They ranged from slightly confused to comatose." Barney learned that an aide was often left very much on her own to carry out the complex care needed for these patients, because "supervision was extremely limited." Chenitz (1983, 238), in discussing the role of the nurses' aide, supports the notion that "nursing home practice was long considered second-class nursing by many" and suggests that "devalued work" must be transformed into "valued work." Also reinforcing the difficulty of nursing home work is an employment tenure study of nurses' aides in nursing homes, in which it was learned that the largest proportion of aides "had terminated their employment within three months or less" (Wallace and Brubaker 1982, 16).

Nurses' aides at Bethany Manor comprised almost three-fourths of the caregiving force. Presently, to be hired at the Manor, aides must possess at least a geriatric aide certificate earned through the completion of a 60-hour course: 30 hours of classroom lecture and 30 hours of clinical experience in caring for the elderly. These educational requirements were mandated by the federal government in 1982; aides who had been hired by the home before that time were "grandfathered" into their positions. New aides receive a one-day general orientation to the home and then are linked up with an experienced aide on one of the units in what is described as a "buddy system." The plan is for the newly hired aide to shadow her senior colleague for several days before receiving her own resident care assignment.

Annie Glover, a 27-year-old geriatric aide who had been working at the home for several years, commented on caregiving activities, stating, "My emotions are more involved than my energy or any part of me." She asserted that the residents "require a lot of understanding because sometimes you might feel that, oh, this man or this woman is over 70 years old and should not be doing this or that, but they are just like children. You have to take a lot of patience. They do not know what they are doing. You just have to take your time to do whatever you have to do for them." Annie added, "There are people that don't have families or don't get visitors most of the time, so they rather enjoy you taking the time to talk to them or be with them to listen to them. Some people feel like talking, but when there is nobody to listen to them they feel very bad, so sometimes I sit with them, I talk with them."

In describing her geriatric aide role responsibilities, Annie explained, "We are responsible for the care of the residents, to see they eat, they are washed, taken care of. We want to sit down, listen to them, talk to them most of the time. We are always short of help, we are always on the run trying to get things done. That's about it. Any change in the patient is reported to the head nurse. She will take care of that." She also complained of the difficulties posed by staff shortages: "The thing that is frustrating is that you feel that more can be done for a person but you don't have time to do it. There are people that get very agitated, and if you have the time you can sit down and take the time to talk to the person, and they might calm down without taking any drugs. But we don't have the time to do that."

Another geriatric aide, Elaine Smith, who has worked at the home for six years, detailed her activities and attitudes: "I care for whatever number of residents are assigned to me for an eight-hour shift. I give a.m. care, do fingernails, feeding, grooming, hair. These residents take a lot of attention and care. You have to be kind to them and be careful. You can't hurry. Some need more attention. No two days or two patients are alike. It can get tiresome, but at the end of the day you really feel like you've done something for someone."

Lydia Jackson, a 30-year-old geriatric aide, had been employed at Bethany Manor for two years and was supporting herself and two daughters on her aide's salary. She had attended a six-month nurses' aide training course and had a certificate in geriatric care. Lydia identified one of her most important responsibilities in caregiving with the elderly as being "very conscious of the skin condition and how to prevent bed sores—turning, keeping them [the residents] clean and dry, rubbing their skin, forcing fluids." She concluded by asserting, "You have to care about the elderly and enjoy helping them, even when they are stubborn and nasty to you as a caretaker." Lydia reported that her favorite thing about working at the home is "making the patients smile." "Sometimes," she said, "I'll spend a lot of time with one person doing her hair or fixing her up. I'll do anything to take the sad look off that person's face."

One of the study investigators met with a small group of five geriatric aides to elicit their attitudes about working at the home. Two indicated that they really liked to work with the elderly residents; the other three considered their work, in the words of one, "just a job." The aides agreed that they got along well among themselves but kept some distance from the charge nurses. One said, "We have to work as a team—it's the only way you can survive this place." Several said the morale wasn't too good, as their work often was not recognized as they felt it should be.

Overall, as the above data and those in other chapters reveal, nurses' aides at Bethany Manor reflect a wide range of attitudes and capabilities. Some, especially those employed for three years or longer, had a real commitment to the elderly and took much pride in their caregiving activities. One commented, "Sure, you take pride, especially like a day when you're short of staff and have nine people to feed, to give a.m. care, to get dressed, to position—you know you have really done a good job. You have accomplished something!" For others, the role of geriatric aide was temporary, a stopgap employment on the way to something better. As a 26-year-old aide explained, "I can do this for now but I sure don't want to do it forever. I'd like to get my nursing [degree] but I don't think I'm the right temperament for old people."

The Nursing Students

Recently schools of nursing have shown a great deal of interest in the nursing home as a clinical placement for student experience. One college found that beginning baccalaureate students benefited significantly from their experiences with nursing home residents: "students' knowledge level increased, their negative bias toward the aged decreased, and there was a reduction in the number of misconceptions they had about the aged" (King and Cobb 1983, 292). Wall-Haas et al. (1983, 6) reported that students obtaining experience in long-term care can gradually gain confidence in their nursing abilities while meeting the residents' needs; they cited five specific benefits of long-term versus acute care for the students' first clinical experience: (1) Because of the nursing home's more stable census, a single client may be followed over time; (2) because treatments are fewer, the student can spend more time with the client; (3) the student has the opportunity to practice a wide range of nursing interventions related to client needs; (4) the student can apply nursing theory and interventions, as nurses are often primary decision-makers in the nursing home; and (5) students learn confidence, which prepares them for the acute care setting.

In addition to baccalaureate-level students employing the nursing home as a clinical site, graduate students are beginning to move into the homes for educational and clinical management practicums; some contemporary educators have strongly advocated doctoral preparation for gerontological nurses (Kayser-Jones 1986; Dye 1985).

A number of baccalaureate, master's, and doctoral students from local university schools of nursing spent time at Bethany Manor to gain both clinical and research experience in gerontology. Several groups of seven to ten baccalaureate junior nursing students worked with cognitively impaired residents on the third floor; the senior-year students were assigned to the skilled patient care area on the fifth floor. Junior students were involved in both group and individual care experiences with the cognitively impaired residents. Some activities included organizing exercise classes with music and balloons, assisting with a "reminiscence" group, and interacting one-on-one with individual residents, with whom the student would attempt to establish a therapeutic relationship. Senior students assigned to the skilled care area worked on assessing patient needs and developing nursing care plans for residents with more serious physical deficits. Several master's-and doctoral-level nursing students also spent time at the home to obtain either clinical or research experience in some facet of long-term care.

As noted in Chapter 1, a number of the baccalaureate group contributed their student logs as additional data for the ongoing case study of the home. Besides describing resident needs, they wrote of their own personal goals and first impressions of Bethany Manor. Some of these students' initial impressions are presented below:

Meg: "My actual first impression of Bethany Manor was that it was a 'big' place. To me it seemed hospital-like rather than home-like."

Cathy: "My first impression of Bethany Manor was positive. The place seems nicely decorated and kept up. My second impression was not so positive. It smells like a nursing home. I was also surprised at the number of people in wheelchairs, especially the ones just sitting there."

Liz: "Many of the residents seemed to be touch deprived and seemed eager to initiate contact ranging from hugs, holding hands and kissing. Their non-verbal communication indicated pleasure at the tiniest touch."

A fourth student, Tracy, wrote extensively and eloquently of her first impressions of the Manor: "Being in a nursing home for the first time in my life, gave me a new and strange feeling, a feeling that life is too short to worry about. One day I'll get to an old age and I'll be called an old woman, which I'm sure is not a lovable term to be given to a human person. Old people should be loved, because they have lived such a long time, surviving all the good and bad. I hope I can help the old women at Bethany Manor, because I feel they need love and they need to be *cared* for and loved. I think old people have much to give but are not given the opportunity."

Other students described their nursing goals during their experience at the home. Sherry asserted, "My own ultimate goal when I care for the geriatric client is to help make the client feel more comfortable in whatever way that I can. Since I have come to realize that the old person is simply 'wearing out' due to aging, there isn't a whole lot I can do to help *cure* his/ her symptoms, *but* I can help make the last of his/her life pleasant and comfortable."

Lisa, another student, observed, "Bethany Manor seems a good place to study the population of elderly emotionally conflicted residents. Being able to study residents in such a large setting is a challenge, as the staff has to work so much harder to individualize care for each one. It will be rewarding to seek out my clients and provide some individual attention for a few weeks."

Finally, Julie, a baccalaureate student, related her reaction to the present research: "Dr. O'Brien spoke to us concerning her case study of Bethany Manor Nursing Home. It was so good to hear her speak of her concern for the elderly and their special needs. I felt myself forming many ideas and beliefs about the elderly while she was speaking. How do people who are elderly feel about death? dying? living? their own life?"

In the main, nursing students at all levels came away from the Bethany Manor experience with either a new or a renewed understanding of the needs of the elderly person in long-term care.

The Teaching Nursing Home Project

The purpose, goals, and basic design of the Teaching Nursing Home Project (TNHP) have been described in Chapter 1. Several project faculty members shared descriptions of their activities in the university-nursing home collaborative project.

Martha Baxter, a master's-prepared nursing faculty member, explained that in developing the TNHP the university school of nursing's administration and faculty had had much interaction with the Bethany Manor administration. She added, however, "We really hadn't had much contact with the staff: the aides, the head nurses and the people we were really going to be working with." Thus, the project faculty were concerned that their initial entrée into the home might be threatening to staff "when suddenly a group from a university come in wearing white lab coats and walking around looking at what they [the caregivers] are doing." Because of this concern a careful and gentle approach to initiating the project was taken. Ms. Baxter continued, "The biggest measure that we took was to tread very gently. We moved in very softly. We deliberately avoided any attempt at aggressiveness. We tried to be not overwhelming; we tried to take a back seat in many things but we continued to make our presence visible as gently as we could. So we would go out in the morning with no specific plan, no specific pattern except to talk with the head nurses, meet the staff, introduce ourselves."

Ms. Baxter described how one of the TNHP staff became accepted by the home staff:

"Jean is an excellent practitioner. As soon as she was able to convince the staff that she knew how to use her hands, her head, that she was clinically capable, they were willing to let her move in. Some people were less willing to go along that rapidly. I can remember one person in particular who ran from us, literally. We were able to identify this person going in the opposite direction. Any time she saw us coming on the unit, she would find a room to go in, she would find something to busy herself with. She was very, very frightened of us. She was a practical nurse, which maybe was part of the problem and she wanted so badly to be an RN, but she just found us a bit overwhelming, no matter how gentle we were with her. However, by the end of the first year she was coming into the office to talk with us and we thought that was major progress. The first day she came into talk with us, we thought we had it made."

A second TNHP faculty member, Nora Kennedy, described her role as primarily that of a gerontological nursing clinician: "I advise on all aspects of clinical nursing care of the residents, and have developed a working relationship with the home's physicians and nursing staff. I think this role will facilitate staff development." Nora described her perception of the home's physicians, with whom she was beginning to work: "Some are very good, like Dr. Parsons. He is excellent. But there is some incompetence. Those who don't come in, who treat by phone. They need to clean up their act."

Bonnie Webb, a third member of the project group, described her primary responsibility as "helping with and consulting in terms of staff development." She added that "another piece of that [role] turned out to be actually conducting the quality assurance program." She described this program as a "self-appraisal program for the entire facility." Bonnie gave her perception of the home's staffing problems: "I think if our staffing were better, which we are trying to work on, I think we would do better. We have a number of stable individuals, but because the staffing is low, there is a lot of turnover, I think, in new people. Those that have been here for a while have a commitment to the place, have somewhat accommodated to that, and do a very good job in the kind of care they give."

Overall, the TNHP staff seemed very realistic about the nursing home's caregiving strengths and deficits. They were optimistic about the project making some significant changes relative to the improvement of care and increased quality of life for residents. They also, however, accepted certain weaknesses, such as limitations on the hiring of staff imposed by budgetary constraints. None of the TNHP staff viewed the setting as ideal; all, however, perceived potential for improvement. Martha Baxter ended her remarks by commenting, "Of course we set goals that are really huge. There is no way that any group of people could achieve all that we wanted to achieve, but I think we have achieved some and we are making movements toward the achievement of others."

Staffing Patterns

The nursing staff pattern is critical in the long-term care setting, which is a "labor intensive industry, because of the impact of the [staffing] decision on costs and on quality of nursing care" (Shukla 1982, 22). To obtain a more accurate profile of staffing patterns and patient care management at Bethany Manor, a member of the research team was assigned to spend several hours before, during, and immediately after the nursing shift transitions, observing and talking to staff. This was done for all three patient care shifts, alternately, two days a week over a six-week period. The observation and interviewing were carried out on the Manor's third floor, which houses 69 moderate to severely cognitively impaired women.

Data collection activities were directed by an observation guide developed by the study's principal investigator. The guide contained such foci as professional level or title and educational background of staff; power and authority among staff (who is in charge and who follows orders); informal relationships among staff (friendships, cliques); stresses during shift change ("call-ins," assignment changes); patient care assignments (who makes them? on what basis are they made? what is the patient-staff assignment ratio? are there "choice" patient care assignments? are there undesirable patient care assignments?); patient classification system on the floor; observational differences among transition times on the three shifts. Data were collected by observation, discussion, and record review. (The Management of Nursing Home Patient Care Observation Guide used is reproduced in the Appendix.)

An overview of the unit's "administration" was reported by the nurse observer: "This unit utilized an RN as head nurse and either RNs or LPNs as team leaders. These team leaders were responsible for administering medications and performing needed treatments in addition to completing required paper work. All other direct patient care such as feeding, bathing and toileting was performed by geriatric aides. The judgement and authority of the team leader was not openly disputed." Third-floor staff for a 24-hour period consisted of the head nurse, (an RN taking graduate courses), one RN, five LPNs, and 22 aides. (These numbers varied somewhat during the course of the study.) Generally the day shift staff consisted of the head nurse, one other RN or LPN, and 10 nurses' aides; evenings were staffed with an LPN charge nurse and five to six aides; nights had an LPN charge nurse and four to five nurses' aides. On one evening shift, several student geriatric aides from a local vocational school and their instructor visited. The student aides spend approximately 48 clinical hours at the home assisting with patient care under supervision.

Although Bethany Manor aides generally did not dispute the authority of the head nurse or the charge nurses, they were observed to function fairly independently. They seemed to work especially well with LPN charge nurses whom they knew, but in one case while working with a "relief" RN, aides were seen rolling their eyes behind her back as she adjusted the assignments. The nurse observer noted that, overall, the aides seemed to "tolerate authority figures" on the floor: "No outright hostility was seen but one day the patient care coordinator wanted to talk to the aides about a problem with the laundry. It took several occasions of bell-ringing and yelling down the hall to get them to come. Several came but were walking very slowly!"

In looking at patient classification, it was found that of 69 residents, many needed nursing assistance for a variety of activities. In terms of mobility, 37 residents were totally dependent, and many of the others needed assistance. Twenty-four third-floor residents required spoon-feeding; only 13 were capable of eating alone; 31 were totally incontinent; 15 had no problems; and 52 individuals were totally dependent for bathing, with only one able to manage on her own.

The aides' shift responsibilities were generally "permanently assigned" and posted on a bulletin board in the nursing station. The permanent assignments were liked by the aides, who reported that that way they could "get to know their patients." Assignments were only changed by the charge nurse if an aide called in absent and her patient had to be reassigned. This sometimes caused grumbling among the staff, depending upon whether the caller was a friend or not. Care assignments generally ranged from five to eight residents per aide. Most residents were grouped by location.

Overall, the aides did not identify any "great" resident care assignments, but in terms of desirability, all agreed that the "white" hall (Bethany Manor's halls are color coded) had the "worst" patients. These patients were described requiring as "complete care": bedridden, total lifts for geri-chairs, requiring total feeding, incontinent, noncommunicating, having contractures. The "blue" hall was reported to be the best. Tangential third-floor duties rotated by shifts; for example, one month the day shift was responsible for the ice cart and linen. Break and lunch times were specifically preassigned.

Informal relationships did exist among the nurses' aides, who seemed to have their special friendships and cliques on each shift. One aide on the night shift had asked for a transfer because she said the other four were "ganging up" on her. One of the other four aides responded that they were only trying to help her and that she "never talks" to them. The nurse researcher was well accepted in her role as observer but reported that her presence did make the "grapevine news" on the 11 p.m. to 7 a.m. shift: "People from other places were calling the third floor to find out what I was doing there. General consensus from the other floors was that I was some sort of 'inspector.' " She added, however, "the aides were very friendly to me and they were quite willing to answer my questions, but they were careful about telling me negative things about the floor. They said the supervisor probably wouldn't like it." Added to the report was a comment: "One aide slept better than most of the patients."

Little social interaction occurred between the nurses and the aides. It was observed that when things slowed down, the groups went their separate ways on the floor to rest or socialize. Although the care providers generally got along fairly well, the Bethany Manor staff did have its interactional ups and downs. On her last night of observing the nurse researcher wrote the following note: "There is a big-time feud going on between the 11-7 aides. The 3-11 supervisor asked me how long I was going to be there. When I told her until 1-2 a.m., she asked me to keep an eye open and let her know if 'anything unusual went on with the aides.' She said she didn't want to be specific since she wanted an objective outsider's opinion. What I saw were 2 distinct groups. Two of the aides kept leaving the area to go to the other side of the hall intersection and whisper. I never heard what they were talking about. There were 2 other aides who just sat at the end of the hall all night while I was there. I spoke to them. They were polite but very quiet."

Finally, the only major difference found between shifts was that during the evening there seemed to be more social interaction between the caregivers and the residents. The observer wrote, "The aides appeared less hurried, not so brusque with the ladies. There was also more non-care oriented conversation though sometimes this tended to be on a child like level—'Aren't you a sweet little thing?'; 'Mrs. L really likes her teddy bear, don't you?' "

In summary, although certain problems did exist, Bethany Manor's patient care management strategies seemed to work fairly well in the stressful situation of caring for the physically and cognitively impaired elderly.

Patient Care Conferences

Patient care conferences led by a nurse clinician were observed during the course of the study. The care conferences were held weekly on each of the five Bethany Manor floors where care was given. State regulations determined patient reviews as follows: skilled care patients once per month, intermediate care patients every three months, and domiciliary care residents every six months. Evaluations of anywhere from six to ten patients were carried out at each care conference; conferences were attended by representatives from nursing (the head nurse of the unit where the conference was being held), social service, dietary, and recreation as well as by the nurse clinician leader. Three case examples demonstrate the nursing problems facing staff in long-term care and suggested resolutions.

Resident: Mrs. Morris   Age: 73   Date Admitted: 1/79

Diagnosis: Breast biopsy–bronchiectasis; generalized arteriosclerosis

Problem #1: Social isolation. She feels no reason for living now that her physical condition is deteriorating. Previously she had wanted always to take care of self; now is becoming unable. She needs to be helped to have a dignified death, still allowed some independence in the dying process. There is conflict between resident's desire for independence and control and physical deterioration. Resident should be offered the right to refuse or accept help with activities of daily living (resident is very private): "My body is ugly and wrinkled."

Other residents, Ms. Clark, Ms. Bond, Ms. McGinnis, now come up to see her and should be encouraged to continue to provide support.

Resident: Mrs. Monaghan   Age: 92   Date Admitted: 12/60

Diagnosis: ASCVD, cerebral ischemia; low platelets, bronchiectasis

Problem #1: Some health hazards related to hoarding; resident needs education and support. She saves food; aide knows her hiding spots. Resident doesn't like baths and keeps many clothes on her and needs bathing. Bed needs to be changed more frequently. She stays in her room; has been here 27 years. Some mornings says she doesn't feel good enough to go to the dining room; tray provided in room.

Problem #2: Frustration with living; says, "I don't know why I'm still living, still here"; but she does lie in bed most of the day (no hope of encouraging her to move if she doesn't want to). Some rectal bleeding; hemorrhoids. Mrs. Monaghan needs to be supported in her need to express frustration. Visits should be encouraged if she will allow it.

During the discussion of Mrs. Monaghan's hoarding, a suggestion was made that the nurse clinician write a brief article for the home's newsletter on the problems related to hoarding of food. For residents who like to keep small snacks, the recreation department will provide tins for cookies and candy. Since the staff could not stop all hoarding, they decided to legitimize it.

Resident: Mrs. Pierce   Age: 89   Date Admitted: 9/83

Diagnosis: Depression, senility

Problem #1: Wanders; confused; incontinent; may hit other residents. May become agitated in afternoon, thinks solarium is her living room. Took Christmas wreaths off doors as "they weren't hung right."

Problem #2: Weight loss; insufficient food intake; forgets to eat if downstairs in dining room. Gets up and leaves dining room. Daughter does not want her to stay on floor; says she will eat sweets. Resident wants to return to floor soon after going to main dining room. Numerous difficulties with family, who do not accept their mother's deteriorating condition. A meeting will be scheduled with Mrs. Pierce's family.

Families of residents were invited to attend care conferences to discuss their relatives if they wished, and a few took advantage of the opportunity. Also, the aide primarily assigned to the resident under discussion was generally called in to give her opinion. These conferences provided an opportunity for interdisciplinary teams to identify and assess significant resident problems and to seek solutions.

Staff Support Systems

Formal staff support systems at Bethany Manor were not strong, although some strides were observed during the course of the study. Early in the research, the geriatric aides and dietary staff began to organize to establish a union at the home. This was a somewhat sensitive topic with the Manor's administrator at the time, who had been used to a more autocratic type of control. In an interview, Duffie (1984, 23) asserts that although the causes of nursing home union organization may vary, "the heart of the problem generally is a failure to manage employees in a fashion that fosters high morale" (*Contemporary Administrator* 1984, 23). Duffie elsewhere (1984, 24) notes that "the key to keeping unions out is successfully implementing effective policy and supervisory development." A number of meetings between staff desiring to unionize and administration were held at Bethany Manor to attempt resolution of staff grievances. Ultimately, however, staff voted to unionize by a very high percentage. Once the decision was accepted by the home's administration, general interest among the staff seemed to recede.

Other staff support systems at Bethany Manor included the monthly head nurse and staff nurse meetings, hosted by the Director of Nursing. The purpose of these meetings, besides the sharing of administrative information, was to elicit staff problems and seek resolutions. (One staff meeting at the Manor has been described in detail under "The Director of Nursing" earlier in this chapter.)

Staff Turnover: The Revolving Door Syndrome

Waxman et al. (1984, 503) report that "one of the most serious and yet often overlooked problems affecting long-term care is the estimated 40-75% annual turnover among nursing home aides." Rantz and Roethle (1984, 187) found that the residents in their nursing home had difficulty remembering who their caregivers were as a result of "staff reassignments that brought a baffling parade of new faces." they add that their annual turnover rate was between 20% and 30%.

High turnover in nursing homes creates serious problems. First it reduces the quality of care given to residents; second, it dilutes productivity and diminishes morale; and third, it is financially costly to the facility (Stryker 1982, 21). It has been suggested that strong orientation programs for all new staff may reduce employee turnover in a nursing home by almost 50% (Tynan and Witherell 1984, 175).

Although Bethany Manor did have an orientation program, turnover was high, especially among the nurses' aides. A 23-year-old aide, who had been working at the home for two years, agreed that the turnover was "much higher than it should be" and described why: "One thing is that the aides are paid basically minimal wages, and they are very rigid in their policies, no flexibility to give the employee a sense of value in many instances. There is just not the incentive to stay here."

Bethany Manor's turnover problem was also graphically reflected in advice given periodically to the study's principal investigator about a potential study subject among the staff: "Interview her quick before she leaves!"

Staff Call-ins: The Weekend and Holiday Syndrome

Bethany Manor nursing supervisors spoke about the "weekend and holiday syndrome" as a cause of unscheduled staff absences. The supervisors' perception was that illnesses and other emergencies seemed to occur much more frequently among staff on weekends and holidays than during the Monday through Friday workweek. Of course, the nursing administrators could not challenge a worker who called in sick simply because the illness occurred on a particular day, but mental notes were made of the frequency of such calls by certain individuals. These call-ins were viewed as an alternative way of getting the day off if the head nurse had not scheduled the staff member for a free day. The weekend and holiday syndrome posed real problems for Bethany Manor, as these days were usually scheduled with fewer staff already to give as many of the staff as possible the day off. The absence of scheduled staff thus sometimes made quality care impossible.

A geriatric aide described the problem resulting from call-ins on her floor of 71 residents: "If people call in sick or on snow days we're in trouble, especially if people who live out in the suburbs can't get in. A lot of times they can't get in, and we just have to work with what we have. We just do what has to be done, the bare necessities. Everybody has to eat; patients who are incontinent have to be bathed. A bath can wait until the next day, but a face can be washed. You just do what you have to do." It should be noted, however, that one winter during the study a very heavy snowstorm hit, immobilizing the local urban area, yet some staff made heroic efforts to get to work trudging through several feet of snow. Also, the sisters, including the Director of Nursing, pitched in to care for the residents when staffing was short.

Staff Attitudes Toward the Elderly

A great deal has been written in recent years about nursing staff attitudes toward the elderly. Two reasons for this interest are, first, the fact that "the rise in the number of geriatric patients who require nursing services has been accompanied by a decline in the number of nurses who are interested in working with this patient population," and second, that "studies of nurses working with the elderly suggest that nurses who have negative attitudes toward them will engage in behaviors which may be detrimental" (Penner et al. 1984, 110). Brower (1985, 27), in a study of 581 RNs, found that "respondents who spend from 25% to 75% of their time with the aged" could best be described as "indifferent." She added that this indifference may result from a sense of frustration due to lack of knowledge of how to solve patients' problems, or from a perception of powerlessness related to inability to make changes in the nursing home setting. Even nursing students have been found to prefer to work with patients of other age groups (Gomez et al. 1985, 6); the patients that students least often desired to work with were those over 60 years of age (Knowles and Sarver 1985, 35). One of the most demoralizing nursing behaviors, undergirded by a stereotyped attitude toward the elderly as children, is infantilization. Dolinsky (1984, 12) asserts that the elderly are "often treated as children, incapable of care of themselves."

A variety of attitudes toward the elderly were manifested by the Bethany Manor staff. Some occurrences of infantilization, although decried by many staff members, did occur. A head nurse explained, "I see the aides here who say, 'This is my baby,' as much as we say, 'Don't use that term,' but if that patient is 'my baby' [to the aide] that patient is 'in'—she really gets well taken care of. They don't really mean it to be putting down the resident. It's like an endearment; it's a positive thing. Or they will say, 'This baby reminds me of my grandmother,' so that resident consequently gets some extra attention."

A patient care nurse clinician shared her perception of Bethany Manor's nursing staff overall: "We have some people here, some of the nurses, who truly do enjoy working with the elderly; gerontology is their thing. I think that we also have a large group of people who work here because of perhaps convenience, and maybe they don't have a whole lot of other options in getting jobs, and perhaps some of the geriatric aides fall into that category, but not all of them. There are some who truly enjoy working with the elderly and I think make a conscious choice to do this, but I would say they are not the majority."

Staff Frustrations and Burnout

In any situation where caregivers work with persons who have little or no hope of recovery, there are frustrations. "Most caregivers are aware of the general 'til death do us part' nature of working with chronically ill patients, and they are prepared for the 'for better or worse' aspects of these relationships. Sometimes, however, the 'for worse' characteristics of the patients or their illness condition seem to overwhelm the interaction" (O'Brien 1983, 85). In working with the institutionalized elderly, aside from chronic illness, there are also the debilitating symptoms of the aging process for caregivers to deal with, such as cognitive impairment and problems with communication. An added problem for nursing home caregivers is the bad press long-term care facilities in general receive. Gordon (1982, 11) suggests that nursing home staff face a serious contradiction: They are "service and people oriented," and feel that they do an important job, yet they are disturbed by the bad publicity nursing homes get. In her article "Today I Came Home and Cried," Walter (1985, 279), an RN supervisor at a nursing home, poses the question, "Can a nurse realize her full potential as a professional in a nursing home?" This question has long plagued and caused frustration for professional nursing staff employed in long-term care. Bethany Manor staff members, both nurses and aides, spoke of their frustrations in trying to carry out their responsibilities as professionals.

One head nurse verbalized her personal frustrations quite freely: "I think the most frustrating thing to me is the fact that I don't have always enough staff. I don't feel I have enough administrative backing either because I don't think the people down in the office, the director and assistant directors, and sometimes even the supervisors, ever really worked the floors or understand all of my frustrations. The other thing is lack of equipment sometime, because you are dealing with fixed-income people and the supplies are limited."

Another head nurse described her staff's frustrations: "The main thing they [the aides] complain of is short staffing. They can't give the residents the care that they are supposed to have, and so much is expected of the aides—to do this and do the other; they just can't get around to doing all the things they really should." An aide expressed her frustration at not being able to give the quality of care she had been taught to give: "You know when it's short, you just can't always do right. You cut corners and the resident suffers. Some days I think, 'Well, I did the best I could.' Other times it really gets to you." She added, "Another frustrating part is the household duties that we are responsible for. The most rewarding is the elderly themselves, the residents."

Another dimension of frustration addressed by many Bethany Manor caregivers was the paperwork. One of the home's nurse clinicians complained, "Working in long-term care is difficult because of the overregulation—you do a lot of nursing 'on paper.' That's one of the things that's wrong with the whole industry." A head nurse reported, "I definitely get more burned out from sitting down with paperwork than working with the residents," and an attending physician admitted, "The paperwork is incredibly heavy. I think I spend more time on paperwork than on talking to patients."

Burnout among nursing home staff members is another area of serious concern for administrators in long-term care. Heine (1984, 14) comments that perhaps what makes nursing home caregivers who work with the same residents for long periods of time so desperate is that usually at least half the residents exhibit confused behavior. They "place an inordinate amount of stress on the caregiver who has to manage and provide nursing care to these residents who also are very dependent in activities of daily living."

Burnout or impending burnout among staff was discussed by a Bethany Manor staff nurse: "After you have been here for a while you do get toward the burnout syndrome. They leave or, like myself, I found myself getting—I love my job and I love the residents—but sometimes I found myself getting to be, I just can't take this. That's what made me think about trying to change my career. Nursing can be a job that would make you just not want to come, you just get so tired." She added, "All the staff have tendencies toward burnout on this floor, but they are dedicated, most of them, even though they feel like 'I can't make this day,' they know they have to and they come because of the residents. They need somebody—you know they need somebody, and if you don't come, who's going to be there? Who is going to do it? I know I have to come. Even though you just hate to think about coming, you come."

The Rewards: "Sharing and Caring"

Winger and Smith-Staruch (186, 31) ask the question, "What boosts the interests of nurses currently working with the aged in long-term care?" They note that some nurses' attitudes toward geriatric nursing improved in direct correlation with their knowledge. In a study of 30 geriatric aides, Fisk (1984) found that nurses' aides perceived their interaction with the residents as providing the greatest rewards in caregiving; intrastaff conflicts were considered most frustrating. A reward for long-term caregivers suggested by one retirement home was development of a career ladder for nursing personnel (Kohn and Biache 1982, 25). The career ladder concept was being considered at Bethany Manor; one LPN head nurse was being encouraged to take classes toward a baccalaureate degree in nursing. Primarily, however, although occasional educational programs were presented, the staff's perceived "rewards" were related directly to their caregiving activities with the elderly.

Ann Snyder, head nurse of an intermediate care floor, described her perception of rewards in long-term care as coming even from small achievements with residents: "Even the rewards of seeing someone who has not been able to feed himself, feed himself, and to know that you helped that patient come to that advancement is a reward in itself." Peg Briscoe, an LPN, spoke of caregiving achievements in the same vein: "Sometimes when a resident is transferred from another floor and they will come down and say, 'We had to feed this resident with a syringe.' Then, after a while, you get this patient able to feed himself or hold a cup or begin to notice things around him; he is aware of his surroundings. That is so rewarding. Then sometimes residents who are alert enough to say, 'Thanks, you really do a good job.' I think this is really good, just coming from that resident, not from your peers but from this resident. Then the little squeeze of the hand when you are talking to them; they'll squeeze your hand and say, 'Thank you.' I think that's really touching, to know that you are helping them. It's something that you have to experience to know the feeling."

Finally, another Bethany Manor head nurse, Melissa Stevens, summed up her feelings about the benefits of working in long-term care very simply: "I think the most rewarding is when a resident smiles and looks up at you and you know that they feel your love. I feel it in my heart really and I do feel good about it."

Coping With Death

As discussed in Chapter 7, the Bethany Manor residents did not treat death as a tragic or unexpected occurrence, or indeed as something to be dreaded or feared. Frequently it seemed that a resident's death was more painful for caregivers than for other residents, in part, of course, because they were losing someone for whom they had cared. Even when anticipated, or as in some cases even hoped for, the death of one's "patient" can leave a caregiver with feelings of powerlessness or failure. Death can also be more difficult for young persons in general, and, as noted earlier, the Manor caregivers (especially the aides) were a relatively youthful group.

In a study examining grief among caregivers following the death of a patient in both a hospital and a skilled care facility, Lerea and LiMauro (1982, 604) found that "approximately two-thirds of the skilled nursing facility personnel remembered experiencing bereavement at the crisis of their geriatric patients." Vickio and Cavanaugh (1985, 349), who studied experience with death among long-term care personnel, also learned that "employees who had experienced a greater number of deaths of nursing home residents reported being significantly more comfortable contemplating death and dying and talking with residents about death." Bethany Manor caregivers generally did find some residents' deaths difficult.

Two head nurses described their feelings about deaths at the Manor. One explained her acceptance: "I learned that I had to cope with it if I had to work here. In a nursing home these residents are in their 80s and 90s; it is inevitable that death is going to come, so I can accept it better here in the nursing home than I could in a hospital setting, but there are cases when you really do have a special feeling for a resident. Then, it's a little hard for me to sometimes to really hold my composure around the other aides when they start to be teary-eyed."

The second head nurse focused upon her concern for the dying resident's comfort: "I feel that if there is a lot of extraordinary means to prolong death—and I don't mean prolong life, I mean prolong death—there is a greater struggle with the professionals and the aides. If a patient is kept comfortable, and it seems to be a very peaceful separation, we accept it better."

Finally, a staff nurse shared her experience in mentoring the geriatric aides and described a recent death at the Manor: "When I first came here it was really funny because a lot of aides had never been involved in deaths and a lot of them were still scared, so I would take them in with me. I would say, 'Come on with me. I'll be there with you. You don't have to be scared.' If a patient died, they would just go to another part of the house, so they didn't have to be there. Just recently one of our residents died and we had all of the aides in there and it was really something. It was heartwarming. Sister was with us and we prayed as a group over this lady. She was 109 years old. All of us on this floor were there and we all prayed together, and she died right as we were all standing there. A lot of the aides said, 'This is the first time I have been with somebody that died.' It was a good experience. It wasn't scary. It was a good experience. It was something that they dealt with, and I feel they will be able to handle it any other time." The nurse added, "The residents help us accept death. I guess they know deep down that that is what they are here for—a place to live, a place to die, and when they die it is no big deal."

Summary: A Caregiver Profile

To summarize the attitudes and behaviors of Bethany Manor nursing staff, the majority of caregivers may be classified according to a broad typology of caregiving consisting of four subcategories: the "career" geriatric caregiver, the "career ladder" geriatric caregiver, the "functional" geriatric caregiver, and the "stopgap" geriatric caregiver.

An example of a career geriatric caregiver at the home is Ms. Walters, a staff nurse who has been at Bethany Manor for approximately eight years. She likes her job, is committed to geriatric nursing, performs well above the average, is planning to further her education in nursing, and will remain in long-term care at the Manor.

Ms. Powell, another staff nurse, is, in contrast, a career ladder geriatric caregiver. She enjoys working with elderly at the home, performs well, and attends school part-time, but is looking for a job in a more sophisticated facility. She plans, however, to continue working in the field of geriatric nursing. She is using her role at the home as a stepping stone to further her career.

A functional geriatric caregiver is Ms. Tuttle, who functions fairly well at the home but does not achieve much beyond her basic assigned duties. She sees her work as "just a job." She will not move up, nor will she move out.

Ms. Coleman, by her own admission, might be described as a stopgap geriatric caregiver. Her purpose in taking a geriatric aide course and coming to the Manor was to get a temporary job when school plans fell through. She is not permanently committed to working with the elderly but will do "what she has to do" as a stopgap measure for survival.

Although a typology has been identified to broadly classify the Bethany Manor nursing staff, individual caregivers within categories may indeed vary in terms of their interest in and care for the residents. For example, a geriatric aide working in a stopgap role may have a very positive attitude toward the residents and perform her duties with excellence, even though her work is done with the knowledge that the role will most probably be temporary. The career geriatric caregiver may, by the same token, become tired or burned out over time and begin to function at a level that provides less than adequate care to residents. In summary, the majority of medical and nursing caregivers attempted to carry out their assigned duties in a manner perceived to support the identified goals of Bethany Manor Nursing Home.

References

Barney, J.L. 1983. A new perspective on nurse's aide training. *Geriatric Nursing* 4(1):44-48.

Black, D.E. 1984. Managing physician services: The integrated approach. *Contemporary Administrator* 7(3):39-42.

Brower, H.T. 1985. Do nurses stereotype the aged? *Journal of Gerontological Nursing* 11(1):17-28.

Chenitz, W.C. 1983. The nurse's aide and the confused person. *Geriatric Nursing* 4(4):238-241.

Contemporary Administrator. 1982. Family physician an answer to aging's health care needs. *Contemporary Administrator* 11(6):19.

Contemporary Administrator. 1984. The drive to unionize long-term care. An interview with L. Traywick Duffie. *Contemporary Administrator* 7(1):22-24.

Dolinsky, E.H. 1984. Infantilization of the elderly: An area for nursing research. *Journal of Gerontological Nursing* 10(9):12-19.

Duffie, L.T. 1984. Union avoidance: Winning over your workforce. *Contemporary Administrator* 7(1):24-28.

Dye, C.A. 1985. Educating leaders in gerontology. Doctoral preparation for gerontological nursing. *Journal of Gerontological Nursing* 11(1):14-16.

Fisk, V.R. 1984. When nurses' aides care. *Journal of Gerontological Nursing* 10(3):118-127.

Gomez, G.E., D. Otto, A. Blattstein, and E.A. Gomez. 1985. Beginning nursing students can change attitudes about the aged. *Journal of Gerontological Nursing* 11(1):6-11.

Gordon, G. 1982. Developing a motivating environment. *Journal of Nursing Administration* 12(12):11-16.

Heine, C.A. 1986. Burnout among nursing home personnel. *Journal of Gerontological Nursing* 12(3):14-18.

Jordan, S. 1983. The nurse in long-term care. *Geriatric Nursing* 4(3):171.

Kayser-Jones, J. 1986. Doctoral preparation for gerontological nurses. *Journal of Gerontological Nursing* 12(3):19-23.

King, P.A., and M. Cobb. 1983. Learning to care. *Journal of Gerontological Nursing* 9(5):289-292.

Knowles, L.N., and V.T. Sarver, Jr. 1985. Attitudes affect quality care. *Journal of Gerontological Nursing* 11(8):35-39.

Kohn, G.L., and A.S. Biache. 1982. Developing a career ladder for nursing personnel. *The Journal of Long-Term Care Administration* 10(4):25-27.

Lerea, L.E., and B.F. LiMauro. 1982. Grief among healthcare workers: A comparative study. *Journal of Gerontology* 37(5):604-608.

Martinson, I. 1984. Gerontology comes of age. *Journal of Gerontological Nursing* 10(7):8-17.

Mezey, M. 1983. Implications for the health professions. *Geriatric Nursing* 4(4):241-244.

O'Brien, M.E. 1983. *The courage to survive.* New York: Grune & Stratton.

Penner, L.A., K. Ludenia, and G. Mead. 1984. Staff attitudes: Image or reality? *Journal or Gerontological Nursing* 10(3):110-117.

Pomerantz, R. 1982. Considerations in the physician's approach. *Geriatric Nursing* 3(5):311-315.

Rantz, M., and L. Roethle. 1984. Who is my attendant today? *Geriatric Nursing* 5(3):187-189.

Shukla, R.K. 1982. Organizational philosophy and nurse staffing: Three-step decisions process. *The Journal of Long-Term Care Administration* 10(3):22-28.

Stryker, R. 1982. The effect of managerial interventions on high personnel turnover in nursing homes. *The Journal of Long-Term Care Administration* 10(2):21-33.

Tynan, C., and J. Witherell. 1984. Good orientation cuts turnover. *Geriatric Nursing* 5(3):173-175.

Vickio, C.J., and J.C. Cavanaugh. 1985. Relationships among death anxiety, attitudes toward aging, and experience with death in nursing home employees. *Journal of Gerontology* 40(3):347-349.

Wallace, R.W., and T.H. Brubaker. 1982. Biographical factors related to employment tenure: A study of nurse aides in nursing homes. *The Journal of Long-Term Care Administration* 10(2):11-19.

Wall-Haas, C., L. Battista, J. Stecchi, et al. 1983. Nursing home placement for beginning baccalaureate nursing students—why not? *The Journal of Long-Term Care Administration* 11(4):3-6.

Walter, A.Q. 1985. Today I came home and cried. *Geriatric Nursing* 6(5):279.

Waxman, H.M., E.A. Carner, and G. Berkenstock. 1984. Job turnover and job satisfaction among nursing home aides. *The Gerontologist* 24(5):503-509.

Winger, J.M., and K. Smyth-Staruch. 1986. Your patient is older. What leads to job satisfaction? *Journal of Gerontological Nursing* 12(1):31-35.

CHAPTER 6

The Ancillary Care Providers

I thank him that brings me a candle...when my sight grows old.

John Donne

Bethany Manor could not operate as a nursing home without the medical and nursing caregivers described in Chapter 5; however, there exists in the home a whole other group of care providers who lend the direction, support, and assistance needed for the medical and nursing teams to function effectively. The groups described here as "ancillary" include administration, social service, physical therapy, recreational therapy, pharmacy, dietary, housekeeping, and maintenance and security. Groups also of great importance in supporting the life quality of Bethany Manor residents are the spiritual caregivers (the chaplain and the sisters) and the volunteers. Although individuals involved in these ancillary services generally do not have direct contact with the residents to the same degree (in terms of amount of time spent) as the nursing caregivers, their roles are nevertheless essential to the well-being of those living at the Manor.

The majority of activities of those involved in ancillary services at Bethany Manor were observed and informally discussed during the two-year period of the study. In addition, individual meetings were scheduled with key persons involved in these caregiving systems in order to better understand their relationship to the life of the home. Those interviewed included two home administrators, an admissions clerk (in the Social Service Department), three social workers, three recreational therapists, two dietitians, a chaplain, and five volunteers.

133

Administration

The formal structure of Bethany Manor's administration is described in Chapter 7. The purpose here is to understand the personal role and experience of the nursing home administrator in relation to resident problems and needs. It is interesting to find in the gerontological literature several accounts of nursing home administrators taking on the role of resident for a time in order to experience personally the burdens and concerns of residents. One example is Bennett's (1980) book, *Nursing Home Life: What It Is and What It Could Be*, in which the author presents an account of how, presenting as a frail alcoholic resident, he had himself admitted to a nursing home, in order to better understand the lives of residents in his own long-term care facility.

A related article is Stacy's (1984, 239) "Resident For a Day," which describes a nursing home administrator's plan whereby some volunteers were admitted to the nursing home as "residents" in order "to supply first hand information to improve the quality of care." Nielsen and Moss (1979, 23, 29) assert, "It can reasonably be stated that the social environment of a long-term care facility is reflective of its administration." They describe the task of "balanced administrator" as one of providing for the development of a community that will possess its own special atmosphere.

During an informal discussion with one of the sister Administrators at Bethany Manor, Sister Catherine Ann spoke to what she felt was the home's philosophy, saying that Bethany Manor "is truly a 'home' for many of our residents where they can live out their days in a religious atmosphere of love, peace, and dignity." Another Administrator described her role in detail:

"The role of the nursing home administrator is changing dramatically. People look at the nursing home administrator as someone who sits behind a desk. That is not true. The administrator has to be a doer. She has to be very, very close to the population and staff. I spend a lot of time doing walk-throughs and meeting with staff. It's rare that I'm in my office. It's not that you don't trust the staff but you have to get out there in the field. You can't make a decision from behind the desk. You do have paperwork—most days my desk looks like a cyclone hit it—but you also channel down responsibilities. Department heads are an extension of administration."

Sister added, "I also spend a lot of time with families. The nurses or social worker could give them the same information, but sometimes they like to go right to the top. The administrator's role is becoming more of a people role, and I keep my door open—an 'open door' policy. A lot of days I think, 'What did I do all day?' I talked and listened to people all day—staff, residents, and families."

Finally, Sister Anna related her role to the contemporary sophistication in the nursing home industry: "It is important that the administrator know the laws and regulations, federal and state. We are overregulated and we must be able to challenge inspectors. We also have to participate in our local organizations and share problems and ideas." Sister Anna ended her remarks by describing the change in Bethany Manor Nursing Home from the domiciliary care facility it was some years ago to a more sophisticated caregiving facility: "The median age of our residents now is 84. Well aged used to come to the home. Now the residents are chronically ill; they require heavy, custodial care. And the turnover in deaths has increased dramatically. The residents are so much older and sicker when they are admitted. Seventy to 80 deaths a year isn't anything. Actually, we're more a geriatric hospital than a residential facility."

Social Services

As might be expected, social services are critical to supporting the care of the elderly in a long-term health care facility. Lewis (1981, 16) reiterates the point that older adults are generally institutionalized for support of multiple physiological and psychosocial deficits: "In fact, the aged requiring institutional care are admitted to nursing homes due to the interaction and resulting exacerbation of complex social, cognitive and physical problems." Silverstone (1979, 49) points out that "provision of social services in homes for the aged should begin with the admission process, carry through to the quality of life for residents, and when called for, facilitate discharge of residents." The intervention of social services is needed for resolution of a number of concerns: physical, social, and financial. The Social Service department at Bethany Manor was very active and involved with the needs of both residents and their families.

One of the social workers, Barbara Nelson, spoke of the importance of her role in regard to the admission process: "We are one of the first people that a resident or a prospective resident meets. Our office is really the initial contact for the family or for the resident. So we really do PR, we facilitate, we advocate, and we provide counseling. We counsel families, we help residents adjust and families adjust to the trauma of nursing home placement. We are always available for any other kinds of problems that may arise throughout the whole living situation." She added, "We provide for the psychosocial aspects of life here, and we provide it to the resident and family. We also, being an advocate to the residents, if staff misunderstand the resident, we are able to explain a lot of things, because we do all the research. We know what's happened prior and even though that information is all written out for staff, we explain it to them at the time of admission."

In commenting on the stresses of social service in the long-term care setting, Barbara observed, "Everyone says this must be a hard job. I never thought of it as being hard. I enjoy it. The only thing that I find difficult is sometimes just dealing with all the little problems that crop up and it has to do with just institutional life. The things that are maddening, like clothing being lost, what I would consider petty things, that's the demanding part of my job, to have to deal with various departments and personalities, difference of opinion and different attitudes. But dealing with the elderly, you know I just never see it as a problem; everyone is a special person." Finally, Barbara explained why she felt that she, personally, could cope well with working with the elderly: "I'm only 29. I look at myself and say, 'Gosh, I have at least another 70 or 80 years.' I'm not close to it [old age] myself yet."

Another Bethany Manor social worker, Helen Kopac, described her role as having a two-pronged focus: "I think there are two sides. There's the counseling side, which has to do with helping residents to get adjusted to the nursing home environment, dealing with family issues if there's family problems. There is also the other aspect of dealing with Medicaid, the very specific things like that. So I think it's kind of a combination. Some of it is Medicaid and those kinds of things, and the other is counseling, roommate problems, room changes, just any kind of thing that might go on to cause a problem." As to working in a nursing home, Helen very strongly expressed her opinion: "You have to like old people. If you don't like old people, you can forget it! You have to be patient in terms of dealing with them slowly. This can be much more problematic than in dealing with a younger population."

A structured group activity provided by a third of the Manor's social workers was "remotivation therapy." Remotivation is a type of intervention used primarily with the cognitively impaired in order to "stimulate individuals to become interested in their environment by creating a link between the objective world and their subjective reality" (Janssen and Giberson

1988, 31). Pat Whiting, a relatively new social worker at the Manor, had volunteered to lead a remotivation therapy group once a week with seven to eight moderately cognitively impaired third-floor residents.

On one winter afternoon a study researcher joined Pat as she gathered her group of eight moderately confused third-floor residents for the meeting and snack in the third-floor dining room. It took about 15 to 20 minutes to assemble the group. Three residents were wheelchair bound, one used a walker, one a cane, and all moved very slowly. One 83-year-old resident, Margaret Gaynor, kissed both Pat and the researcher as they arrived and said, "Well, I think it's a good thing that you're here—I hope it's worth your while. I like to come to the groups because otherwise I'm away from people so much. I don't leave this floor much." All of the residents except two were able to give their names.

After thanking the group for coming, Pat suggested discussion of a food topic, fruit and its preparation, using pictures and charts. She read the poem "Johnny Appleseed" and showed pictures as she went along. Some residents said that they remembered "Johnny Appleseed" from school, and a discussion ensured about how everyone best like to prepare and eat apples. Several residents reminisced about how they used to have apples or apple pie at home. Two residents' comments wandered in and out of reality ("My mother always helps me make apple pie at home," from a 90-year-old), but this seemed to go unnoticed by the group, as did the fact that one resident sitting next to the researcher kept taking her hand and kissing it. Overall, the group appeared to enjoy their meeting and discussion; simple though it was, the group interaction provided sociability and a chance to leave one's room, and stimulated cognitive functioning.

Physical Therapy

Bethany Manor employed a trained physical therapist part-time to meet the therapy needs of residents as prescribed by their physicians. Mr. Norton, who had been with the home for five years, was credited with accomplishing some "stellar" feats in terms of such activities such as straightening long-term contractures. He also helped a number of residents to maintain their mobility by teaching them the use of canes, walker, and wheelchairs. Although Manor physicians prescribed physical therapy fairly frequently, it was resisted by some residents, who considered the activity too strenuous. For others apathy was a problem. Mr. John Carter, an 87-year-old left lower leg amputee, had been fitted with a prosthesis and crutches, which he soon refused to use. When his physician asked why, he replied, "I have no need to walk."

Recreational Therapy

The recreational program in a nursing home has as a primary goal moving the resident "toward a level of functioning that has some similarity to a lifestyle developed at an earlier time in life" (Riskin, 1979, 61). Recreational therapy of some sort for all residents, regardless of physical condition, was a part of the care plan at Bethany Manor. Recreational therapy could involve anything from sensory stimulation carried out at the bedside of a severely physically and cognitively debilitated resident to shopping trips or picnics in the local community for the more mobile group. Some social activities in the home planned by the Recreation Department included a sensory stimulation group, exercise class, a creative interaction group, ceramics class, a "French Festival," movies, art class, ice cream socials, holiday celebrations, and sing-alongs.

In discussing credentials, one member of the Manor's Recreation Department staff noted that she had "a Bachelor of Science in Recreation, specializing in the therapeutic improvement of clients." Another staff member, Jean Terry, reported "I went to the university and majored in therapeutic recreation." She added, "I would say most nursing home activity directors do not have a degree in therapeutic recreation. I feel they should. Some of them have been nursing aides for a long time and then they promote them to recreation director. That's fine; they may have a lot of experience, but my personal opinion is that I really do believe that a degree in recreation or recreation therapy is really appropriate." Jean described her role as follows:

"I am responsible for 230 residents' recreation needs. Residents here probably fall into three categories. We have residents here who we just provide a service for. They come and they go to the programs they wish to participate in, but we don't have to have any actual therapy with them. They are pretty high functioning and they seem to know what they want, and we don't interfere with their decision-making process and their leisure time.

"Then there is another group that has special needs. They are unable to communicate their leisure needs to you, so you almost have to look back at their past and you have to make a general assessment of what you think they would like to participate in. That is really providing therapy, simply for the matter that they need socialization, they need to be around others, and they are incapable of doing it on their own.

"Then there are those who are the shut-ins and reclusives. They prefer to stay in their rooms. For them we simply let them know what is available, and we may even provide certain things for them to try it out."

Jean summarized some of the formal activities: "We have movies, guests who come and entertainment, piano concerts, sing-alongs. We also have trips out into the community. That's a really important part of the program. When I got here there were hardly any trips out, maybe just to the [shopping] plaza on Fridays, but I really feel that's a big, important part of recreation because it's getting the residents back out into the community. When you become institutionalized there are a lot of things that they feel aren't available to them any more, and one of those things is the community trips and the community itself. I really try to get many residents out on these trips."

Finally, Jean Terry spoke of her frustrations as a recreational therapist at the nursing home: "I like it here and I really enjoy my job, but I just feel sometimes that there are a lot of residents I am missing due to time and staffing; we don't reach everybody. I wish I could and that upsets me sometimes. We will go to a care planning conference and someone will say, 'What about this lady?' and it is somebody who has slipped through the cracks. It makes me feel I wish I could reach more people, but due to the staffing and budgets I don't."

Another Recreation department staff member, Joanne Davis, described her work with the cognitively impaired residents: "I am not sure to what degree they can understand. I just discuss things with them. Maybe I will tell them the day's activities and go over the date and time and the place, tell them who the president of the United States is, orient them to reality. I always start by telling them who I am and what department I am with, but then I am not sure if they do understand. Some of them, like Mrs. O'Boyle, she recognizes my face but whether she puts the two of us together as in recreation and my name, I don't know." She added, "Hopefully, I can provide them some therapy and socialization."

Some of the recreation department's social activities attended during the course of the study included bingo; "happy hour"; exercise class; numerous holiday parties such as Christmas, St. Patrick's Day, and Valentine's Day; sing-alongs with the cognitively impaired group; a balloon launch to celebrate the beginning of "Older Americans Month"; and a resident's 100th birthday party. Often a large number of residents attended these affairs; some were brought by aides, the sisters, or other residents, and some were able to navigate on their own. The residents' degree of participation varied notably. At Mrs. Ursula Wiggens' 100th birthday party, some residents visited with their friends, a few danced with the staff or other residents, but most just sat quietly enjoying the band music provided for the occasion. One wheelchair-bound resident, Mrs. Valassi, said, "I'm sitting near the door in case I want to get our of here"; Mrs. Sheehan reminisced about her family in Ireland; Mrs. Lizotte fretted that she hadn't gotten to Mass that morning; and Mrs. Mary Didion, a charming 87-year-old resident, chided the researcher, "You haven't come back to see me; I should have brought my big stick." It was observed that the majority of residents responded well to individual attention; many, however, appear too timid to reach out on their own either to staff or to other residents.

An arts and crafts program can result in increased self-worth and a new outlook on life for nursing home residents *Contemporary Administrator* 1984). Although Bethany Manor did not have an occupational therapy department, one long-time nursing home aide manned a small handicraft department that was enjoyed by many residents. Activities such as sewing and painting provided afternoon pastimes for those who made their way to the basement shops.

A Recreation Department staff member commented that resident activities such as crafts have had to be modified at the Manor over the years because of the population's physical and cognitive decline as a group: "There are old wounds in this place. People used to make so many beautiful things here. Now when residents come in they are unable to do the things they used to do at the home, crafts and handiwork. They are a lot sicker when they get here so we have to plan accordingly."

The change in Bethany Manor's population was a theme echoed frequently by long-term staff. A physician with many years experience at the home observed that 15 to 20 years ago residents were much "healthier" and that the Manor was then more of a domiciliary entity than an intermediate care facility. A Director of Nursing reported that some years previously residents could travel outdoors freely and many even gardened, an activity few could presently manage. Thus, the current crafts department offerings consist mostly of activities such as making yarn animals, making quilt patches, knitting coverings for coat hangers, sewing and stuffing small dolls, painting ceramic figurines, and needlepoint. Nevertheless, some residents derived much pleasure from their craft work. Miss Anna Conway asserted, "I love working here. She [a recreational staff member] gives me tasks to complete and I don't mind doing them for her. She never makes you feel rushed; she never asks, 'Why didn't you finish this?' You get to do so much here and the time just flies by for me. There are some [resident] ladies who say that the days are so long. It's because they don't do anything with their time."

Pharmacy

Bethany Manor employed two consultant pharmacists, experts in drug therapy, who provided the residents' medications according to a unit dose system, maintained 24-hour delivery of drugs seven days a week, and issued a monthly newsletter with updates on the latest drugs. The pharmacy consultants sat on the Manor's Pharmacy Committee and also provided educational programs for the home.

At a Sunday afternoon Family Circle meeting (the Family Circle was described in Chapter 3), Mr. Goldman, a Bethany Manor pharmacist, discussed his company's resources and services relative to such points as 24-hour coverage for the home, knowledge of federal and state regulations for the handling of medications in nursing homes, procedures for delivery and administration of home medications, computerized records of all residents' prescriptions, cost-effectiveness; the unit dose system, handling of physicians' orders, and Medicare and Medicaid reimbursement. Finally, Mr. Goldman noted that one of the pharmacists regularly attends both the nursing home's Infection Control Committee and the Pharmacy Committee meetings. The Pharmacy Committee consists also of the Administrator, the Director of Nursing, the Medical Director, the Director of Social Services, and the Dietitian.

At one meeting during the study, the primary topics discussed by the pharmacist included federal regulations for the prescribing and handling of "schedule 2" drugs (narcotics and stimulants, sedatives), and the state directive for a computerized program to provide needed documentation for Medicaid reimbursement. Finally, to expedite delivery and documentation of these drugs, Mr. Goldman promised that the pharmacists would come to the home periodically to orient new staff.

Dietary

Nutrition and aging are reciprocal. "Aging affects nutritional needs, and level of nutrition affects the process of aging" (Patten 1982, 141); also the "nutritional needs of an older person have a major impact on health and well-being" (Bailey and Cerda 1984, 67). Nutritional deficits or excesses in the elderly may be manifested in the skin (Neldner 1984) and in other tissues and organs and may result in significant deleterious physiological changes. Thus, the dietary department is most important in a long-term care facility devoted to the care of the older individual.

One of Bethany Manor's registered dietitians, Sue Hill, described her role: "Mostly, we are concerned with assessing the resident's nutritional status to make sure that it is being maintained adequately. It is vital to them coping with other kind of stresses to have adequate intake, so I do a lot of assessments, trying to find how well they are eating, what types of things they like to eat and don't like to eat, what changes dietary can make to improve their status." She added, "I review the charts to see if the residents have any special needs and to see what the background has been like, if they have always been underweight, if they have always been a poor eater. From that I will go talk to the patient."

Some specific dietary problems reported by Miss Hill included dehydration, related to some residents' inability to ask or reach for water; difficulty in chewing many foods, especially meats (even when tender or chopped); personal dislikes for some nutritious foods included in the menu; and a number of resident's preference for snacks, which they sometimes kept in the rooms. She observed, "The majority of them have snacks in their room. So often when we find that they are not eating much from their trays, we are very quick to say, 'Let's give them a supplement.' The problem with that is it just increased the problem with them not eating their food. A supplement should be given at a time when there are not other means to get them to eat, and then it should only be used as a supplement and not as a total replacement, with the eventual goal of getting them back on regular food. Then you are sure that they are getting the fiber and all the nutrients that they really need. It makes them feel more like a person, too, to eat food, and not like a sick person who has to drink their nourishment."

Miss Hill also described mealtime at Bethany Manor as a very important event for some residents: "It's the highlight of their day, it really is.

When something goes wrong, some people, it upsets them an awful lot. I just spoke to a man about 10 or 15 minutes ago. He was upset because the meat was very tough and I asked him, 'Did you talk to your server? Was she able to get you a substitute?' He said that he had mentioned it to her and she mumbled something and walked away. He was very upset and he had a real right to be."

The nursing home had a problem with high turnover among dietary attendants. Two dietary aides, ages 19 and 22, commented that the work didn't promise much in terms of their future. One reported having worked at the home for over a year and said she enjoyed working with the elderly; the younger aide had been at the Manor less than a month and said he would only stay "for a little while."

Housekeeping and Laundry

Housekeeping services at Bethany Manor were originally managed by the home; however, during the course of the research, a change was made to contracting for outside services. One reason for the management change was to ensure continuity of services, which had previously been a problem because of high staff turnover. The homes' laundry, which came under the direction of the housekeeping services, also posed management problems in terms of both staff attrition and the periodic disappearance of residents' laundry. Spicer (1982, 13) asserts that indeed "special problems occur with in-house laundry facilities in nursing homes." Some of these include hoarding of linens, overuse of linens, missing items, and high temperatures around the heavy equipment.

At Bethany Manor, two female members and one male member of the housekeeping staff were assigned to each floor on the day shift. Although some staff members had little or no history at the home, a number had worked at Bethany Manor for some time and had developed friendships with residents. On several occasions housekeepers were observed assisting residents to move about their rooms or directing them to the elevator or the dining room. One female housekeeper was overheard saying to a wheel-chair-bound resident, "Now why didn't you tell me you wanted to get out to the elevator? You know I would have taken you down." Residents frequently greeted the housekeeper by name and made positive remarks about "how nice" they kept the home.

Maintenance and Security

"Plant maintenance is crucial in the operation of the long-term care facility" (Spicer 1981, 14). The Maintenance Department at Bethany Manor consisted of the department head, Mr. Clarence McKown, and about six to eight full-time maintenance employees. The department, whose offices were located in the basement of the home, seemed continually busy.

A dimension of the Manor's general maintenance responsibility was nursing home security and the force of security personnel. "The main causes of accidents involving the aged are well documented: medication effects, confusion, unfamiliar environment, hearing and visual impairment, the effects of illness and the normal aging process" (Finkelstein et al. 1984, 47). In the nursing home setting many safeguards against these occurrences are built in to the physical and social environment. At Bethany Manor, severely confused residents were housed whenever possible on one floor, which had alarms attached to exit doors to alert staff when residents wandered (although some did occasionally escape via the elevator). Medications were carefully checked by professional nursing staff to avoid error, and the impairments of the aging process were considered in designing the personal and communal spaces used by residents. As an added measure of security, however, Bethany Manor, which is located near a large urban area, maintained a force of security guards around the clock: two on each eight-hour shift. Their usual activities focused on determining the appropriateness of visitors to the home and patrolling the grounds at night. Aside from these inspections, the guards were on call for any security-related emergencies occurring throughout the home.

At a meeting of the home's department heads, Mr. McKown cited one of his recent problems: A night shift security guard had been reportedly using the home telephone for personal calls lasting a half-hour to 45 minutes. The group determined that in the future all personal calls to staff needed to be directed first to a department head or supervisor. It was also requested that employees not tie up pay telephones as they are in place primarily for resident use.

Chaplaincy and Spiritual Support

Because Bethany Manor is publicly recognized as a home with a strong religious philosophy, spiritual support, especially the provisions of religious services, was a priority for many residents. Because of the Catholic character of the home, a full-time priest-chaplain was in residence. One of the chaplains (there were several over the course of the study), Father Mike Harrity, described his role as consisting primarily of overseeing the provision of religious services to the residents: Mass and the Sacraments, counseling, and sick call visits to those who were bedridden. Father Harrity added that he had a number of assistants in providing religious care to the residents:

"We have other individuals who are involved. We have a permanent deacon from the Archdiocese who has been ministering here for seven or eight years, and he is very effective and very devoted to the residents. He comes one evening a week just for the purposes of going around and visiting. He also assists on Sunday with the liturgy and helps distribute Holy Communion. The priests who are over at the local priests' residence are very good about covering Masses for us if I am away or if we are short. You see, there are two scheduled Masses here every day, 7:30 and 9:30. The sisters are also all commissioned as Eucharistic Ministers, and on Sunday they assist with Holy Communion. Sister Ann is very good. She has, on occasion, also distributed Communion on the floors. She usually leads the Rosary every day. We have Rosary devotions six days a week, Monday through Saturday."

In discussing the difficulty of working exclusively with the elderly, Father Harrity commented, "Oh, it can get to you, because you are in a facility that, almost by definition, when the residents come, they are going to remain here until they go to a hospital or to Gate of Heaven [a local cemetery]. It's the downside of life and that can be psychologically, I think, depressing when you are constantly in a nursing home." Father added, however, that he did have personal support from other priest colleagues, some of whom were involved in similar chaplaincy work. He also discussed his inclusion of the confused residents in religious rites:

"Even patients who are pretty much out of contact, they are still able to make the sign of the cross, they are still able to say prayers they learned when they were three or four years old. It is one of the things that goes last, as far as memory is concerned. Well, at least some basic religious tenets that they held on to, because they were so deeply ingrained, and you will find patients who have great difficulty remembering most things and whose memory for current time sequences is almost completely gone, but who will recognize the Eucharist and are very devout, will receive [Communion] very piously, and I think it is very meaningful to them."

Finally, Father Harrity confirmed the investigators' early perception that death was not something feared by most residents and indeed even welcomed by some: "Some really long for death. I don't mean they are suicidal, it's not a question of being self-destructive, but they are just weary and tired and they would just like to go home to the Lord. There doesn't seem to be any kind of apprehension or anxiety or fear or dread."

The Volunteers: Bridge to the Local Community

Volunteers are an important part of the ancillary support system of a nursing home. "Traditionally, they lead bingo and sing-alongs and assist with arts and crafts and visitation" (Holmes and Everline 1984, 9). Bethany Manor had a very active volunteer organization consisting of two subgroups: adult volunteers and youth (teenage) volunteers. The adult volunteer program is open to all persons, male and female, over the age of 18 who are able to volunteer time on a regular basis. Adult volunteers participated in such activities as visiting with or reading to residents, delivering mail, presenting movies or slide shows, helping with bingo or other recreational activities such as outings, writing letters, escorting residents to activities in the home (e.g., beauty salon, physical therapy), and helping with arts and crafts. The youth volunteer program was open to students 14 years or older who had finished ninth grade. Youth volunteers were expected to work a minimum of two hours per week during the school year and could visit more often in the summer. Their activities consisted of helping staff with the serving of meals and other nourishments, escorting residents to treatments or other activities, helping at social activities, writing or reading letters for residents, and visiting those who were bedridden or confined to their rooms.

The home's volunteer office was also in the process of revitalizing a Bethany Manor Guild, the goal of which was to assist the sisters and staff through sponsored programs and special events. Besides the Manor's own volunteers, a number of local organizations such as civic groups, churches, and schools provided support and assistance to the residents. Some of their activities included music appreciation, a slide show (England's cathedrals), a Catholic Daughters' Bingo, Sierra Club visitors, "Exercises with Suzanne," a Ladies of Charity Halloween Party, Irish dancers, and a Kiwanis Club sing-along.

Bethany Manor volunteers were very articulate in describing their personal satisfaction with nursing home activities in which they were engaged. One adult male volunteer commented that he found great personal satisfaction in doing "little things" for the nursing home residents, now that he was retired, and he added, with a chuckle, "My wife likes my doing it, too. It gets me out of her hair!" A female volunteer stated, "I can have patience with old people because they are so grateful. If you say, 'Hello,' they grab your hand, they won't let you go. They just want to talk or you don't have to talk. You just have to sit there and they look at you like they are just so happy you stopped by. You have to hold their hand, shake their hand, kiss them. They do like to hold your hands." Another woman described her reason for volunteering at the Manor: "The problem is some [residents] never receive any family, their friends, nothing—no one ever comes. They need someone to smile, to say, 'How are you doing?'" She added, "I never just walk in their rooms. I always knock because that's all they have. I always knock as if I were going into their home."

Several teenage volunteers also spoke about working with the elderly at Bethany Manor. Michael, a 15-year-old, described his activities and those of several friends: "Mainly we just visit residents but sometimes we do different projects. Right now a few of us go round and stamp people's clothes so they don't get lost in the laundry, and earlier a few of us played the piano—we had a piano recital. I guess it's just getting people involved, talking to them, making them more sociable." Michael added, "Some of them, when you first meet them, it is very difficult to talk because you have to find out what they want to talk about. Once you get to know them and you come back every week and you get your routine, who you are going to visit, it is a lot easier, because you know what they like and things they like to talk about." Another 15-year-old, Tim, explained what he thought his weekly visit meant to the residents: "A lot of the residents are very grateful for any attention. The ones who remember you, that adds something to their lives. There is something good in their life as part of their routine, something to look forward to and that there is somebody who, to some degree, does care about them, thinks about them."

The Foster Grandparent Program

The most recently established volunteer program at Bethany Manor was the Foster Grandparent Program. In discussing the relationship of the elderly to children, Cheek (1982, 252) points out that "the need for tenderness does not diminish with age." The Foster Grandparent Program was described in a Volunteer Department report as follows: "Fourth, fifth, and sixth grade children have made their way into the hearts of Bethany Manor residents for the past five weeks now as part of an intergenerational companion program known as 'Foster Grandparents.' The fifteen children and their adopted grandparents meet each Thursday afternoon from 2:45 to 4:00 p.m. in the auditorium. Their activities include everything from shared arts and crafts projects and checker games to story reading and strolls around the home."

One of the foster grandparents expressed her delight in the young lady with whom she had developed a friendship: "She's coming this week and I'm going to teach her how to stitch these flowers. She said they don't teach her anything like this at the school. We had some cakes at lunch and I saved her some." As the study was drawing to a close, the Foster Grandparents Program appeared to be working well for all involved.

Summary

It should be noted that the labeling of the care providers described in this chapter as "ancillary" is in no way meant to understate the importance of their activities in the lives of Bethany Manor residents. The word "ancillary" is derived from the Latin ancilla, meaning servant or helper, and it is the ancillary group who indeed provide the aid and support critical to maintaining a positive quality of life for members of the nursing home community. The facility's Administrator sets the tone for all home activities in terms of philosophical and policy issues. The social workers provide strong undergirding support for critical incidents in the lives of residents and their families: admission, transfer, hospitalization, discharge, death, and any unexpected crises that occur. The Recreation Department assists residents in making their days at the Manor more meaningful and satisfying. The Pharmacy Department supports residents' physical and sometimes behavioral needs through chemical intervention and manipulation. The Dietary Department provides food for nutritional and psychological satisfaction—both essential to life. Housekeeping and maintenance support the residents' quality of life through the provision of a pleasant and safe environment. The chaplaincy offers spiritual support and intervention if needed. Finally, the volunteers provide the residents' a most important and much-needed bridge to the local community.

References

Bailey, L.B., and J.J. Cerda. 1984. Diagnosis and treatment of nutritional disorders in older patients. *Geriatrics* 39 (8):67-71.

Bennett, C. 1980. *Nursing home life: What it is and what it could be.* New York: Tiresias Press.

Cheek, M.V. 1982. My friend David. *Geriatric Nursing* 3(4):252.

Contemporary Administrator. 1984. Hillhaven's 'arts with elders': Not your basic arts and crafts. *Contemporary Administrator* 7(1): 43-44.

Finkelstein, H., P. Barnett, and H. Myers. 1984. Safeguarding the residents. *Contemporary Administrator* 7(11):47-49.

Holmes, E.A., and D. Everline. 1984. The use of volunteers in social group work as remotivation leaders. *The Journal of Long-Term Care Administration* 12(4):9-12.

Janssen, J.A., and D.L. Giberson. 1988. Remotivation therapy. *Journal of Gerontological Nursing* 14(6):31-34.

Lewis, K. 1981. Three approaches to social services. *Contemporary Administrator* 4(11):16-19.

Nielsen, S., and T. Moss. 1979. The administrator's role in the long term care facility. In *Long term care of the aging. A socially responsible approach,* edited by L.J. Wasser, 23-29. Washington, DC: Division of Long Term Care, Health Resources Administration, Department of Health, Education, and Welfare.

Neldner, K.H. 1984. Nutrition, aging and the skin. *Geriatrics* 39(2):69-79.

Patten, S.E. 1982. Nutrition and the elderly: A cultural perspective. *Geriatrics* 37(1):141-145.

Riskin, C. 179. Activity programs in homes for the aged. In *Long term care of the aging. A socially responsible approach,* edited by L.J. Wasser, 55-61. Washington, DC: Division of Long Term Care, Health Resources Administration, Department of Health, Education, and Welfare.

Silverstone, B. 1979. Providing social services in the long term care setting. In *Long term care of the aging. A socially responsible approach,* edited by L.J. Wasser, 49-54. Washington, DC: Division of Long Term Care, Health Resources Administration, Department of Health, Education, and Welfare.

Spicer, W.A. 1981. New ideas advance plant maintenance. *Contemporary Administrator* 4(4):14-15.

Spicer, W.A. 1982. Mastering the laundry. *Contemporary Administrator* 5(12):13-16.

Stacy, C. 1984. Resident for a day. *Geriatric Nursing* 5(6):239.

CHAPTER 7

The Nursing Home
as a Social System

one must observe the proper rites...

"What is a rite?" asked the Little Prince.

"These are actions too often neglected," said the fox.

Antoine de Saint-Exupéry, The Little Prince

On entering Bethany Manor, one is struck with an immediate sense of paradox that might be expressed in the question, "Is this place, this nursing home, truly a 'home,' or is it rather an 'institution' "?

Because of the facility's physical size and the number of persons who reside there, the concept of institution seems initially to be more appropriate. A formal reception area complete with a switchboard and a nearby security desk support the thought. On the human side, however, a visitor is touched by the warmth of the greeting received from one or several nursing home residents sitting on the porch (in clement weather) or in armchairs in the front lobby. There is indeed a sense of home in the comfort and familiarity of exchange with which guests are received, and in the territoriality established by residents in regard to favorite chairs or favorite places to "take up the watch." Rarely is a nursing home visitor without a word of greeting, a comment or two about the weather, or a bit of advice or direction if the visitor is unfamiliar with the home.

What, then, constitutes the "world" of the nursing home? What is its character, and whence is derived its spirit and its presentation of self? How are its joys, its sorrows, its sufferings, and its rewards, the myriad actions and reactions that make up the fabric of everyday life, woven into a tapestry that can be labeled, "nursing home life"?

Bethany Manor is a microcosm of the larger society, with its own unique culture and subcultures—generational, racial, religious, and ethnic. The home provides the resources for physical, emotional, and spiritual sustenance. Bodily needs are met through the provision of adequate nutrition and facilities for physical care, as well as for special medical attention, when it is required for more productive and/or more comfortable continuation of life. Activities such as occupational therapy and structured social interactions—happy hours, teas, parties, movies, guest performances—provide the residents with means of occupying their day.

Informal social interaction is promoted simply because of the density of the group. The presence of large numbers of elders housed in the same physical facility provides an opportunity for friendships to develop that might elude the older person living alone or with family in the community. The population density and the structure of the life are seen as a negative characteristics for some residents, however. One of the most difficult things to accept, especially for residents who formerly lived alone and who maintained significant autonomy in their lives, is the institutional atmosphere of the nursing home.

On the central question of whether Bethany Manor is really a home or really an institution, most respondents, both residents and caregivers, reported that the Manor contained elements of both. Frequently responses were related to the respondent's own life-style preference. If a resident was used to living with a large household (e.g., an extended family with children, grandchildren, pets), the nursing home was viewed predominantly as a home. Such respondents were used to a home that included at least some type of schedule for meals and social activities, as well as the sharing of facilities, in order to accommodate a diverse number of household members. In contrast, the respondent who was used to living alone or with only one other person tended to view the nursing home more as an institution. These residents had often been used to a life-style in which such activities as mealtimes and sleep could be changed at will, as could general household or personal activities. One's daily schedule was under one's own control. Retsinas (1986, 24), in her sociological analysis of a nursing home, notes that "to think of the nursing home as a possible home, we must discard the family-institution continuum." She adds that we must recognize not how the home fits the archetypical institutional model but how indeed it deviates from it.

To address the question of home versus institution in more depth, the Bethany Manor case study adopted the conceptual orientation of social systems analysis (Loomis 1960). In the social systems framework, elements, processes, and conditions of actions of social systems are identified and described in a "processually articulated structural model" (PASM; Loomis 1960, 8). This model focuses the analysis on those variables central to social system structure, which include beliefs (knowledge), sentiments (feelings), goals (ends, achievements), norms (standards), status roles (positions, functions), rank (hierarchial allocation of roles), power (control), sanctions (reward or punishment), and facility (environment) (Loomis 1960, 8). This model provided the research with a broad conceptual base appropriate to the evaluation of a complex social entity such as the contemporary nursing home.

Goals of the Home: Philosophy and Administration

Bethany Manor is a private metropolitan long-term care facility (i.e., nursing home), providing three levels of care: domiciliary, intermediate, and skilled. The home is a 230-bed residential facility with a staff that includes the Administrator and her assistant, a physician Medical Director and visiting staff physicians, registered nurses (MSNs, BSNs, AAs, and diploma graduates), licensed practical nurses, nurses' aides, religious caregivers (primarily priests and sisters), social workers, numerous support staff members (physical therapist, recreational therapists, dietary aides), and volunteers.

Bethany Manor was founded in the late 1950s to provide a home where aged residents could receive 24-hour professional nursing care and other supportive services to meet their physical, religious, and psychosocial needs. The goals of the home are to provide these services in an atmosphere of love and respect for the aged and infirm, stressing restorative nursing and multidisciplinary planning (*Teaching Nursing Home Project*, p. 3).

The home was established as a nonprofit corporation supported by its local Catholic diocese and administered and partially staffed by a community of religious women whose primary mandate is care of the aged and the infirm. The philosophy of care is conceptualized in the home's ethical code or "Credo" of patients' rights which concludes with the statement: "We must afford the individual the opportunity to withdraw from the demands of life, as needed, with honor, comfort and dignity." Bethany Manor's Credo also addresses protection of the resident's self-esteem and individuality and supports the freedom to continue self-determination in the major aspects of personal life. Nursing home administrators frequently cite attempting to respond to residents' individual personal needs as a critical variable in nursing home care (Spicer 1982, Miller 1984).

The Manor's sister Administrator directs and coordinates all activities of the home in keeping with the policies of the Board of Directors and in accord with federal and state regulations. The Board of Trustees exercises general management and control of business affairs. It reviews all home policies, enters into contracts, and prepares annual capital and operating budgets (*Teaching Nursing Home Project*, p. 3). The Assistant Administrator directs the work of such departments as security, purchasing, food service, housekeeping, maintenance, volunteers, and social service. The Director of Nursing oversees the organization and implementation of all nursing services. The professional nursing staff assumes responsibility for directing, coordinating, and providing care. The physician Medical Director has responsibility for administration of patient care services and acts as a medical representative of the home in the larger community. Approximately 40 physicians practice in the facility, with each resident having a personal physician. Dentists and podiatrists are under contract and visit residents as needed (*Teaching Nursing Home Project*, p. 4).

The home's major committees include the Executive Committee, the Utilization Review Committee, the Administrative Review Committee, the Patient Care Policy Committee, the Infection Control Committee, the Pharmacy and Therapeutic Committee, the Institutional Planning Committee, the Social Service Committee, and the Fire and Safety Committee. Figure 7-1 presents a simplified version of Bethany Manor's organizational chart.

The Physical Environment

Bethany Manor is an attractive, five-story, red brick building, which is both fire retardant and air conditioned. It is entered from a semicircular drive, which is the termination of a longer driveway connecting the facility

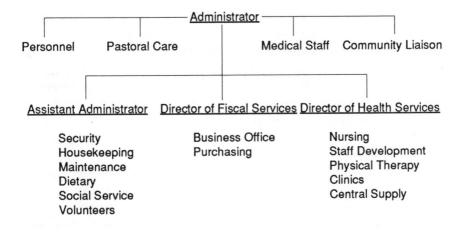

Figure 7-1 The Bethany Manor Governing Board (Trustees).

to the neighboring urban community. The grounds are spacious and well kept, with numerous shade trees and benches and chairs for the residents' outdoor enjoyment.

The home has 187 single bed/sitting rooms or bedrooms, 18 two-bedroom suites, 1 three-bed ward, and 1 four-bed ward. The ground floor (basement) contains an activity area with a 300-person seating capacity, a recreation room, a coffee shop, a cocktail lounge, a ceramics craft room, residents' laundry, a beauty shop, and several storage areas. The first floor consists of the chapel, visitors' parlors, administrative offices, the boardroom, the main resident dining room, the Dietary Department, and the employees' dining room. Also on the first floor, 17 domiciliary care residents are housed, most of whom require little assistance with activities of daily living other than the administration of medications. These residents are all ambulatory and have moderate control over their own daily routine.

The second, third, and fourth floors consist primarily of residents' rooms, nursing stations, utility areas, and communal dining rooms. Also found on the second floor are a conference room, a physicians' office, and the Physical Therapy Department. The fifth-floor facilities include a 20-bed skilled patient care unit with nursing station and utility rooms as well as private residence quarters for the sisters.

Bethany Manor's second and fourth floors, housing 53 and 71 residents, respectively, provide intermediate care for individuals whose physical condition necessitates such attention as assistance with bathing and dressing, assistance with eating, care of hair and nails, and a variety of medical treatments. Many of these residents are wheelchair bound or on bed rest. The third floor, also considered an intermediate care unit, with facilities for 69 residents, is unique in housing the majority of the home's cognitively impaired group. Exit doors on this floor are provided with alarm systems to prevent confused residents from wandering off without the staff's knowledge. Gaffney (1986) stresses the importance of all nursing homes providing a less restrictive environment for the cognitively impaired resident while providing for their safety. In studying a home subpopulation who were labeled "wanderers," the following concerns were reported: Residents frequently wandered out of sight of staff within the building; much staff time was spent tracking residents; wandering residents often disturbed bedridden patients by entering their rooms; and residents attempted to go outdoors inappropriately dressed (Gaffney 1986, 94). Door alarms were found to be a useful protective mechanism.

The fifth floor of Bethany Manor was organized and staffed to provide for the needs of residents whose physical deterioration, either temporary or permanent, required skilled care, including more sophisticated medical and nursing procedures.

Although the Manor's building is almost 30 years old, it is functional, well maintained, and clean, and presents a pleasant ambiance. This was frequently commented upon by residents, who were especially sensitive to new aesthetic additions to the Manor—holiday decorations were always a topic of discussion and pleasure. Andreasen (1985) discusses the importance of nursing home design in terms of meeting both the resident's functional and aesthetic needs, observing, "The environmental design and structure of any extended care facility must be suited to the disabilities of the elderly if it is to meet their needs" (Andreasen 1985, 19). She adds that aesthetic additions or changes, especially in regard to color, should be made to suit the resident's physiological needs (e.g., vision changes) rather than those of the owners or administrator.

The Technical Environment

The equipment and supplies at Bethany Manor, although not ultra high-tech, are generally of good quality and adequate for the care of the residents. Although one does not find such equipment as the Flexi-care bed presently advocated in some quarters for the bedridden geriatric patient, comfortable beds with adequate clean linens are available, as well as varieties of chairs and couches suited to particular needs. Obviously, equipment and supplies vary with the type of care carried out on the unit, with the more highly medical-technological materials available on the fifth-floor. Although certain communal areas such as the dining room and sun porches have small luxuries such as color television sets and comfortable armchairs and sofas, the home's basic physical and technical environment is decidedly functional—the reflection of its institutional aspect. Most of the small, homey touches—a personal television set, framed photographs, an attractive lamp, brightly colored pillows, or a hand-crocheted afghan—are brought to the nursing home by the residents or their families. The majority of residents who are cognitively aware of their surroundings make studied attempts to color their world homelike in the semi-institutional physical environment of Bethany Manor.

A 90-year-old female resident, Mrs. Mattie Shackelford, reported that although she was able to add some personal touches to her room on the fourth floor, she would have liked to have more. She noted the difficulty of having to give up treasured possessions: "That table and chair are all I have in here, and the stool. They wouldn't let me bring anything else so I gave it all away. I had a lovely rocking chair and they wouldn't let me bring it. It was 150 years old and now it's gone." She added with resignation, "They gave me that [armchair]. It's all right, it's better than nothing."

The Psychosocial Environment

The psychosocial environment of Bethany Manor reflects not only the overall character of the home as semi-institution, but also several different characters related to the facility's subculture and differing levels of care. In general, the psychosocial interactional milieu of the home demonstrates both institutional and homelike characteristics. Following Goffman's definition of "institution" as "a place of residence and work where a large number of life-situated individuals, cut off from the wider society for an appreciable period of time, together lead an enclosed, formally administered round of life" (Goffman 1962, i), perhaps the most significant and, at times, most difficult aspect of nursing home life is its formally administered nature.

Miss Pritchard, a 93-year-old resident who was both ambulatory and alert, commented on the difficulty of the home's schedule. She said, "Sometimes you'd just not like to get up for breakfast in the morning or get your bath right then, but if you don't you'll miss it. People sit in their wheelchairs outside the dining room sometimes for an hour waiting to eat. You just can't do things when you want to here at all and it's not very private." She added, "I suppose it's for the best, though. With so many of us here, I mean, it's about all you can do."

Besides the difficulty of adjusting to the structured nature of life at the home, some residents also found the more public aspect of life at Bethany Manor trying. One third-floor resident who said when asked her age, "I'm around 300 years old" (later she said that she had been born in 1902), and admitted that she found being forced to interact with other home residents very hard. She stated, "I am what you call a loner because I am not companionable with very many people. There are not many people that I want to talk to." This resident also commented on her more recent inability to control her own life in the home because of physical disabilities: "I was very independent and did everything for myself until really just since I have been down on this floor. When I was on the fourth floor I was still doing quite a lot for myself, and that was very nice. I liked the fourth floor. Then you come down here. Most everybody down here is crazy as a june bug. I haven't lost my mind yet, and it is very trying to be with people that are crazy all the time. It's depleting. There is no inspiration for anything."

Gubrium (1975, 3a) in his study of "Murray Manor" also found that the institutional character of the home caused difficulties for residents in terms of privacy. He reported, "When patients don't work to maintain private places, they are not likely to have them any longer. This does not mean that they aren't desirous of them."

Many of the other cognitively alert study respondents at Bethany Manor also commented on the distastefulness of having to interact with cognitively impaired residents in the home. Fear of "becoming crazy" seemed of much more concern to the study group than fear of death, death being considered a more accepted and nonstigmatizing part of life at Bethany Manor.

Certain respondents did, however, view the nursing home more as a small community or "home" than as an institution, following an under-standing of home as a social unit whose members are "bound together by a shared sense of belonging and by the feeling among its members that the group defines for them their distinctive identity" (Broom and Selznick

1963, 31). Mrs. Little, a 78-year-old second-floor resident, described her situation and her feelings this way: "I got rid of my home and my car and my little dog. I couldn't get out so it's a right sad thing, but this is home to me now. I'll be here until I'm gone. I have no place else to go. My nieces and nephews are good to me but I'm not going to move. I'm comfortable here and they're good to me—that's the main thing. I wouldn't like it at all if they weren't."

Some residents treated their rooms as their own private territory, as that part of the institution that was home. Miss Catherine Turner was such a resident. A research team member described a visit with her:

"Miss Turner saw the opportunity to have a new face to talk to and invited me to her room to see her new desk. She was very proud of the new piece of furniture and wanted to share her joy with someone that would care. She invited me to try out her chair—this was my invitation to stay a while.

"We talked for almost an hour about her relatives, her stroke, and her feelings about Bethany Manor. Miss Turner had been at Bethany Manor for eight months—this is her first nursing home placement. She is from New York and moved to the area to help her brother and his wife through a short illness. She suffered a stroke and did not want to be a burden on her relatives. She had never married nor had any children. She called herself an 'old maid' but stated she was lucky she had something to fall back on and was not a financial burden on her family.

"Miss Turner reflected on her life and her current situation. She was frustrated when names and events would not come to recollection due to her stroke. She was tearful as she talked of how wonderful her sister-in-law is and how helpful she has been in helping her take care of herself following the stroke. Her right arm has not regained full range of motion but she continues to exercise it.

"We discussed life at Bethany Manor. She was pleased to have a private room. She had a small radio but no TV. She spent most of her time in her room listening to classical music. She stated she goes to bed early (7 or 8 pm) and sleeps soundly. She invited me to take a look at her "back yard." Her window view is of the back court yard of the facility. There are lovely flowering trees and green grass. The boundary of the courtyard is a line of huge trees that according to Miss Turner are simply beautiful in the Fall.

"For the hour we spent together, it seemed as if I was in her 'home'— she was pleased to have a guest!! She thanked me for coming in and apologized for taking up so much of my time. She and I returned to the nursing station. Another resident stated, 'You were with her for over 45 minutes; every time I start talking to someone, somebody takes them away. Now you can come and visit my house!' "

Kayser-Jones (1981, 27), in her comparative study of two nursing homes, points out that long-term care facilities are conceptually considered " 'homes' for disabled elderly people" and asserts that "In order for the institutionalized person to be integrated socially and enjoy a meaningful life, it is desirable to create an environment within the institution that approximates that of an older person in the outside world."

At times, residents' opinions of the character of the nursing home reflected ambivalence. Mrs. Brundage, an 86-year-old first-floor resident, stated, "Well, of course this is my home. It's the only place I've got now. And the people here—my friends—are my family. But then, it's not really a home, you know. I mean not exactly like my home used to be. You can't do just everything you want, like make a cup of tea for somebody, but you can still do some things like home and keep some [of your] things with you."

One reason why a number of residents seemed more content to accept the nursing home as their permanent home was physical disability. An 80-year-old respondent, in commenting that Bethany Manor was her home, observed, "It has to be . . . I can't walk, I can't stand up. My knees have arthritis. Other than that I am perfectly healthy. The doctor was apologetic about it and said, 'I wish I could get you to walk, but if you do, you will be on the floor.' That scared me to death, so I sit in the chair. You can get used to anything if you live long enough." The nursing home's institutional restrictions were also more easily accepted by residents whose physical condition prevented self-care.

A number of individual and small group friendships or cliques were forms of informal social interaction observed during the course of the study. These informal relationships served to decrease the sense of loneliness and alienation resulting from the institutional nature of the facility and to promote a "family-like" atmosphere. An 86-year-old female resident, Mrs. Anna Dempsey, had for several years looked after her younger sister Rosemary, who was also a nursing home resident. After Rosemary's death, Mrs. Dempsey adopted a wheelchair-bound resident, Alice, and proceeded to call her her "sister." She took care of Alice as she had her natural sister, making certain she got dressed appropriately in the morning, wheeling her to the dining room for meals, and seeing that she ate everything. Mrs. Dempsey commented, "I take care of her. I get up and go all about my business and help her, too. Of course I'm 86 years old and I'm getting a little tottery but I get there." A 76-year-old female resident commented, "I'm still pretty active and can get around and I have my friends here. We play cards and go to happy hours. We sort of have our own little group and we keep each other in the know about things going on around here, like when they were going to strike for a union—we've got a pretty good grapevine."

The Grapevine

Interestingly, although the Bethany Manor grapevine was not easy to track formally, both residents and caregivers alike (including the sisters) reported that it was very active and seemed to be a source of lively interest to all concerned. Frequently members of the research team picked up important bits of information about new home policies, security matters, staff activities, and resident problems through informal chats with residents who had access to the nursing home's grapevine. If a new sister or other staff member arrived at the home, he or she was carefully assessed in terms of both physical appearance and demeanor much as any new arrival in a family might be examined. These initial informal evaluations were generally favorable, perhaps because there was indeed a vested interest in new arrivals being a source of positive influence in the social environment of the home. If a negative comment was made, the potential offender was usually considered innocent until proven guilty.

This type of attitude seemed to exist in regard to the behavior of all nursing home staff as well as newcomers. Although residents sometimes complained about the attitude or behavior of a particular staff member, they would often follow up with a comment such as "But sometimes she's really OK," or "They just have too many of us to take care of, or "The others are really very nice." The research team got the distinct impression that residents really had two hidden or subconscious agendas, the first being an attempt to put the best face on their situation, which they knew probably could not be changed immediately or dramatically, and the second relating to fear of retribution or retaliation should word of criticism reach the ears of those with authority or power. Sometimes during tape-recorded discussions, residents would request assurance (which was given frequently) that their comments would be anonymous. One researcher wrote the following note after completing a meeting with a very bright and alert 95-year-old resident: "As you can hear, Mrs. Anthony is very hesitant to say anything which might be construed as criticism. She asked several times what was going to be done with the information, and I explained it over and over. When I turned off the tape recorder, she spoke more freely."

Staff-Resident Interaction

Interaction between staff and residents at Bethany Manor took on both a formal and an informal character depending upon such variables as the setting, whether the topic was central to the interaction or activity, the time of day or year (e.g., night or evening shift, holidays), the personality of the individuals involved, and the length of time the persons interacting had been members of the nursing home community. On the fifth-floor skilled care unit, where the more seriously ill persons living in the home were considered patients rather than residents, staff-patient interaction was decidedly of a more formal nature. In this setting, care needs were serious and sophisticated, and many patients were too ill for the light-hearted type of joking, teasing, or cajoling that might be used to encourage the more functional residents. Fifth-floor patients also tended to be short-term, their illness either resolving to a state indicating transfer to another floor or terminating in death.

Few fifth-floor patients could be interviewed for the study because of the gravity of their condition. However, one 74-year-old gentleman, Mr. Jack Norman, who was on the unit for treatment of severe diabetes and peripheral neuropathy, did discuss his interaction with the caregiving staff. He commented, "The nurses and aides up here are more professional because the patients are sicker and they need more attention. I think they [the staff] have to know what they're doing. They don't kid around with you so much like downstairs. They're too busy, too."

An RN who had served for sometime as head nurse on the fifth floor commented, "The patients are more ill up here. They come back from the hospital sicker. That has to do with DRGs [diagnosis related groups]. With DRGs, they [the hospitals] are discharging patients sooner, and I do think nursing homes are going to have to change, provide more skills, and think about the number of special staff. I never used to see someone with a new fractured hip. Now they are in and out [of the hospital] within a week. That is so unusual compared to a couple of years ago. They would be in the hospital three weeks.

Resident-staff interaction on the second, third, and fourth floors of the Manor took on a less formal nature, in many instances, especially if the topic of the interaction (such as dress, hairstyle, or social activities) was less serious and if the staff member and resident were well known to each other. Frequently first names were used between residents and aides, with charge nurses being more formally addressed as Miss or Sister. The head nurse of one of the semiskilled units admitted that she did not spend as much time with the patients as she would like to: "I try to get into the [resident's] rooms as much as I can, but the desk keeps me tied up most of the day. There are [physicians'] orders, residents' assessments, assignments—the paperwork in a nursing home is endless."

Most residents reported basic satisfaction with their interactions with staff, although some did admit to problems with individual staff members. An 82-year-old fourth-floor resident, who was wheelchair bound, spoke of her unit: "I think on this floor we have a fine group of aides and nurses. We have a top nurse on this floor, Sister Barbara, a wonderful nurse and a wonderful religious. She knows how to get around these difficult people ... knows her busines...The evening shift is good, very good, and the night shift I don't know because I don't see them."

Another 84-year-old fourth-floor resident also asserted that she got along well with "the nuns, the nurses, and the aides." She frequently articulated the fact that it was she who had sought to enter the nursing home and that she was grateful to be there. She stated, "Well, I just feel it's their job and they are trying to do the best they can, so I never argue with anybody. If there's any question, I do what they want. It's their job. I keep repeating to these people [other residents] who are so upset, 'I asked to come here.'" She continued, "I've never had any difficulty. They've all been very pleasant to me. I've never had—the only run-in I've had with one girl, she insisted—don't put this in, is this being recorded?" The resident continued with her story, the tape recorder having been turned off, about being psychologically pressured to take a treatment that she did not want and having to call her physician to intervene. She asserted, however, that the situation was resolved to her satisfaction, and added, "They were nice about it, too." As noted earlier, frequently a subject was hesitant to criticize a particular individual or describe a specific situation because it might jeopardize his or her status as a "good resident" in the home.

One variable that clearly seemed to affect both how residents felt about staff and how staff related to the resident was that of history (length of time) of the relationship. Residents seemed to be able to tolerate a number of perceived failings in a nurse or an aide if they knew the caregiver well and had received good care in the past. One study subject described one of her long-time aides this way: "Sometimes she's a little slow and she forgets to do what I asked her, but then she comes in and puts her arms around me and gives me a big kiss. She really cares, and with me caring means everything." The concept of caring as a resident priority is supported by Grau's (1984,

15) study of nursing home residents, in which 66 percent of the approximately 59 subjects valued "kindness and caring" as the most important qualities of their nurse. One respondent asserted, "A nurse should be kind, speak gently, love much and laugh often."

An 86-year-old resident of the Manor's fourth floor complained about a new aide: "I talked to Sister Celeste about how this new girl had been very impudent to me and downright awful to me. She threatened me. She [Sister] said she wouldn't have that and evidently spoke to her because she did mend her ways." The resident said she did not know the new staff very well but did not see much use in complaining to them. She stated, "I'm doubtful that they pay much attention. They come and go a lot. They listen to you and sound sympathetic. They say, 'Yes, yes, we will take care of it,' but you are just an 'old thing' and they don't do anything about it." The same resident, however, praised a nurse who had taken care of her for several years: "I used to have a nurse who would do all that [nursing care] automatically, and she knew just what to do and how to do it. She's been out for over two months with phlebitis. They said she would probably be back in April. I hope so. She was grand."

Staff-resident interaction on the third floor differed from that on the other four nursing units, because of the fact that almost all of the residents were cognitively impaired. The relationships on this unit centered around complete resident dependence upon the caregiver, with little or no feedback provided to the staff member. Findings from observations and interviews with cognitively impaired third floor residents are discussed in Chapter 2 and confirm that only minimal attention to the staff member is paid by this group. In contrast, caregivers on the cognitively impaired unit were frequently observed attempting to give positive feedback and reinforcement to confused residents. A charge nurse on the unit during the tenure of the study commented on the difficulty of staff-resident interaction with her resident population: "My staff is special. I think I have the most special staff on this floor, because we are dealing with total care of a patient, day in and day out, and not much response. I have one resident whose aide—and I have told her over and over again—deserves a halo. She [the aide] is called a bitch every single morning, and this lady accuses her of taking things. All right, the resident probably can't control what she's saying. Therefore, [I tell the aide] we have to be professional and we have to accept her verbal assaults." She continued, "I tried to change one of the aide's assignments around one time because the load was too heavy, and I wanted to give her some of the residents that walk versus some that are totally bedridden or that require just lifting into a chair. Well, it became a big battle. They didn't want to give up their people. They get attached. You should hear them, 'I have to get her a dress for Christmas.' 'You call up somebody. She needs stockings.' It shows that they care."

The head nurse commented also on the personal things her aides did for the residents: "I have one aide that went and got her pocketbook one day. I said, 'What are you doing?' She said, 'Well, her family won't bring lipstick and she doesn't look pretty without it.' She was using her own lipstick. I have another aide who went down to the bazaar and bought a whole bunch of jewelry and mouthwash and stuff, so she would be sure to have it for her residents. They [the aides] are very attached, and I think basically the third floor has the most unique aides in the whole house because they have to deal with constant confusion."

Finally, staff-resident interaction on the first floor of Bethany Manor might be said to be of an almost collegial nature, as the domiciliary residents basically care for themselves. Home staff support their care only in such areas as monitoring of vital signs (blood pressure, temperature, if needed) and the administration of medications. Thus, the interaction is kept to a minimum. It is pleasant but superficial. One 86-year-old gentleman, who had recently been moved from the first floor because of a physical disability resulting in his being unable to walk, noted that on the first floor he had been happier because he was more in control of his life and not "at the mercy" of the staff. He added, however, that he was learning to cope, stating, "When you are learning to box, you've got to learn to roll with the punches." A 76-year-old first-floor resident, Miss Alberton, stated, "The staff here are very nice but, you know, I take care of myself. Maybe someday I'll need them but for now, the less I have to see them, the better because it means I'm OK."

Social and Cultural Incongruence

As understood by the social scientist, "culture" refers to an individual's total social heritage, the "knowledge, beliefs, customs and skills. . .acquired as a member of society" (Broom and Selznick 1963, 52). Culture influences one's attitudes and behaviors in relation not only to oneself but also to others both in one's immediate environment and beyond. Expectations and behavioral norms for both self and others are derived from the cultural heritage. For the older person, cultural beliefs and customs are deeply ingrained in the concept of self and in the daily operationalization of life philosophy. To violate those beliefs may cause serious trauma not only to the elder's self-concept but to his satisfaction with life as well. Snyder (1982, 19, 25) suggests that long-term care institutions must create culturally supportive environments if they are to promote patient adaptation and growth. Snyder argues that "recognition of cultural influences on behavior can enhance relations between staff and residents" in the long-term care setting.

A variety of social and cultural differences existed in Bethany Manor between the caregivers, especially the nursing home aides, and the patients. Because the home was a private, Catholic facility with a long history of service in the urban Catholic diocese where it was located, many white, lower-middle-income to middle-income families of Irish and Italian descent considered the Manor as a place where they would be well cared for in old age. Thus, the waiting list was consistently filled with applications from this local population. A number of study subjects reported that they had come to Bethany Manor because a former family member or friend had lived out the final portion of his or her life at the Manor. Some residents had been frequent visitors to the home in their younger days. Catholics were especially drawn to the home because they "trusted the sisters" and felt that their spiritual needs could be met at Bethany Manor.

In contrast, the majority of nurses' aides, the direct caregivers, were from a nearby metropolitan area with a largely Black, Protestant population. Most were from lower-income to lower-middle-income homes. Whereas most residents were high school graduates, with a few having achieved either professional experience or a college degree, the majority of aides were ten to twelfth grade graduates of inner-city schools.

Thus, social and cultural differences, especially in regard to such variables as language and music, sometimes caused serious tensions on both sides of the staff-resident interaction. Residents reported that aides spoke to them sharply in a loud manner (occasionally using obscenities), which was particularly offensive to an older person accustomed to respect from younger family members and acquaintances. Residents also complained that the younger aides would sometimes come into their rooms and change the radio station to "their" music, which the residents found "harsh and irritating." One second-floor resident observed, "They're rough and ready here. They think nothing of coming in and turning on your radio—it's not our kind of music—it's hard to take." Another "very Irish" female resident even commented on the new Administrator:

"Now, of course, there's all this that we have to get used to, because a new 'mother' [title for the sister Administrator] has come and they don't call her 'Mother' any more. You probably have heard that. She is very tall. Sister—oh dear, that's one thing about my mind, I can't remember quickly—Sister Margarita. She goes by 'Sister' instead of 'Reverend Mother,' so that has been a little hard to change for us, too. Now they are all called just 'Sister.' You see, well, I always knew Mother Ann Teresa was Irish. This lady [Sister Margarita] is very kind and good to us but she is Italian. There are little bit of differences that you find in later years of accommodating yourself to people of different nationalities. It comes up too in our friends around here. We seem to go back to what we were raised in our families and friends. My father was born and raised in Ireland. I haven't anything against Italians, and Sister Margarita has been very kind to me. She let me bring all my furniture up here."

The aides, for their part, felt that at times the residents were domineering or patronizing, either ordering them about as servants or treating them condescendingly, which was particularly insulting to the aide who was attempting to be professional. Occasionally, racially colored remarks were directed at nurses' aides, and these were very difficult especially for the younger women to deal with. A head nurse whose unit had many confused residents noted that this was a particular problem: "They [the residents] sometimes give racial slurs, too. A lot of racial slurs. I spend a lot of my time discussing this with the aides. You've got to remember that you've got people [the residents] who perhaps grew up during segregation. You've got people who perhaps had servants and they are not necessarily being derogatory. It was their way of life and you have to accept that. Also, for the music, you don't play rock-and-roll music with Michael Jackson, you play Guy Lombardo or something like that, that was their era!"

Communal Places

Much of Bethany Manor's social life takes place in the home's communal places: the main dining room, the unit dining rooms, the lobby, the chapel, the sun porches, and the hallways. Residents report that mealtime is looked forward to not so much for the food as for the conversation and companionship. Some residents find a fulfilling volunteer activity in helping the wheelchair-bound residents to the dining room. Ninety-year-old Martha Callahan reported that she always took several people from her unit to the dining room at lunchtime, a task that gave her much satisfaction. Mrs. Callahan added that the food itself was not really important: "I am never hungry. I have been on a special diet ever since I have been here, but still they pile my plate up and I can't eat it all. I just leave it on the plate. Sometimes, the food is really good, sometimes it's not really cooked, but you can't do anything about that."

Eating in the large main dining room was sometimes stressful for residents who preferred more privacy. In the words of 82-year-old Miss Ellison, "I go downstairs for midday meal and evening meal. Candidly, some people are quite annoying. Although I don't look nervous, it does bother me. There's some tension there, and when you eat you shouldn't have tension. It does something to your digestion. It's not people's table manners. It's their physical ailments." She also confessed that although she knew it was "good for her" to get out of her room and go to the main dining room for meals, she really enjoyed breakfast more—a meal which she was allowed to take in her room.

Mrs. Alma McGuire, a first-floor domiciliary care resident, described her "troubles in the dining room": "I'm so upset. It's just so difficult at our table. You know Mrs. Schmidt. Well, she's so deaf. She doesn't hear at all and I try to talk to her. I say things about six or seven times, but she still doesn't hear me. Then at our table there's Mr. Johnson, too. He' so confused. He wants to talk all the time, but you know you can't understand a word that he's saying. He keeps moving his things all over the table and taking up all the space and you know those tables are so little."

Mrs. Agatha Preston, a second-floor resident, described her feelings this way: "What's the food like? We'd better not go into that. The price of food has gone up everywhere, and I tell these people that fuss a blue streak, 'Nobody paid me to come to Bethany Manor.' I came—I sound awfully preachy, but I'm not—but personally I came here of my own accord. Nobody forced me to come. I had to try and get in. Food doesn't mean that much to me, so I just eat what I'm given. I think for an institution, as you might call it, it's very good food. I've been at the same table since I came here and that's what I enjoy—being with my friends."

Another primary communal place for social interaction at Bethany Manor was the main lobby. The lobby was nicely decorated with a variety of armchairs and couches and was always "dressed up" for the holidays. Perhaps the best feature of the lobby was that it was immediately adjacent to the Manor's main front entrance—essentially the only entrance for visitors and newcomers to the home—and thus provided an excellent site for the activity of watching, which is discussed later in this chapter. Home residents not only had the pleasure of visiting with each other in the lobby but also achieved the secondary gain of being able to see who came and went during their visit. Important grapevine information was gathered about such topics as whose family was visiting, what patients went out to the eye doctor's office or for an x-ray, which sisters had the day off (sister nurses who had a free day frequently changed from their white to dark clothing and went out to do errands), what students or faculty were at the home, and even whether members of the research team were working. One resident, who spent many hours socializing and watching in her "own" chair in the main lobby, not so gently (though admittedly with a twinkle in her eye) chastised the study's principal investigator for being away from the home for a period of time: "So, where have you been, Dr. O'Brien? Off taking a vacation? We certainly haven't seen you around lately!"

Another pleasant facet of the main lobby was that even if a resident was sitting alone, there was always someone coming or going through the front door with whom to pass the time of day—a greeting, a word about the weather, a teasing comment, or maybe even a longer chat if the visitor had time to stop and talk for a while.

Directly off the lobby was Bethany Manor's chapel, which was a communal place considered very important to many residents. In fact, a primary reason why many Catholic residents chose to come to the Manor was the fact that the home had a chapel providing daily Mass and other Catholic services. A number of residents expressed their feelings about the importance of the chapel: "It's so wonderful to have daily Mass right here. You don't ever have to worry if it's icy or snows. You just come downstairs."

"The chapel is why I came here. You can go in and pray whenever you want. You know prayer is a real consolation when you get old."

"I looked for a Catholic home with a priest and a chapel. This made me decide to come to Bethany Manor."

Other communal places in the home that were frequently used for social interaction included the auditorium, where special parties or holiday festivities were held; the unit sun porches and dining rooms; and the hallways. For residents who were unable to freely leave their floor because of cognitive or physical disabilities, the hallways and sun porches became important communal places, and often one's "territory" was carefully guarded.

In a study of common behavior patterns of nursing home residents in public areas, Brent et al. (1984, 88, 192) discovered that a multiplicity of diverse activities were demonstrated, ranging from very active behavior, such as social interaction, helping others, and game playing, to extremely passive behaviors, including thinking, observing, daydreaming, and sleeping. The investigators concluded that a "great diversity of needs among residents must be accommodated within the physical setting of the nursing home" and that the physical environment of long-term care facilities should be organized and planned to meet such needs.

Territoriality

"Territoriality" was a very important dimension of life at Bethany Manor Nursing Home. For as many as seven, eight, or nine decades, most of the residents had been establishing "territory" in their personal worlds— some in private homes, some in apartments, some in individual offices at the workplace, and most relative to a multiplicity of personal possessions. Yet on entering the Manor, as discussed in more depth in Chapter 4, very few possessions may be retained. Personal space or territory is clearly at a premium. It was observed that many residents went to great lengths to establish their territory. Residents' rooms were frequently decorated with small objects from home. Eighty-six-year-old Mr. Charles Romanoff proudly showed some small items, which he described as "wedding presents for my father and mother." He added, "See that vase? That's also from the old home. I also have two Currier and Ives pictures. I really enjoy them." Residents established territory in regard to their wheelchairs also, which often contained such items as satchels to carry personal belongings or brightly colored blankets or afghans. Territoriality was temporarily established in the communal places, with certain residents opting for a special lobby chair whenever possible or a specific place in the hallway to park a wheelchair. It was with the residents' rooms, however, that territoriality was most dramatically manifested and most important to the occupant. Such territoriality was also directly related to the concept of "transfer trauma," which is detailed in Chapter 8.

Roosa (1982, 242) conducted a survey to identify residents' perceptions of territory and privacy in one 386-bed nursing home. She concluded that "all residents need some territory or space to call their own," as the contemporary nursing home is a social institution that attempts to assume the character of "home" by housing those persons who are no longer able to manage their own individual homes. Several other observations from Roosa's work included the following: Residents need a variety of places where they can be alone; not all residents want private rooms—some enjoy a compatible roommate; locks on private room doors increase residents' control; and "staff attitudes and behaviors are crucial to residents' privacy." The concept of territoriality is also generally considered to include or be closely associated with that of personal possessions. In his classic work *Asylums*, Erving Goffman asserted that institutionalization of an individual was characterized by a loss of property or possessions (1961, 14), and Millard and Smith (1981) discovered that the nursing home resident's loss of personal goods frequently resulted in a devaluing of the individual. Although it is admittedly difficult, simply from a physical and environmental standpoint, to allow the nursing home resident to keep or accumulate a multitude of possessions, the retention of certain treasured and memorable items should be encouraged. It has been suggested that some possessions that might be retained in the institutional environment of the home include "pictures, painting, photographs, bureaus, bookcases, bed spreads, quilts, blankets, lamps. . .or any other 'reasonable' items that have meaning for the individual" (Holzapfel 1982, 158).

The import of territoriality at Bethany Manor might well be exemplified by the case of Miss Virginia McCarthy, a 76-year-old single Irish Catholic resident who had been admitted to the home's domiciliary care unit several months before the study's initiation. Miss McCarthy had worked until her retirement, at age 62, as an administrative secretary for a local government agency. She had never married and had very little family, and none in her immediate residential area. She had lived alone and been very independent for all of her adult life. Miss McCarthy was quite active in her postretirement years, occasionally doing typing to pick up a little extra money but spending the majority of her time involved in volunteer work with a Catholic group that coordinated such activities as prayer meetings and visiting the elderly in their homes or nursing homes. Miss McCarthy had been a frequent visitor to Bethany Manor before her own admission. During the several years before admission to the home, Miss McCarthy's health began to deteriorate, specifically in the areas of hearing, eyesight, and ambulation. Her physician told her that she had a mild case of diabetes, which would necessitate a modification of diet and possibly oral medication. She also had a more serious condition of hypertension and was overweight.

Recently Miss McCarthy had become quite depressed. She had also begun to manifest multiple physical problems. She had an episode of shortness of breath requiring oxygen, and she had several falls with her walker. Thus, it was determined that Miss McCarthy needed to move from the domiciliary area on the first floor to the fifth-floor skilled care area where her physical needs could be attended to. Miss McCarthy was very upset when informed of the move. She described it as a terrible shock: "I just can't take a shock like this. This [she gestured around her first-floor room] has been my home for the past year. I had one shock when I had to come here. Now this is just too much." She began to sob: "You have to be a zombie to live here. I just hate it up there [the skilled care unit]. I hate it. I'll never see any of my friends."

On the day of the move, Miss McCarthy continued to be very depressed, alternately crying and sullen. She had an abundance of clothing and small possessions of every variety to be packed for the transfer. She began to sob disconsolately, then angrily asserted, "I don't know why you're doing this to me. If somebody else puts these things away up there [on the fifth floor], it will just be months until I find anything. That's what happened to me down here. When someone else puts your things away you can't find anything. I hate it. I just hate it. You don't understand—they're not your things. You don't know what it's like. They're all I've got in this world." After a few minutes she started to sob again and said, "Do what you want— I don't care. I might as well just walk out of here and wander around until I die. It doesn't matter anymore."

Privacy

Privacy is another concept related to territoriality. In extensive interviews with 60 nursing home residents, Roosa (1982, 242) found that almost 50% of the respondents identified emotional release as an important correlate of privacy: "Privacy 'calmed' them [the residents], made them 'more comfortable and secure,' or 'provided a breather.' In short, privacy gave them respite from stress, for example, 'watching a roommate die.' " The need for privacy was articulated in different ways and to differing degrees by Bethany Manor residents; the variations were in part related to their differing life experiences. As with the discussion of the nursing home as home versus institution, study data reflecting the residents' need for privacy showed that those such as Miss McCarthy who had lived independent, autonomous lives were much more sensitive to and troubled by their perceived lack of privacy as nursing home residents than were residents who had lived out their adult lives surrounded by large families. More often the latter enjoyed the companionship of other residents and were for the most part not troubled by having to share a room or common facilities.

Mrs. Mary Sheehan, a charming 77-year-old mother of seven, observed, "Oh, it's lovely here. You just have the nicest people to visit with and you never feel alone. You know, darling, it's just grand and you never had to be afraid."

Roommates did become a problem, however, when one of the individuals was confused. Mrs. Theresa McClosky, the daughter of a resident, complained of her frustration at constantly trying to keep up with her mother's clothing needs only to find on the next visit that recently bought items were missing or being worn by her mother's confused roommate, Mrs. Watkins. Mrs. McClosky told the nursing staff that she really would not mind bringing some things in for Mrs. Watkins, but that it hurt to come to the home and see her mother, who had been a meticulous dresser during her more active days, wearing an old sweater while Mrs. Watkins wore the new one brought last week. Mrs. McClosky added that she had gotten a special pair of shoes for her mother that would give needed support, and that morning she had discovered Mrs. Watkins wearing them. Mrs. McClosky expressed her frustration: "What can I do? I can't take the shoes off of her feet. Maybe she doesn't have any others. But why couldn't she have taken one of mother's old pairs?"

This was a distressing problem for the Manor staff also because Mrs. Watkins was indeed severely cognitively impaired and totally unaware that she was taking things that did not belong to her. Her roommate was herself mildly impaired and not concerned about preventing the "borrowing." As is discussed in Chapter 3, families of Bethany Manor residents sometimes had greater difficulties than the residents in accepting the lack of privacy their loved ones faced in the home, yet frequently the physical or mental deterioration of the resident had left the family captive to institutionalization as a last resort.

For some residents, however, the experience of having roommates or the development of nursing home friendships was a positive experience, especially if they had been lonely before admission to the home, as was Miss McCormick:

"I got to the point where my parents died and I wasn't married and my girlfriend died and I was in an apartment. I worked for 30 years for the government and it was too lonely. I didn't know what to do with myself when I was retired, so I talked to my girlfriend's husband, who suggested this place. It was a godsend. I am contented. I have every reason to be, because the people are nice, the place is nice. I have been very fortunate, because I didn't have anybody, really, a family. I was an only child. I have a couple of friends that check on me once in a while, and they are there if I need them. That's the main thing. I sound like Pollyanna, don't I?"

Touch

Touch is central to the art of caregiving (Langland and Panicucci 1982). The elderly person has a great need for effective or meaningful touch because the deterioration of other senses such as sight and hearing limits experiential capabilities; it is argued that "lack of meaningful touch" makes the already lonely elderly individual become increasingly more isolated (Huss 1977, Seaman 1982).

The concept of affective touch was found to be an important feature of interaction among residents, as well as between residents and staff members and between residents and visitors at Bethany Manor. Members of the research team frequently commented on the fact that residents touched their hands and hugged or kissed them when they visited. One interviewer concluded her notes on a conversation with a very alert 95-year-old female resident with the comment, "I got a big kiss and an invitation to 'please come and see her again.' " Research data collectors reported that they could have spent many more hours with the residents, who both figuratively and literally welcomed them with open arms.

Residents were sometimes observed to hold hands or touch each other's hands when walking together, and residents and staff were frequently seen hugging or touching, especially the very young staff and the very old residents. It seemed that once a person had passed into that developmental stage labeled "elder," certain norms of society imposed upon adult members relative to such variables as touch and personal space no longer held. In the general hospital or even in a long-term rehabilitation center where the majority of patients are young to middle-aged or "younger older" adults, hugging and kissing between staff and patient might be considered undue familiarity and not appropriate to the professional relationship. In the nursing home, no one appeared to find such physical familiarity outside the norm.

Touch was also observed to be a central means of communication on the third floor of Bethany Manor, where the cognitively impaired residents were housed. Although a resident often could not understand the words or even gestures of a staff member, they seemed almost universally to respond to such actions as a touch on the arm, the taking of a hand, or a warm hug. One of the third-floor charge nurses reflected on the importance of touch for the confused residents: "Touch is as important as anything. You don't have to say anything, really, but the idea is give them a hug. Everybody needs a hug. . . . We need that love, that touch, and families, I think, are afraid [to touch or hug] sometimes."

A third-floor resident, Mrs. Martha Callahan, a former RN who was mildly confused, made these comments to her research team interviewer: "I like sitting here holding your hand. When you get old like me you're not worth much. Especially your mind. I was a nurse, you know, and I know that when you get old, things just sort of fall apart. I think my health is pretty good. It's my mind that's the problem and that's just not very funny. I just don't remember things like I would want to. It's hard to be useful when you don't even remember where you are." Mrs. Callahan went on, "All my life I've done things for other people. I don't like not being able to do for myself. I'd like to remember your name. I'm sorry. I know you've told me before and I should remember, but I don't. But I'm glad you're here."

Another head nurse spoke of the importance of "psychological" touch, of "getting to know" the residents. She said, "they like to be close to you. They like to know if you are married and if you have children. I think that is their way of getting just a little bit closer to you and feeling like one of the family. They like to get to know you personally, so you have to open up to them as you ask them to open up to you. They are assessing you at the same time. I think it helps extra, almost like a bond. It helps them trust you, because if you are willing to give them a little bit, they figure they can give a little bit, too." One of the home's recreational therapists added, "I go and talk to the residents. I hold their hand. That's what they want me to do. I try to get close to them."

The "Work" of the Resident

Rituals and Activities of Daily Living

Another question the researchers proposed in attempting to examine the life career of the nursing home resident was, What is the "work" of the individual residing at Bethany Manor? That is, what makes a resident want to get up in the morning, and what occupies the rest of the day?

It was anticipated that residents, especially those more newly arrived, would find it stressful to have to give up former work activities and would have a great deal of free time on their hands. Hooker and Ventis (1984, 478) note that indeed both the "loss of a work role and the corresponding increase in amount of unstructured time" for the retired older person can be stressful and a source of problems, and Moss and Lawton (1982, 121) reported study findings that indicate that "there is a great deal more discretionary time in the lives of older people than in younger people."

During the course of the Manor study, numerous activities were identified as serving to occupy individuals' days. These included reading, letter writing, watching television, visiting, walking, crafts, recreational therapy, organized social activities, and trips for shopping or other outings. However, as with most members of the larger society, the home residents needed and wanted a personal "plan of the day" that would give some structure and sense of security to their lives. In order for this plan to be individualized beyond the Manor's established schedule of activities revolving around rest, nutrition, and bodily hygiene, most residents manifested a set of unique and individualized "rituals" of the day.

Mrs. Agnes Stratton, a delightful 84-year-old partially wheelchair-bound but very busy resident, described her rituals:

"Strangely enough the days pass quickly. I can't quite explain it but of course there're always things at church to go to. Everyone to their own. I've formed a little routine. I sleep well at night. First thing in the morning—my eyes aren't too good, so I don't read—I get washed in my room. I can get around a little and do all my straightening up. Then, I have my breakfast, and sometimes after, I go to church or to some activity. Then later I have things to read and letters to write. I don't think I'll ever get caught up. I'm way behind in my letter writing. And I try to keep up with the news on TV. My routine works for me but it might not work for everybody."

One of the serendipitous methodological findings of the Bethany Manor study was the fact that the researchers did not, as expected, have a totally accessible and available population of subjects in the nursing home group. Although the majority of residents approached agreed to be involved in the study, and indeed enjoyed the discussions and requested the researchers to return, data collection times often had to be carefully timed to fit a resident's busy schedule. This was brought home to the research team quite early in the study when a resident rather imperiously informed a potential data collector that she would be happy to meet with her "at an appointed time" but that she had a number of things planned for that particular day and was not just sitting around "waiting for a visitor."

The residents' "rituals" might almost have gone unnoticed unless one or another was interfered with or disrupted. Then heaven help the offending resident or staff member who, perhaps quite innocently, interferred with an important element of the sometimes long-standing and important (to the resident) routine. One of the oldest (97 years) and most senior residents (26 years at Bethany Manor) was Mrs. Maggie Scott. Mrs. Scott was known as a delightful lady, a pleasure to care for, who made no undue demands on the staff and was very well adjusted to life at Bethany Manor. It was whispered on the grapevine that, being the senior resident at the Manor, she knew everything about everybody—all of the sisters and staff who had ever been at the home. Or at least she had known; maybe she had forgotten a bit now.

Mrs. Scott had a ritual. Although she was quite capable of getting out and about in her wheelchair (when she chose), and did so for the noon and evening meals, Mrs. Scott took breakfast privately in her room and had done so for the past 26 years. During the course of the study a new nursing supervisor arrived at Bethany Manor. She also had her "rituals," one of which was to immediately operationalize ideas for change. One of her first recommendations was that all residents capable of doing so go down to the main dining room for breakfast—this included Mrs. Scott.

When the word reached her room, the gentle, gracious Mrs. Scott displayed a character slightly milder than that of Attila the Hun. She fussed, fumed, and threatened in protest to walk or wheel herself down to breakfast in the Manor dining room stark naked to the embarrassment of everyone in sight. Suffice it to say, that Mrs. Scott became the first exception to the nursing supervisor's edict on breakfast attendance in the first-floor dining room.

Taking the Watch

As suggested, researchers attempted, through both observation and interview, to get at the "work," or that which filled the days of the Bethany Manor residents. Although there were, as described, the formally scheduled nursing home projects and patients' personal "ritual" activities, one work function not specifically identified by residents but observed by the research team and discussed by Bethany Manor staff members was "watching." Residents, especially those who were more fragile physically, had difficulty hearing or speaking, or were cognitively impaired, often spent hours in either the main lobby or the ward porches or hallways "watching."

"Taking the watch" sometimes involved watching the interaction of other residents, sometimes that of staff or visitors with other residents, and sometimes watching just involved seeing who came and went from the home or from a particular floor. Although such watching might not involve any formal or informal interaction with others, it seemed to give the residents some sense of belonging to the group and a lessening of loneliness. Miss Catherine James was an 81-year-old resident who had been very active and well known in the home until a recent stroke left her mildly asphasic and wheelchair bound. Because of difficulty speaking she no longer sat in the front lobby where she had formerly greeted visitors. Miss James did, however, station her wheelchair right at the busiest hall intersection of her nursing unit each morning so that she could, as she haltingly reported, "still keep an eye on things." Even though she spoke little, Miss James still received lots of greetings from staff and visitors. This type of interaction was acceptable to her in her deteriorated physical condition. She also had found work. She asserted, "I do an important job here on this floor. I sit in the corridor and observe what's going on. I know everybody. Some of the [residents] get confused and don't know where their rooms are. I make sure they get back to their rooms."

It was also observed that the third-floor cognitively impaired residents seemed to find satisfaction in watching. Although their response could only be intuited from researchers' and caregivers' observations, it was felt that these residents did indeed seem less restless and more comfortable when they were able to be with and watch others.

Two mildly confused residents spent a great deal of time watching in the main lobby. One, Mr. Thornton, guarded the front door and became very agitated if a visitor or resident left it open too long. He talked extensively about the home and the residents, explaining, "This is a population problem, people living 'til they're so old.' Geriatrics is a new study that they have in the schools." Suddenly the front door traffic captured his attention and he abruptly ended the conversation by saying, "I'm not going to talk any more now but we can talk again. It was nice to talk to you." Mr. Thornton returned his full attention to the watch.

Mrs. Harcourt, who is both confused and disoriented, sits in the lobby from after breakfast until the evening meal, with a break for lunch. She stated, "I sit here so that I can keep an eye on things."

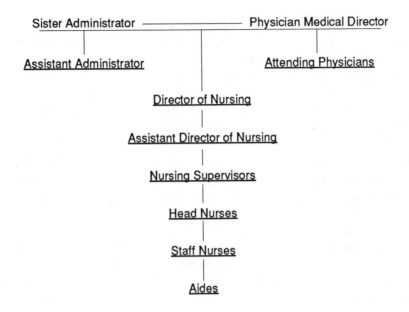

Figure 7-2 Hierarchical Set of Status Roles.

Power

Authority and Decision Making

Perhaps one of the most difficult aspects of life at Bethany Manor for many residents was the abdication of authority and control over many aspects of their lives. Clearly, most power in the nursing home resided within the authority of the staff—the administrators and caregivers—whose roles and functions follow delineated patterns based on the division of labor.

A hierarchical set of status roles was demonstrated for health caregivers, with power and control progressing in a vertical fashion (see Figure 7-2).

Although the home's Medical Director and attending physicians are not always physically present at Bethany Manor, they remain symbolic authority figures as controllers of the residents' medical management. The medical staff were also perceived by some residents to be the primary source of authority. Residents sometimes directed their complaints (or threatened to do so) to their physicians rather than to members of the in-house staff. (The structure and process of the Bethany Manor complaint system is presented later in this chapter under a discussion of "Stresses."

The question of residents' power is difficult to address summarily, even after a scientific examination of life at Bethany Manor. Obviously, for the confused or cognitively impaired resident, what power there was resided in the hands of a legal guardian or conservator. For the cognitively alert resident, both the perception of power and control and actual autonomy varied notably, depending to a great extent on the individual's physical and psychological capabilities. Some residents did indeed feel in control of their lives at the home. Mr. Frank McArthur, a 73-year-old lifelong bachelor residing on the domiciliary care unit, asserted, "I certainly am in control here. I do what I want and I go where I want. If I want to skip a meal or something like that I can do it, and my time is pretty much my own, so it's not like being helpless. But then I get around OK—not all these people here can do that."

Another male resident, an 86-year-old who had formerly been housed on the domiciliary unit, spoke of the decrease in control since his move to an intermediate care area: "All my life I have been a very independent person. That's been my trouble. But downstairs it wasn't too bad. I could do my thing. Now up here I get bossed around but I still have control over some things. Anything I don't like, I tell them about. I don't hide a thing. Since I have been here I have had two different big fights with people. I'm a very easygoing person when left alone, but if I am aroused, I am another person. If I think I am right I will just stand on my two feet, talk about it and give my say-so."

In contrast to the responses of these two gentlemen, a female resident complained that she felt she had no control over her life as a nursing home resident. Mrs. Mary Talbot's perception centered on her physical disabilities: "I don't have any control over my life in this place. How can I? I don't see or hear well anymore. My feet have problems and I don't walk steady, even with that old thing [walker]. And there's all those crazy old people here, and you never know what they're going to do. One day Annie, you know her, Mrs. Annie Shelby, she walked right into my room and hit me. But what can I do about it? Nothing."

In the past the nursing home has been viewed as a place where residents are devoid of any freedom or control. In his analysis of nursing home residents in the United States, Moss (1977, 12) identifies a "catalog of fears," included in which is "the fear of losing liberty, identity and human dignity." Moss cites the New York Civil Liberties Union's critique of nursing homes: "They virtually abolish privacy, stifle individuality, deify the values of order and discipline and enforce arbitrary and discretionary rules. Viewed as a policy, these institutions can only be described as totalitarian." A decade later, however, although admittedly residents' fears remain, many contemporary nursing homes at least attempt to consider the resident's need for control to the degree they are capable of exercising it. Ryden (1983, 130), in a study of intermediate care nursing home residents, found that perception of control was a key variable related to morale and that perceived control did indeed exist among some residents.

Resident Councils

Many contemporary long-term care facilities for the elderly have "resident councils," and Bethany Manor was no exception. For several months prior to the study there had been a relatively active council at the home; however, activities and interest seemed to have died out during the study period. Several key informants who had themselves been active council members identified reasons for the council's demise. These included:

Apathy on the part of Manor residents—one informant reported that it was "always the same people" who attended the meetings and did all the work

Disagreements among the members who did attend the meetings—"nobody could every agree on things"

Finally, a leader who only did "what he wanted" and "never paid any attention to the other residents."

Grover (1982, 6), in her discussion of the formation of resident councils and coalitions (groups of councils), summarizes the benefits of such activities by suggesting that groups do much to "prevent, minimize and eliminate the problems of group living and the effects of institutionalization. They serve to bring people together in a common bond to the benefit of all. They develop a community spirit of mutual help, and aid in preserving an attitude of independence among residents that nourishes both their physical and mental well being."

Bethany Manor's staff were attempting to encourage the residents to renew and strengthen the council and to bring it back to usefulness as a mechanism for discussing resident problems and issues of concern.

Legal Issues: The Resident's Bill of Rights

Bethany Manor's administration subscribed to the "Patient's Bill of Rights" developed by a state association of health care providers. A copy was given to each resident on admission. Articles in the bill related to such areas as respect and dignity for the individual, adequate care, confidentiality of condition, freedom from mental and physical abuse, a reasonable response to requests, a procedure for grievances, and the retention of personal possessions.

At the Manor, legal issues with which the residents or the home was faced generally revolved around such matters as the settling of residents' previous financial affairs or the payment of the facility's bills if not covered under Medicare/Medicaid. Timmreck (1983, 9, 13), in examining legal considerations for the nursing home resident, asserts that despite the introduction of the patient's Bill of Rights, the legal status of nursing home residents is a gray area and suggests that this may be due, in part, to such factors as lack of policy, staffing problems, and "simple lack of awareness on the part of the patient, staff and administration." Timmreck concludes that nursing home staff must become aware of the legal ramifications in such areas as care of a resident's possessions, the patient's right to refuse treatment, and the use of detention and restraints. At the Manor these issues seemed fairly well understood, as is described in Chapter 5. Many residents had a personal lawyer to handle their affairs, and for some the conservator was legally identified as next of kin.

Social and Recreational Activities

Bethany Manor has an active Department of Recreation, which provides for a multiplicity of social and recreational activities for residents. A number of these activities center around such interests as music, games, parties, and pets. A survey of the home's "Calendar for the Month" over the two-year data collection period identified a variety of activities such as bingo, shopping and educational trips, guest singing and instrumental groups, teas, holiday parties and picnics, music appreciation sessions, slide shows, ball games, happy hours, movies, friendship circles, dog shows, nature walks, ice cream socials, and remotivation groups. Residents' attendance at these activities varied widely and was related to both interest and physical or cognitive deficit. For major home activities such as the Christmas tree decorating party or the St. Patrick's Day party, as many residents as possible were brought to the auditorium, the more fragile being assisted by staff, visitors, volunteers, or more able-bodied residents.

On a Sunday before Christmas, a large holiday party was held in the home's basement auditorium. Approximately 100 residents attended, many in wheelchairs, dressed in their holiday best. Interestingly, both the band members, who donated their services to the party, and the volunteer organizers appeared to be in the "young older" (or "older young") age group, with gray to white hair being the most visible symbol. The only young to middle-aged attendees were the Administrator of the home, some Recreation Department employees, a researcher, and several of the sisters. A few of the ladies got up to dance, including Ms. Smithfield, a 100-year-old resident. Most just sat and enjoyed the Christmas music. There was not too much visiting at the tables of eight to ten residents. Part of the lack of conversation appeared due to the fact that many residents have hearing impairments. Some also are confused. It seemed that many were content just to sit and watch. Although some residents sang along with the band, others did not seem to have the energy, being more content to listen than to participate. One of the residents, Mrs. Maggie Scott, commented, "I've been here at Bethany Manor 26 years in the same room. I really am ready to go."

Frequently Bethany Manor residents related either their physical progress or degree of deterioration to the social and functional activities they were or were not able to engage in. Mrs. Peg McCracken, a sprightly 77-year-old who was temporarily residing on the fifth floor following surgery, described her life at the home this way:

"Every day I go down and sit in the lobby after lunch 'til Rosary. Sister Ann always says the rosary every day at four. It's nice in the lobby because there are people there. I wanted to go to Mass this morning but they weren't able to get me dressed in time. They get busy, you know. Sometimes there are too many patients and not enough nurses. I've been sick a lot lately. Ever since my gall bladder surgery I didn't do very well. My feet get numb and I can't walk right. I go to therapy everyday but sometimes you just can't do the things they think you can. Sometimes I can take the top off the milk carton so they think you can always do it, but sometimes you can't—even if you try and try. I go downstairs every week to bingo but sometimes I'm too slow. When somebody gets bingo I can't get my things off the board fast enough for them. I thought, 'What if I can't play bingo anymore? Then what will I do?' Maybe God will take me. My niece wanted to come and take me for dinner today but I told her no, that I'd be a burden on her. She would have to help me and it would just be too much on her, but she still wanted to anyway."

Residents of the home seemed to find satisfaction in the opportunity to do things even if the activities were not actually carried out. One study respondent observed, "Oh, it's wonderful here because there are so many different things to do. I don't usually go to social functions—I get too tired—but it's nice to know that I could if I wanted to."

Social Meaning of the Holidays

Holidays were an important focus of nursing home life at Bethany Manor from the perspective of administration, staff, families, and many of the cognitively aware residents. Keddy and Young (1984, 43) pose the question "Do [nursing home] residents enjoy, ignore, or simply go along with special celebrations?" They respond, according to their survey, "all three." To better understand the meaning of the holidays at Bethany Manor, the study's principal investigator spent several hours at the home on one of each of the following holidays during the two-year course of the study: Christmas Eve, New Year's Eve, Thanksgiving, Easter, and Valentine's Day.

Perhaps what strikes one most on observing the holidays at Bethany Manor, especially major holidays such as Christmas and Thanksgiving, is the fact that the daily routine of necessary caregiving goes on—"business as usual"—without interruption. The sometimes routinized chores of bathing, feeding, and changing of severely disabled residents are modified, however, at least a bit, by the festive air of the home's holiday decorations and music from the residents' televisions and radios. On Thanksgiving Day when a special turkey dinner was served by the Manor's sisters, geriatric aides on the fourth floor took special care in seeing that the ambulatory residents were dressed up to look their best before going downstairs to the main dining room. Several residents seemed to delight in having their holiday appearances admired by staff and other residents.

The nursing home also tends to be quieter on the major holidays, many residents having been taken out by their families. It can be difficult for those left behind. On an Easter morning, Mrs. Maeve Carty, a fifth-floor resident, spoke about previous holidays: "My son and daughter-in-law always took me home for dinner on the holidays, but then last year he died and I can't expect it anymore. She's so good to me and she wanted to come and take me by herself. She said, 'Oh, Mother, you must come,' but I said, 'No, it's too much trouble—to get me in the car and out of the car, and with all you have to worry about.' So this is where I have to be and I accept it." Another resident, Mrs. Anna Gittings, described the holidays as not quite as important as they used to be: "After a while the days all run together, and each day here is about the same as the next. They do try to make the holidays special for us. It's nice to have a little festivity, but that's more for the young than for us."

In looking at Bethany Manor's monthly newsletter, one finds a multiplicity of organized social and recreational activities scheduled around the holidays, such as Ladies of Charity Valentine Party, Children's Center Easter Egg Hunt, Harvest Fair (at Thanksgiving), Labor Day Barbecue, Oktoberfest, Christmas carolers, and Catholic Daughters Christmas Party. Although many residents did indeed enjoy these activities, one got the feeling that at least as much enjoyment and satisfaction, if not more, was derived by the organizers. Some residents seemed to attend the festivities more to please their hosts than to please themselves.

Music of a variety of types and renditions was enjoyed by the Bethany Manor residents. Those who could not see well often kept small radios tuned to a favorite station. Music was central to most of the religious chapel services, with a choir provided by the sisters. Holiday parties usually were supported by the presence of a visiting choral or instrumental group, and occasionally, in-house sing-alongs were organized by the Manor's Department of Recreation.

Music is advocated as therapeutic for a variety of illness conditions and also as a calming element to reduce the stress associated with severe anxiety or depression. Nordeck (1981) reported that music therapy sessions with the physiologically and psychologically frail elderly in one nursing home resulted in marked improvements: "Patients seemed more alert, were less incontinent, had increased mobility, and improved in personal appearance" (Kartman 1984, 29). Music therapy has been described as a "useful tool" for the alleviation of depression and stress experienced by geriatric patients; as a mechanism for providing meaningful relationships and activities for the elderly nursing home resident (Guerin 1982, 170); and, finally, as a means of establishing cohesiveness within a nursing home group, to enhance the self-esteem and self-expression of its members (Glynn 1986, 10). Music clearly was used as therapy at Bethany Manor.

Pets

The Manor did not have a consistently active pet program for its residents, although periodically pets were brought to visit and dog shows were held. The home did adopt a Labrador retriever puppy during the period of the study. At first, Blackie delighted some of the residents, but later he began to frighten a few as his puppyhood began to diminish and his size increased. Miss McCarthy commented that Blackie had just gotten entirely too "big for his britches in this home," but others seemed to enjoy his somewhat rambunctious meanderings through the Manor's halls and often stopped to pet him or rub his ears.

Frank (1984, 30) admits that the introduction of a pet into a long-term residential setting may require "reorganization of routine and a somewhat different philosophy of treatment." She adds, however, that pets may make contributions to institutional life by adding interest, warmth, and humor to the setting. The nature of the facility and the physiological and psychosocial abilities of its residents need to be considered and planned for in selecting nursing home pets (Sukosky 1982, 16); however, such planning seems worthwhile considering the conclusions of Barnett and Quigley (1984, 7) that "the psychosocial climate of long-term care facility and residents can be enhanced by the presence of animals" and those of Banziger and Roush (1983, 527), who found that pet activity with birds improved residents' self-reported "control, happiness and activity."

Although Bethany Manor's dog did at times cause a modest disruption of activities, the pleasure his presence gave residents and staff seemed to mitigate the wrath of any who might have been disturbed.

Reminiscence

Reminiscing was found to be a favorite pastime among residents at the Manor. Through reminiscence, losses could, to a degree, be regained through the vicarious experiences of sharing a previous joy or success. Residents were content to spend long hours regaling the researchers with tales of their past lives, both happy and sad. One theme that seemed to emerge frequently was that of the resident's childhood. It was as if a generation had been skipped; rather than talking of their own children and their developmental activities, study respondents frequently moved back in time to the era of their parents. An 86-year-old mildly confused, yet very active resident spent the better part of an hour-long interview session describing her childhood home in great detail, the various antics of her siblings, and her parents' philosophy of childrearing. A 95-year-old fourth-floor resident remembered, "I was born in 1890 in Virginia–way back in the sticks. My mother had eight children and how she could give us something to eat I don't know. My mother went to the store once a year. Of course we always had a hog and a cow and things like that to eat. And a vegetable garden and we all worked to help, but we had very little school education. But we lived by The Book and did what we were told."

The importance of reminiscence is supported by Holzapfel (1982, 156), who explored its relationship to personal possessions for the institutionalized elderly: "Reminiscing appears to lend continuity to the older adult's self concept through which they can trace the path of their development through time and can identify moments that were of central importance." Johnson et al. (1982, 21), who employ reminiscence as a methodology in group therapy in a nursing home, explain that reminiscing is used in their groups "as a vehicle for sharing and communicating with others about meaningful relationships." Reminiscence is also encouraged as a way for caregiving staff to learn more about the past and present anxieties and fears of the elderly (Hamner 1984, 81). Students and faculty from a nearby university periodically organized structured reminiscence groups for the Manor residents; these were generally attended with enthusiasm.

Stresses

A number of stressors in the social system of Bethany Manor have already been addressed: the social and cultural differences between residents and staff, the residents' loss of autonomy and control over daily activities, and the difficult interaction of cognitively alert and cognitively impaired residents.

Noise

Another stressor identified by some residents of the home was noise. One 77-year-old complained that television sets and radios were "played too high" and that "staff spoke in loud, rough voices" to residents. The staff response was that because so many residents suffered from hearing deficits, they had become used to speaking loudly and turning up televisions. One aide commented, "We have to yell at these people all day long because they don't hear if we talk normal. When I go home my children say, 'Please, Momma, you don't have to talk so loud,' and I say, 'Oh, I forgot you're not old.' "

Two second-floor residents complained about noise. One spoke of the sun porch: "My room is near the day room, but the television there is always so loud that I can't stay in my room." The other spoke about nighttime noise in the home: "I go to bed early and have a pretty good sleep until the night crew come on, the aides, those are girls who are very rested and ready to talk loud and laugh and jabber. I have asked the nurse if she could please tell them that they don't have to talk so loud and whistle. Two of them the other night came over here to, I think, change this patient and banged up the sides of the bed and had a big talk while they were doing her. Then they clanked it down, the bed side, and one of them whistled all the way down the hall. Absolutely unnecessary at night."

The Elevators

Another stressor that Bethany Manor residents and staff universally agreed constituted a problem was the fact that the home had only two elevators, only one of which was large enough for several wheelchair patients at a time. Thus, some residents, especially those in wheelchairs, stayed away from social activities held in the basement auditorium or on the first floor because of anxieties about road trips.

In his participant observation study of nursing home life, Clifford Bennett (1980, 94) learned that the elevator was a frightful place for many elderly residents. He reported, "They become apprehensive when it travels between floors and wonder if it will stop at the right place. Some residents get the feeling of claustrophobia." Bennett added that often, because of such anxieties, residents needed a staff companion to accompany them on the elevator and had to make "travel reservations" in advance. A conclusion of his study was that "elevators limit patients' freedom and independence considerably."

Frequently a whole string of wheelchair-bound Bethany Manor patients could be observed lined up waiting for an elevator after a meal in the main dining room, a chapel service, or a holiday entertainment. One wheelchair-bound resident, arriving at the fourth floor after having dinner in the first-floor dining room, commented, "My goodness, it's half-day's work to get back up here. Sometimes I think we should just all stay on our own floors." Another wheelchair resident sitting in the hall outside the elevator responded, "It's not for me. I used to wait for those elevators, and wait and wait and wait, but now I'm afraid if I go down, there won't be anybody to bring me back up, so I stay here on the fourth floor. I just live up here."

Mrs. Peg Lansing, an ambulatory but somewhat fragile 82-year-old, gave her reason for leaving the fourth floor infrequently as related to the elevator: "Every day has its little things you have to think about. Getting on the elevator, getting off the elevator with all these canes and things. You have to think whether you are going to bump him or her or he is going to bump you. There's a lot of that. You have to keep your wits about you, you really do. You don't want to bump someone who is going to fall down or bump their chair. You have to be on your own and be ready. I am proving to myself that I am, but I don't want to have too much worry." When asked by one of the researchers, "Do you stay in your room because you are worried?" Mrs. Lansing replied most decidedly, "No, I stay in my room because I *like* my room!"

Clearly, life in the nursing home is more limited for the wheelchair-bound patients. However, a number of ambulatory residents "adopted" one or more of their wheelchair-bound wardmates and took on the responsibility for escorting them to meals and social activities. When special holiday functions or religious services were held, the sisters and volunteers from the outside pitched in to transport those in chairs.

Previous studies document the fact that most nursing home residents, like those of Bethany Manor, accept a degree of stress as a matter of course in nursing home life. Stein et al. (1985), in studying 223 newly admitted residents in 10 nursing homes, found that most residents expressed ambivalence about being in the home and had a general state of anxiety about nursing home life. Gorden (1985) predicts that multiple resident concerns might be elicited employing a modification of the Holmes and Rahe Social Readjustment Rating Scale.

Complaints

Bethany Manor has a very specific policy regarding complaints, which is presented to the resident and family upon admission to the home. The statement of procedure reads as follows:

Under the provisions of Title X, relating to the Resident's Bill of Rights, the Resident has every opportunity to exercise his/her right to present without fear of retribution, any Legitimate Complaint.

It is the choice of the Resident to make his/her complaint to the Home orally, by telephone, mail, office visit, or direct outreach by staff.

All Legitimate Complaints will be filed and record of such and action taken will be kept for inspection. Such complaints do not need or require the Resident's signature.

The Resident, Relative or Representation shall be given the opportunity to present complaints to:

The Sister or the Nurse

The Facility's Staff

The particular Department of Complaint

The Social Service Staff

Other Persons

If the Resident chooses, the complaint may be presented to the Administrator or her designee.

When a Resident makes contact with Administrator or any other member within the home, the legitimate complaint shall be resolved within four (4) working days.

Manor residents did avail themselves of the complaint procedure; however, complaints seemed to be made more frequently through informal channels than through a written communication or visit to the Administrator. Occasionally a resident made the complaint to his or her physician, but more usually the concern was raised with the head nurse or with one of the sister nurses. One research team observer's concluding note read as follows:

Freedom to voice complaints is encouraged by Bethany Manor policy. Some residents have exercised this right by complaining to their families who in turn bring these complaints to the Nursing home Administration. Those who don't have families, voice their complaints to the charge nurse. Sometimes, the problem can be resolved. My basic feeling is that the residents have freedom to talk to people about how they are being treated.

Patterns of Medical and Nursing Care

Patterns of medical and nursing care involving specific details of physician-resident and nurse-resident interaction have been presented in Chapter 5. These patterns of staff attitude and behavior, however, also have implications for the social life of the nursing home. According to the theoretical concept of symbolic interactionism (Mead 1934), individuals generally respond in the manner in which they think others, especially significant others, expect them to. Thus, nursing home residents' attitudes and responses often mirror those of their significant caregivers. When a physician or a nurse treats cognitively alert nursing home residents with dignity and respect, and with the expectation that they are valuable and contributing human beings, capable of some degree of control over their lives, the residents are stimulated to respond in that manner. Mrs. Kate O'Hara, a 73-year-old second-floor resident, admitted that "when people treat me nicely, I try to respond that way and I'm the same here. Most of the nurses do act like that and I try to act that way back. And Dr. Swanson is so good to me. He always comes in and asks if I need anything and says, 'Don't worry, if you do, just have the nurses call me and I'll take care of it.' You can't help but be nice when people are nice to you."

When, on the other hand, a bright and alert but perhaps physically disabled resident is treated like a child, he or she might begin to respond in that fashion. As one 78-year-old widower put it, "You know, you come in here—you've given up your home and your things, buried most of your family and friends, and you just need a place for a little peace at the end of your life. But just because you can't get around doesn't mean your brain has gone soft! Sometimes they treat you like the 'elevator doesn't go all the way to the top floor,' so you figure, what the hell, if I'm going to be treated like a two-year-old, I might as well act like it—kick up my heels a little bit! Why not?"

The phenomenon of staff treating the elderly as children, or "infantil-ism," was reported by Kayser-Jones (1981, 39-40) as consisting of such behaviors as authoritarian scoldings; harsh commands to do something or to stop a certain behavior; issuing of threats; addressing of residents in familiar terms such as "honey," "baby," or "mother;" and the giving of stuffed animals or dolls as gifts. With the exception of the stuffed animal gifts, these behaviors were on occasion, although not frequently, observed at the Manor. The most usual offense was that of an aide calling a resident "dear" or "honey." Head nurses tried studiously to avoid such familiarity, generally addressing a resident by Miss, Mrs., or Mr.

Norms of Resident Behavior

In order to identify standards of behavior at Bethany Manor, staff were asked about the behavior of residents and other staff, and residents were asked about the behavior of staff and other residents.

Staff members were somewhat hesitant to label residents as good or bad. As one nurse put it, "Well, you know, I don't like to put labels on people but I can say there are some people who will really just go on and adjust to life here, and then there are some others who don't at all." She continued:

"The residents who sort of take the life as it comes and don't try to fight it—like always wishing they could do this or do that or be some place else—they really are a lot easier to work with and do a whole lot better. They like living in the nursing home—sort of accept it and just go with it. Some people, though, it's just hard for them. Maybe they were really independent before, and now it's hard to be told everything to do, especially if you don't think the person telling you knows so much. Like some of our residents will say, 'Well, she's just an aide; she can't order me around!' One man said, 'That little girl isn't even dry behind the ears yet, so why should I listen?'"

One of the Manor aides commented, "Some residents are really nice and try to do right and treat you right—that's the way it should be, but then there are others who think God put you on earth to wait on them. They don't even know to say 'thank you'—that makes working here a real pain."

Residents also talked about the attitudes and behavior of other residents quite freely. Such information dominated the Manor grapevine. A 91-year-old fourth-floor resident commented on the difficulty of having to be with confused patients, who she said really didn't belong on her floor. Mrs. Hopkins described her perception of some of the residents: "It probably looks nice here, but you have to live here to know what it's like. It's not like my home. Mrs. Flaherty and I complain when we get together. Some people won't fight it because people think you're senile—they pat you on the head and say, 'We'll take care of it.' It's hard to have that happen. But you know a lot of the people around here are really squirrelly, the people in their 90s. As I said, I can't blame them. When I was younger I thought anybody in their 70s was really off the beam."

Mrs. O'Connell, an 88-year-"young" resident who had been at Bethany Manor for seven years, had decided opinions on the norms of behavior for the home's residents (as well as decided opinions upon most aspects of life at the Manor—the transcript of Mrs. O'Connell's first study interview ran to 54 typed pages. The research team data collector complained to the principal investigator, "I know you warned us not to tire the residents—but it was Mrs. O who wore *me* down in that session!"). Mrs. O'Connell observed that at Bethany Manor the residents must get dressed every morning and never wear robes to breakfast. "For everyone," she stated, the most important behavior was "manners": "Yes, manners. You know, with old ladies, they are very apt to appear in a robe sometimes, not always, but you notice that kind of thing. I don't think they have the vigor now to dress themselves in time, or they don't see that their petticoat shows, and it's sad, because you don't like to go up to one of those ladies and say, 'Let me pull your skirt down because your petticoat is showing.' You don't know how they would take that so you accept that. Sometimes their hair is a little messy but the hair is not too bad here. We have a very nice girl, do you know her? Alice? She is very nice, a very lovely person with old people. She is always doing their hair up, washing it. So that, I think, nowadays means a lot for a person's appearance. They can be old, with an old face, but they have perky hair."

Norms of Staff Behavior

Residents were somewhat tentative in commenting on staff, most particularly on staff deficiencies, for fear of retaliation. One of the study data collectors concluded her observations with the following note: "When there are no staff members around, residents seem to feel free to verbalize feelings of isolation, lack of understanding of their physical needs as well as their emotional needs. A few residents verbalized to this researcher that only a few aides have treated them with patience, understanding and respect. The predominant label for the nurses' aides who don't pay attention to the needs of the residents is 'lazy.' "

Mrs. Stark, a perky 92-year-old on the home's fourth floor, described her feelings about the staff more positively: "Oh, they're all so good to me here. They really treat me nice—at least most of them do. That's the way it should be but not everybody...most of the girls, they bathe me, fix my bed and give me a hug. I don't know what I'd do without them. I just couldn't make it."

Another resident reported that she felt that "good" staff really tried hard to take care of all the residents' needs, "even the little things like fixing your hair and your room." She added, "They give me the best they can give me considering they are shorthanded and they also get the minimum wage. That makes me feel bad because they don't feel happy. Some of them think I'm a nice person, and some of them think I'm a nuisance because I require so much care, being disabled. There's one aide, she's unhappy here, she shouldn't be doing this kind of work. When she is taking care of me she's a little deficient in what she does. She wants the money but she doesn't like the work."

Miss Bessie Coleman, a long-time second-floor resident who was known to be somewhat unhappy with the staff, stated her case regarding Bethany Manor standards as follows: "Good nurses are the ones who are well trained and well organized. I don't like the way they haven't trained the nurses well and they talk to you something scandalous. You would think that you were paying them—well, you are paying them, but they just tell you where you get off and what you do. They just make you think that you've got to mind them about everything. It just gets your goat. And they are so rough."

A neighbor of Miss Coleman shared her opinion about how she thought the staff should take care of the patients: "I think we have some splendid nurses, very, very good people. Some of the aides are coming in from different countries, different backgrounds, can't speak very well, and you have one aide that is rude to the patients. That I can't condone at all, the manners of some of the aides. Others are just lovely girls." She added that the caregiver's attitude was most important to the nursing home residents: "Some of them are very nice to old people, and old people respond to kindness. They really do. It might take a little longer time but it's worth it."

Finally, a concern raised by several long-time residents was the high staff turnover, which resulted in the residents constantly having to get to know new caregivers. One resident put it this way: "Whatever nurse you have, the trouble is, you don't have the same nurse. They change and every nurse you have is a different one. They don't give you a chance to ever get friendly with the aides. On the fourth floor where I was before, I was friendly with the aides and they were real intelligent girls, smart and good company. I enjoyed them. I don't have that here. I have nobody to talk to. That's why I'm running my mouth off to you."

Staff members also made observations about the attitudes and behavior of other caregivers. A charge nurse observed, "You know, my aides are not very highly educated, most of them, but I see a lot of progress here. Sometimes they talk to the residents in ways they shouldn't and treat them like they're children, but they don't ever abuse them or hurt them. You have to remember what the aides' salaries are, and the kind of work they have to do, which isn't pleasant, especially for young people. I try to raise them up, encourage them to be professional, but it's an uphill battle, I can tell you that."

A more senior aide, who had worked at the Manor for many years, commented, "This work with the old is not cut out for some people. Some of these young girls, they get an attitude and they get nasty with the residents. I tell them, 'If you don't like it, then go get a job at McDonalds. You shouldn't come in here with an attitude.' "

Sanctioning

Negative and positive sanctions are imposed in both directions in staff-patient interactions. Staff may punish or reward a patient verbally or by some activity in return for perceived good or bad behavior. By the same token, residents also rewarded or punished staff members appropriate to the resident's opinion of the caregiver's attitude or actions. Sometimes staff members delayed in answering a resident's call bell if they felt that the resident was a "crock" or just "bugging" them about nothing. Staff members also verbally criticized residents when they felt, as one aide put it, that they "just don't do right." No physical abuse was observed or reported during the Bethany Manor study; however, a degree of verbal abuse was noted. Residents who were perceived as "pleasant," "nice," "kindly," or "no trouble" were rewarded with a pleasant greeting or a hug from staff members.

Residents were generally hesitant to impose negative sanctions on staff, feeling that they would be powerless if retaliation occurred. As one resident put it, "I just grit my teeth and bear it. It's best not to ruffle any feathers." Residents who had good feelings toward staff were generous in their praise and positive feedback. Often resident comments such as, "Thank you, darling, you're so good to me," or "Bless your heart, you're just grand," were overheard being made to staff.

Religion

The meaning of religion and spirituality in the lives of Bethany Manor residents is discussed in Chapter 2; in this chapter, religion as a cultural tradition is treated as a social vehicle for adjusting to and coping with nursing home life. It was suggested earlier that many Catholic residents came to the Manor because it was perceived as a Catholic home, with a number of formal religious rituals such as Mass, the sacraments, the Rosary, and Benediction available and accessible to residents on a daily basis. In a review of the home's monthly calendar the following religious activities were identified: daily and Sunday Mass, Confession, Rosary, Benediction, Vespers, Confirmation class, Bible study, Marian year prayers, religious lectures, Gospel singing, and choir.

The importance of the home's religious milieu was pointed out by one of the head nurses, who had worked in several other nursing homes: "I don't think I ever realized the importance of it until I came here. Very seldom do you see a nurse in a hospital or many facilities sit down and say a prayer with a patient. I don't think it's done that much, especially when someone is dying. They do it here. The patients here seem to have the feeling that God is going to take them and that is Okay. They feel at peace."

Several residents expressed their feelings about Bethany Manor's formalized religious culture. Seventy-six-year-old Mrs. Schaffer observed, "I came to Bethany Manor because of the sisters and the chapel. Daily Mass is so important to me, and I couldn't get out at home unless somebody came to pick me up. Now I can go every day, but even if I'm sick, Father will bring me Communion. It's the best part of this home."

Another resident noted, "I might sit around the lobby for a bit or go into church, the chapel. It is so lovely to have the chapel in this building. I don't have to go outside, in any weather; we have Mass in the chapel. In Lent now we have the Rosary and then we have Benediction. So the day goes along very well. I have an awful lot to be thankful for. . . and such a chapel! Do you know that they told me that the statutes of St. Joseph and the Blessed Mother are wood carvings. Beautiful, just beautiful. And the chaplain assigned here—oh, he is a terrific priest. He is just everything. He is bright and he is cheerful and he is funny and he speaks beautifully. He has a beautiful vocabulary. He is just precious."

Non-Catholic residents of the home also occasionally participated in Catholic religious services for social reasons, for example, to attend funeral services for former residents. Pastoral caregivers of other denominations visited members of their church periodically for personal support and counseling. One Baptist resident commented that she was going to ask her minister to help organize a Gospel choir at Bethany Manor.

Ethical Dilemmas

The approach to the termination of one's life has become a complex matter in the contemporary health care facility. Most institutions have specific policies relating to the issue of "code" (artificial resuscitation) versus "no code" (a "do not resuscitate, or DNR order). These policies address such issues as physician orders, patient and family wishes, and legal ramifications for the facility. Institutionalized patients no longer "die"; they "arrest" through either failure of cardiovascular functioning (cardiac arrest) or cessation of breathing (respiratory arrest). If either of these conditions occurs in a health care facility, staff must act to resolve the problem or the patient's life will cease. The decision to act or not to act may be fraught with difficulties related to the patient's overall condition and the perceived quality of life the patient will have if he or she survives. Therefore, most large health care facilities today have standing ethics committees whose members are on call to evaluate such situations and provide advice and guidance, legal as well as ethical, to staff and families. Helm (1984, 21), a registered nurse and a lawyer, observes that since death is now a "hi-tech issue, institutions have not only physiological but sociological factors to consider: considerations include not only whether the patient can live but under what conditions or artificial support systems should the patient be forced to live. The value or quality of such a life . . . the benefits to be obtained by further treatment, and the resultant costs . . . are pertinent factors in the decision."

Ethical dilemmas at Bethany Manor were generally not as complex as those encountered in, for example, the large, contemporary, highly techno-logical intensive care unit of hospitals. Dilemmas in the care of the residents revolved around such topics as DNR or "no code" status for a patient; the use of extraordinary means, such as major surgery or ventilatory therapy, to prolong survival; and the resident's wishes regarding life and death versus those of the family. On admission, each new resident is asked to examine and consider signing the "Christian Affirmation of Life," a statement on terminal illness published by the Catholic Hospital Association. The statement is based on the Christian philosophy that "through death life is merely changed and not taken away; and also, that death need not be resisted with every possible means" (Catholic Hospital Association, 1982). The philosophy is also grounded in the belief that patients have the right to choose what will be done for them as death approaches. Although the affirmation statement is not a legal document, it is a reflection of moral persuasion indicating an individual's wishes regarding treatment for terminal illness. The affirmation statement reads as follows:

To my family, friends, clergyman, physician, and lawyer:

Because of my Christian belief in the dignity of the human person and my eternal destiny in God, I ask that if I become terminally ill I be fully informed of the fact so that I can prepare myself emotionally and spiritually to die.

I have a right to make my own decisions concerning treatment that might unduly prolong the dying process. If I become unable to make these decisions and have no reasonable expectation of recovery, then I request that no ethically extraordinary means be used to prolong my life but that my pain be alleviated if it becomes unbearable. ("Ethically extraordinary means" signifies treatment that does not offer a reasonable hope of benefit to me or that cannot be accomplished without excessive expense, pain, or other grave burden.) No means should be used with the intention of shortening my life, however.

I request that my family, my friends, and the Christian community join me in prayer and sacrifice as I prepare for death. I request that after my death others continue to pray for me, that I will, with God's grace, enjoy eternal life.

Most Bethany Manor residents do sign the affirmation of life statement, and it is attached to their chart kept in the nursing station.

Death and Funerals

Attitudes toward death, one's own and that of others in the home, was a key interest in the examination of the resident's life career at Bethany Manor. It was also a topic that the investigators felt must be treated with great sensitivity and care. Before initiating the study, the research team agreed that, lest a respondent be disturbed by a direct conversation about death, the subject would be dealt with indirectly only in terms of discussing a resident's expectations for the future. It was determined that if indeed a resident initiated conversation about his or her future death or the death (past or future) of other nursing home residents, then the subject might be pursued cautiously to elicit more detailed feelings and attitudes. Data collectors were advised to discontinue any discussion of the topic and to refocus the conversation should a respondent seem to become anxious or disturbed by it. At the study's conclusion it was determined that the research team's concern had been virtually unfounded. Almost without exception, Bethany Manor study subjects raised the topics of their own future death and those of family, friends, and other Manor residents. It was learned that death was indeed an integral part of life at the home, and funerals were, in a sense, religious celebrations that many residents attended and spoke about among themselves. Death and funerals were important grapevine topics.

Much is written about death in the nursing home, a number of contemporary authors suggesting a hospice-type approach as most appropriate. Hinnant (1981, 14) advises that the goal be to "provide maximum quality of life until the dying person reaches [the] moment of last breath." It is suggested (Wagg and Yurick 1983, 503) that the elderly person may "welcome death as a relief from suffering or believe that death will reunite them with loved ones," but although the patient may not fear the condition of death, he or she may indeed be anxious about the dying process. Thus, it is advised that a staff member be prepared to serve as a "helping agent." The caregiver might serve to neutralize the perceived negative connotation of death prevalent in contemporary society (Mullins and Merriam 1983).

Selected excerpts from Bethany Manor residents' comments display a variety of sentiments toward death. Mrs. Angela Rinaldi, an 86-year-old fourth-floor resident commented that her life was deteriorating and she did not expect to live much longer:

"I go to bed at eight p.m. and get up at six. They have entertainment but I don't feel up to it. My eyes aren't good; I'm not too much into [sitting in] the hall. I'd like to get the news, though. You know I think I'm getting antisocial. I have one friend who comes once a month. My other friend doesn't have a car, and she doesn't like to ask people to use the gas to come over here. Lately, I have the feeling I'm sinking and people say, 'Oh, you're not going to die.' When I see the samples around here, I say, God forbid. I think 85 is enough to live and I made 86. I don't have a reason to live but I'm afraid to die. I think that's human nature. I don't know if it's worth it to keep on this earth. The earth is all upset out there. They're worried about the third world war."

Other residents, in contrast, had no fear at all of death. Miss Conoboy stated that she was totally at peace: "It's really time, you know, for God to take me. I've lived 87 years—they were good years—and I tried to do the best I could. I cared for my mother until she died and now I guess it's my turn soon. I'm really not afraid. I wish He'd come soon because I get so tired."

Younger residents focused more on the deaths of others at Bethany Manor. Miss Shaughnessy, a 72-year-old single lady, spoke about a close friend at the home who had recently died:

"Did you know Mrs. Gates? She lived a couple of doors down. A very nice Irish woman. She died, just about two weeks ago. I just couldn't get over it. She and I were like peas in a pod. On Sunday we went to Mass together. After lunch we would come up and she would say, 'I am going to put my stuff away.' About three weeks ago, or maybe four, she was failing, and her nephew was down and he said, 'I think she is failing.' She was the nicest lady. She was an elderly lady but she was very good. She felt pretty good when she got up in the morning, and the girl that was with her said, 'I left her so happy this morning,' then that night she took a heart attack and died. That was it. When I got up in the morning I said, 'What's the matter?' She said, 'Annie Gates passed away.' She really just passed away very quiet and her nephew said she had a very quiet death. No fuss. She was very peaceful and a very good Catholic. I haven't gotten over it yet. Every day she would come and sit and talk...I can't make it up with new friends, can you?"

Another resident spoke about her attendance at funerals at the home:

"If it's a person I've never known until she dies, I am very apt to go to the chapel for the observance of death, but I don't dwell on it. We had this awful condition at our table. This woman came to live here and she had one leg. She was one of the bravest people I have ever known. Her children were scattered. Here she is, alone, at this nursing home. She was very alive, very dressy, and very brave for the condition she was in. She could not walk. Not much *joie de vivre* but she knew how to handle it. She wasn't asking for pity for one minute.

"She sat at the table with us and all of a sudden she got very sick. They took her to the hospital and she died. We missed her but she's much better off. She worried about it but she was a very buoyant woman, wore very big earrings, not to be jazzy but just as an outlet. She couldn't walk, so she would buy a very colorful dress and wear lots of jewelry.

"If we wanted to, we could still see her in that chair, but we don't, because you can't. Another woman died the next year, at our same table. They come and they go. When that happens you move over with the next one."

Finally, a head nurse on the fifth floor (the skilled care floor) spoke of her perception of residents' deaths at Bethany Manor: "One of the things here that I think helps us deal with death is the fact that this is a religious nursing home. I think the staff have a hard time to deal with it, especially if someone really suffers, lingers on, but it is nice to have the nuns and the priests, to be able to call on them to come and say prayers. You feel like you really help someone die comfortably. I personally hate to see anyone die alone. I would rather have someone in there [with the dying patient] a lot, however long it takes to sit with them and hold their hand."

Researchers attended funerals for several residents during the course of the study (most funerals were held in the Bethany Manor chapel). Usually at least 40 to 50 residents, several aides, staff nurses, and as many of the sisters who were able attended as a support to the group of family and friends who were present.

Summary: Bethany Manor—Home or Institution?

At the study's initiation, the question was posed: Is Bethany Manor Nursing Home truly a "home," or is it rather an "institution"? It was anticipated that elements of both would coexist at the Manor; however, it was thought that one system might predominate, that is, that Bethany Manor would be discovered to be either a home with some characteristics of an institution or an institution with a homelike dimension reflected in certain attitudes and behaviors. At the conclusion of the study's two years of data collection, no definitive answer can be claimed. As the respondents' comments demonstrate, individual residents differed in how they perceived the nursing home, and these differences were frequently related to the respondents' own previous life-styles. Those residents who's former lives were more solitary and autonomous found that the experience of suddenly being thrust into the midst of a large "family," necessitating give and take in terms of fellow residents' personalities and behavior, could be trying at best and outright traumatic at times. Also, having to follow a schedule for such activities as mealtime and sleep frequently posed a difficult adjustment. These individuals generally perceived Bethany Manor to be an entity quite different from their former concept of "home"—to be an institution.

For residents whose previous life-style had not been as radically dissimilar from the home's large-group, structured atmosphere, Bethany Manor's character more closely reflected that of a home. Those residents who had experienced life in large, extended family situations, with several generations cohabiting, were better able to cope with the home's institutional characteristics. Stresses related to sharing of facilities, establishing a schedule for sleep and meals, and interacting with a variety of personalities, although admittedly magnified in the nursing home setting, were more easily dealt with.

Staff members who were asked to describe Bethany Manor frequently gave responses such as "it is really an institution–it has to be, but we try to make it as much like home as possible," or "with this many people in one facility, it has to be institutional, but it really is the residents' home. Most of them don't have any other." One caregiver captured the heart of the issue. She said, "Bethany Manor is whatever we and the residents make it!"

References

Andreasen, M.E.K. 1985. Make a safe environment by design. *Journal of Gerontological Nursing* 11(6):18-22.

Banziger, G., and S. Roush. 1983. Nursing homes for the birds: A control-relevant intervention with bird feeders. *The Gerontologist* 23(5):527-531.

Barnett, J.C., and J. Quigley. 1984. Animals in long-term care facilities: A framework for program planning. *The Journal of Long-Term Care Administration* 10(4):1-7.

Bennett, C. 1980. *Nursing home life: What it is and what it could be*. New York: The Tiresias Press.

Brent, R. S., E. C. Brent, and R. K. Manksch. 1984. Common behavior of residents in public areas of nursing home. *The Gerontologist* 24(2):186-192.

Broom, L., and P. Selznick. 1963. *Sociology*. New York: Harper & Row.

Catholic Hospital Association. 1982. *Christian Affirmation of Life. A statement on terminal illness*. St. Louis, MO: Catholic Hospital Association.

Frank, S. J. 1984. The "touch of love." *Journal of Gerontological Nursing* 10(2):29-35.

Gaffney, J. 1986. Toward a less restrictive environment. *Geriatric Nursing* 7(2):94-95.

Glynn, N. J. 1986. The therapy of music. *Journal of Gerontological Nursing* 12(1):6-10.

Goffman, E. 1961, *Asylums*. New York: Anchor Books.

Goffman, E. 1962. *Asylums*. Chicago: Aldine Publishing Company.

Gorden, G. K. 1985. The social readjustment value of becoming a nursing home resident. *The Gerontologist* 25(4):236-398.

Grau, L. 1984. What older adults expect from the nurse. *Geriatric Nursing* 5(1):14-17.

Grover, R. M. 1982. The impact of resident councils. *The Journal of Long-Term Care Administration* 10(4):2-6.

Gubrium, J. 1975. *Living and dying at Murray Manor*. New York: St. Martin's Press, p. 36.

Guerin, M. E. 1982. Come sing along with me. *Geriatric Nursing* 3(3):170-171.

Hamner, M. L. 1984. Insight, reminiscence, denial, projection: Coping mechanisms of the aged. *Journal of Gerontological Nursing* 10(2);66-68.

Helm, A. 1974. Debating euthanasia: An international perspective. *Journal of Gerontological Nursing* 10(11):20-24.

Hinnant, C. H. 1981. Hospice approach in long-term care. *Contemporary Administrator* 4(8):14-16.

Holzapfel, S. K. 1982. The importance of personal possessions in the lives of the institutionalized elderly. *Journal of Gerontological Nursing* 8(3):156-158.

Hooker, K., and D. G. Ventis. 1984. Work ethic, daily activities and retirement satisfaction. *Journal of Gerontology* 39(4):478-484.

Huss, A. J. 1977. 1976 Eleanor Clarke Slagle Lecture: Touch with care or caring touch? *American Journal of Occupational Therapy* 31:11-18.

Johnson, D. R., S. L. Sandel, and M. B. Margolis. 1982. Principles of group treatment in a nursing home. *The Journal of Long-Term Care Administration* 10(4):19-24.

Kartman, L. L. 1984. Music hath charms. *Journal of Gerontological Nursing*. 10(6):20-24.

Kayser-Jones, J. 1981. *Old, alone and neglected*. Berkley, CA: University of California Press.

Keddy, B., and D. Young. 1984. The meaning of holidays in a nursing home. *Geriatric Nursing* 5(1):43-46.

Langland, R. M., and C. L. Panicucci. 1982. Effects of touch on communication with elderly confused clients. *Journal of Gerontological Nursing*, 8(3):1522-1525.

Loomis, C. P. 1960. *Social systems. Essays on their persistence and change*. Princeton, NJ: D. Van Nostrand.

Mead, G. H. 1934. *Mind, self, and society*. Chicago: University of Chicago Press.

Millard, P. H., and C. Smith. 1981. Personal belongings—a positive effect? *The Gerontologist* 21:85-90.

Miller, W. 1984. How I made Millens Manor merrier. *Contemporary Administrator* 7(10):56-60.

Moss, F. E. 1977. *Too old, too sick, too bad*. Germantown, MD: Aspen Systems.

Moss, M. S., and M. P. Lawton. 1982. Time budgets for older people: A window on four lifestyles. *Journal of Gerontology* 37(1):115-123.

Mullins, L. C., and S. Merrian. 1983. Nurses react to death anxiety. *Journal of Gerontological Nursing* 9(9):487-492.

Nordeck, M. A. 1981. The healing power of music therapy. *Contemporary Administrator* 4(11):26-29.

Retsinas, J. 1986. *It's OK, Mom. The nursing home from a sociological perspective.* New York: Tiresias Press.

Roosa, W. M. 1982. Residents' views: Findings of a survey. *Geriatric Nursing* 3(4):241-243.

Ryden, M. B. 1984. Morale and perceived control in institutionalized elderly. *Nursing Research* 33(3):130-136.

Seaman, L. 1982. Affective nursing touch. *Geriatric Nursing* 3(3):162-164.

Synder, P. 1982. Creating culturally supportive environments in long-term care institutions. *The Journal of Long-Term Care Administration* 10(1):19-28.

Spicer, W. A. 1982. Where residents get what they want. *Contemporary Administrator* 5(12):17-18.

Stein, S., M. W. Linn, and E. Stein. 1985. Patients' anticipation of stress in nursing home care. *The Gerontologist* 25(1):88-94.

Sukosky, D. G. 1982. A special friend to many. *Perspective on Aging* 10(4):15-24.

Teaching Nursing Home Project. 1981. Grant application submitted by The Catholic University of America School of Nursing, September 29, 1981.

Timmreck, T. C. 1983. The nursing home resident: Some legal considerations. *The Journal of Long-Term Care Administration* 11(2):9-13.

Wagg, B., and A. Yurick. 1983. Care enough to hear. *Journal of Gerontological Nursing* 9(9):498-503.

CHAPTER 8

A Typology of
Long-Term Adaptation to
Nursing Home Life

Often the test of courage is not to die but to live.

Vittorio Alfieri, *Oreste*

The Survivors

How often have we heard the remark, "She didn't live long after they put her in that home!" In certain cases, even for Bethany Manor residents, this was true. Many variables might be associated with such brief nursing home stays: the resident's physical condition on admission, the absence of a supportive social system, or even simply the lack of will to live. During the course of this research, Miss Catherine Flaherty, an 89-year-old poststroke and hip fracture patient, was admitted to the home. Miss Flaherty was a retired government executive secretary who had lived a very satisfying and independent life in her retirement years. Although she lived alone, she had many friends and was very involved with her church and with helping those in need. Indeed she had been a frequent visitor to Bethany Manor over the years.

Miss Flaherty had virtually no family left, most of her friends had died, and so she was admitted to the Manor's fifth floor for care after falling and breaking her hip. Although her condition did not seem critical, she rapidly deteriorated physically and mentally and survived in the nursing home for only five weeks. Because of her incredibly active life-style (Miss Flaherty was still volunteering for the church in her 80s, one might speculate that she did not have a strong desire to continue her life in a nursing home. In fact, a staff member who cared for her observed, "She just didn't seem to care about living in here."

In contrast to Miss Flaherty, Bethany Manor had many "survivors." Miss Agnes DeGraff had lived at the home for 27 years and was still doing quite well, although at 97 she herself admitted that it was "about time to go," and one assumed she did not mean to another living situation. Generally, however, with the passage of the years, multiple physical and psychosocial changes and problems intruded in the lives of the survivors.

Eighty-four-year-old Mrs. Julia Crowley, who had resided at Bethany Manor for seven years, reported that she had no serious illnesses but that aging had taken its toll on her body: "I am very careful of my eyes because I have had two cataracts removed, so I have to wear these glasses all the time. Any my feet aren't very strong for heels, so I have to wear this flat kind of shoe. Otherwise, you know when you get older, you tighten up here, loosen up there. It's just the process." In contrast, 78-year-old Mr. Ackernecht described multiple physical problems:

"I get this arthritis in my neck sometimes when I hold my head in one position, it makes me worse. I have got it in my shoulders and arms and wrists. I was getting bent over more and more. I have something wrong with my hand. I am sleepy all the time. In fact, I was sitting here saying the rosary and I go to sleep, let the rosary slip out of my hands. I did that twice this morning. I am almost blind and I've got this monocular deterioration. My eyes water awful and that dries and leaves like sand. Then they have trouble getting it out around the eye. I am a mess."

Physical Deficits Over Time

Myriad physiological problems can and do afflict the resident of a long-term care facility over time. Selected problems addressed here are those observed fairly frequently at Bethany Manor during the course of the research, including chronic fatigue, foot problems, infections, and skin changes (decubitus ulcers).

Fatigue

Mitchell (1986, 19) asserts that "fatigue is accepted as an almost universal symptom of aging." In the nursing home, daytime fatigue may be increased as a result of interrupted sleep patterns. Although there is no specific number of sleep hours mandated to ensure adequate rest, "a person over the age of 60 usually needs only 6-7 hours or less," and naps may be included in this time (Schirmer 1983, 17). It does, however, usually take the elderly person longer to fall asleep, and if awakened during the night, which may happen in a nursing home because of noise created by ill or confused residents, he or she may have more difficulty returning to a sound sleep. Older persons also often display a pattern of "excessively early arousal in the morning" (Quan et al. 1984, 42). Inadequate sleep may result in decreased energy and alertness during the day. Clark (1985, 143) reports that fatigue and sleep changes in the nursing home may be related to such factors as "inappropriate physical restraints, sedative, or confinement" or result from "changes to unfamiliar surroundings and alteration in usual bedtime routines." A Bethany Manor resident spoke about fatigue: "Frankly, I don't feel like doing anything. I just returned from lunch and usually I sit and prop my feet up and sleep until supper time. After supper I go to bed. It's not a very happy kind of life. I am so weak. I have arthritis and I have a swelling in my feet and ankles—edema. I have to take a pill which sets me urinating constantly."

Social history data for the Manor revealed that 47 (20.4% of the residents were identified as suffering from chronic fatigue prior to nursing home admission; for many the condition seemed to worsen for reasons related both to the environment and to the aging process.

Foot Problems

It has been observed that "many of the frail elderly have learned to cope with their illnesses, but they and their families often do not equate immobility with inadequate foot care" (Chung 1983, 213). Helfand (1982, 49) argues that to avoid disabling foot problems the elderly must be cared for with three primary goals: "reducing pain, restoring maximum functional ability, and enabling the patient to retain the restored function." Preadmission social history data from the Bethany Manor group contained a multiplicity of references to and comments about already existing foot problems. Such remarks as "poor feet," "painful feet," "foot problems," and "can't walk very far because feet hurt" abounded in resident and family statements. One 79-year-old resident elaborated, "My feet don't take me where I want to go anymore. I guess it's to be expected, so I've had to limit my activities accordingly." The social history forms documented 34 (14.8%) of the resident group as having had serious foot problems prior to admission.

Infections

Infections of various types are endemic to any institutional health care setting. However, in a long-term care facility where residents have basically adapted to the usual bacterial strains of the institution, infections seem more often associated with the aging process in general than with the environment. Spicer (1982, 7) suggests that "inside nursing homes the infection control war is waged ceaselessly by dedicated housekeeping, laundry, nursing and dietary staffs." Indeed, Bethany Manor had its own Infection Control Committee, which met monthly to discuss issues relating to the control of resident infections in the home. Members of the committee consisted of the home's Administrator, the Director of Nursing, the House-keeping and Laundry Department head, the Medical Director, the head of the Maintenance and Engineering Department, and two external consultants: a pharmacist and a pathologist. At one committee meeting, discussion focused on several topics. The first was indwelling catheters in use by residents (the reported number was 14: four to prevent urine retention, six to prevent skin breakdown, two to promote skin healing, and two residents recently admitted with catheters). A discussion ensued about whether or not catheters should be used to prevent skin breakdown and who should determine when they are to be removed. No urinary tract infections were reported; six residents were, however, on prophylactic antibiotics.

Some other concerns discussed were the need for bacterial cultures on environmental areas such as dishwashers, ice machines, and drinking fountains; a decreased temperature in one walk-in ice box; the recent county dietary inspection (no major problems were identified); the upcoming state inspection of boilers and other maintenance equipment; and deaths. The Bethany Manor report for the past quarter documented 17 deaths (three in the hospital, the others at the Manor). The following causes were identified:

stroke, myocardial infarction, congestive heart failure, cerebral thrombosis, respiratory failure, pneumonia, and general visceral collapse (due to natural causes related to aging).

Two notable infectious processes observed at Bethany Manor during the study were pneumonia and urinary tract infection. Pneumonia in the older person can become a critical situation. As Hill and Stamm assert (1982, 40), "in the elderly, bacterial pneumonias predominate and, if left untreated, often result in death." The Manor patients who developed pneumonia or an impending pneumonia were usually transferred immediately either to the hospital or to the home's fifth-floor skilled nursing unit where intravenous antibiotic therapy could be administered.

The majority of elderly in a long-term setting are also at risk for urinary tract infections (UTIs) due to such factors as "inadequate hydration, immobility, chronic disease, poor hygiene and toileting and urethral catheters" (McConnell 1984, 361). UTIs were a common problem at Bethany Manor, one that the staff discussed and worried about frequently during patient care conferences. However, no UTIs were identified among presently catheterized residents at the Infection Control Committee meeting. Some suggestions for avoiding these infections in the future were made, one being the use of new silicone catheters, which have an antibacterial agent in place where the catheter is connected to the drainage bag. It was also agreed that retention catheters would be frequently cultured.

Skin Changes (Decubitus Ulcers)

Related to the use of catheters to prevent skin breakdown was the topic of decubitus ulcers. Although there are varying degrees of change from one individual to another, aging significantly affects the skin's structure and function: "The skin becomes parchment thin, wrinkled, dry and scaly; the nails become more brittle and grow at a slower rate," and the hair becomes thinner and may lose its color (Porth and Kapke 1983, 158). Some common problems include skin tags, keratoses or wartlike lesions on the skin, and vascular lesions. A more significant potential skin problem for the bedridden or wheelchair-bound patient is a decubitus ulcer.

The decubitus ulcer or bedsore has for years been the bane of the nursing home caregiver. Nursing home "scandals" reported in the media generally "led to the widespread notion that these facilities are 'houses of bedsores' " (Stompor 1984, 28). This is inaccurate; however, it has been reported that an estimated 30% of nursing home residents do develop some type of pressure sore (Fowler 1982, 680) related to the immobility associated with fragile skin and sometimes a history of poor nutrition. Even in excellent nursing homes where staff take great pride in the quality of their care, as reported by Tooman and Patterson (1984, 166), an alarming number of decubitus ulcers can develop. The absence, presence, or healing stage of a decubitus ulcer was frequently included as part of the Bethany Manor daily patient reports and the monthly patient care conferences. The nurses' aides especially took great pride and satisfaction in reporting improvement in resolution of a resident's pressure sore as a reflection of their skillful and attentive nursing care. Head nurses and the patient care clinician were quick to reward the aides with complimentary remarks in order to reinforce their hard work.

At the Infection Control Committee meeting, the Director of Nursing reported that presently 11 residents had decubitus ulcers, mostly on the buttocks, hips, or sacral areas (the 11 residents had a total of 16 specific ulcerated areas). The decubiti ranged in diameter from 1.2 to 6 cm approximately. It should be noted, however, that preadmission social history data identified 18 (8%) of the Manor population as having "skin problems" prior to coming to the Manor; four were identified as having already developed decubitus ulcers.

Alzheimer's Disease

Alzheimer's disease or Alzheimer-type dementia was probably the most commonly identified specific diagnosis other than "senile dementia" among the cognitively impaired residents at Bethany Manor. Social history (admission diagnosis) data indicated that 44 (19%) of the newly admitted residents had been assigned an Alzheimer's label (15 of these had Alzheimer's disease; the other 29 were diagnosed with Alzheimer-type dementia or syndrome), prior to admission, sometimes in combination with a multiplicity of other conditions such as arteriosclerotic cardiovascular disease (ASCVD), hypertension, osteoarthritis, or coronary artery disease. Twenty (9%) of the residents were diagnosed with organic brain syndrome, 13 (6%) as having chronic brain syndrome, 32 (14%) with senile dementia, and 15 residents were labeled "confused." One of the home's senior physicians commented that it was often very difficult to diagnose individuals as having Alzheimer's disease without the appropriate pathological data to specify the condition; hence the labels "Alzheimer-type dementia" or "Alzheimer-type syndrome" were sometimes used. The Report of the Secretary's Task Force on Alzheimer's Disease (Department of Health and Human Services [DHHS] 1984, 19) noted that the "definitive diagnosis of Alzheimer's disease is based upon the observation at autopsy or biopsy of large numbers of neurofibrillary tangles and senile plaques in the cerebral cortex of clinically demented individuals." It has been observed that the behavioral hallmark of Alzheimer's disease is "memory loss, especially for recent events" (DHHS 1980, 2). Other symptoms may include inability to concentrate, anxiety, irritability, agitation, withdrawal, lack of judgment, disorientation, anger, and depression (DHHS 1980, 2-3).

The etiology of Alzheimer's disease is unknown, but because the disease sometimes occurs in more than one member of the same family, a genetic factor is suggested (Williams 1986, 22). Rousey (1984, 49) asserts that many authorities consider Alzheimer's "as a distinct entity, different from senile dementia," with onset identified "prior to the age of 70 and senile dementia placed after that." Palmer (1983, 87), however, reported that "recent clinical investigation had identified few pathological differences between senile dementia and Alzheimer's disease" and that the two are considered one disease entity by some. Alzheimer's disease is more common in women than in men and generally has an insidious onset, ultimately leading to death in approximately five to ten years (Gwyther and Matteson 1983, 92). Approximately 50% of "dementia" patients over 65 years have Alzheimer's disease (Roach 1985, 77).

Alzheimer's patients at Bethany Manor presented a variety of symptoms and in varying stages. Mrs. Sylvia Valentino, an 87-year-old diagnosed with Alzheimer-type dementia, had been admitted to the nursing home four years earlier because of "mental confusion" and "unreasonableness." She was described as being "confused, depressed, very forgetful, easily fatigued." Her judgment had become poor and she had occasional temper outbursts. Her daughter and son-in-law could no longer cope with her in their home. Mrs. Valentino resided on the third floor where she could have the freedom to walk about, which she did incessantly. She appeared to like companionship, and although her responses were often incoherent or unintelligible, she appeared to love touch and enjoyed hugging or holding onto someone's hand. Mrs. Valentino responded positively to any kind of attention.

In a much more advanced stage of the illness was Mrs. Adams, a 75-year-old, bedridden Alzheimer's patient being treated for decubitus ulcers on her back and heels. Mrs. Adams had been cared for at home by her husband and daughter until a fractured hip three years ago hospitalized her and necessitated transfer to the nursing home. Presently she was almost nonresponsive verbally and only minimally responsive to touch or the attention of others. Her lower extremities were contracted from immobility; food and fluid intake and elimination were poor. The nursing goals for Mrs. Adams were basically comfort-oriented measures, adequate nutrition, and the prevention of further skin breakdown. Her family, although faithful, found visiting very difficult because of Mrs. Adams' continued deterioration.

Alzheimer's disease in the early stages is most stressful for the patient, who retains enough cognition to be aware that the mind is failing. A second floor resident, Mr. Butler, complained, "It bothers me. I'm losing my memory. I forget my room number. . .how would you like that? I'm 83 years old. Before you know it you have lost 40, 50, 60, 70 years! It's old age, that's what it is." Alzheimer's in the later stages causes the greatest distress for family members, who must stand by helplessly while a loved one slowly regresses, both mentally and physically, before their eyes. Mrs. Cunningham, whose husband was in the advanced stages of Alzheimer's disease, explained her feelings: "It hurts so bad. . .after a while you just go numb. You have to, you know, to make it. Now it will be a blessing when he goes— it's been so long."

Mobility: Wheelchairs, Walkers, and Canes

After a significant time in a long-term care setting, mobility is necessarily lessened by physical (and sometimes psychological) deficits related to the aging process. Bethany Manor residents employed a variety devices such as wheelchairs, walkers, and canes in order to support their mobility as long as possible. Wheelchair use limited mobility significantly in the Manor, as in many nursing homes, because only one of the home's two elevators could hold multiple wheelchair-bound residents.

Mrs. Lucy Karrat, a fourth-floor wheelchair-bound resident, explained her anxiety about using the Manor elevators: "We go down to the first floor for our meals. We go down on the elevator. That's one thing I have such a fear of—the elevator. There's nothing to it, but I'm afraid I'll get on maybe by myself and something will happen. I haven't really tried to go alone. I always wait until I know there's someone going down." Mr. Wilson, a second-floor resident, commented, "I don't like going to activities on that elevator. I don't know. It's a long way for me to come back upstairs."

A Manor patient care nurse clinician described the importance of wheelchairs to some residents: "Wheelchairs sometimes become personal space. People keep all their things that are near and dear to them in wheelchairs. Sometimes their personal space is their wheelchair, perhaps more so than their rooms. Their personal space becomes constricted, smaller and smaller." A staff nurse also gave an example of the importance of her wheelchair to one resident, Mrs. Moran: "She told me about how they took her wheelchair and washed her chair and she couldn't get up for a whole day. This is her entire life, that she sits in a wheelchair. The way they lose control is unbelievable. What happened, they got mixed up and so they cleaned it twice in one week and she was frantic. It's the connection with the world for some of them, their transportation."

Walkers and canes posed less of a problem in the elevators and did serve to increase residents' mobility a fair amount. Eighty-six-year-old Mrs. Martina Simms reported, "The walker has made a great difference. Before that I couldn't go anywhere at all" and Mrs. Anna Gittings commented, "It [the walker] really does help because I can scarcely walk. I am really ashamed when I walk. I go limping along so." Social histories revealed that prior to admission a number of residents' mobility was already limited: 31 (13.4%) were bedridden or chair-bound; 40 (17.3%) were wheelchair bound, 32 (13.9%) needed the assistance of walkers to move about, and 30 (13%) used canes to stabilize an unsteady gait. In addition, 25 (10.9%) of the residents were described as slightly unsteady on their feet, and 66 (28.7%) as "slow" walkers.

The Manor's physical and recreational therapists made serious attempts to encourage at least some type of exercise for the residents in order to stimulate psychosocial interests as well as promote physical health. Lonnerblad (1984, 93) in discussing exercise asserts that "vigorous measures are needed to counteract infirmities that force increasing numbers of aged to depend on others." Johnson (1985, 137) notes that "exercise is the most powerful therapeutic tool to aid in keeping people functional for as long as possible—hopefully until the moment of death."

Finally, several residents explained their reasons for limiting their own mobility. Mrs. Delaney said, "I have never been out of this building since I came in, except last year I had a fall and they took me to the hospital in an ambulance, but that's the only time I have ever been out the front door. I don't care to go out in this condition. If I was able to walk around the grounds, I would like to walk around, but I can't do it. I don't want to be shoved around." Miss Graham stated, "I might be taken sick and disturb the people and I don't go to any activities." Miss Hollings said, "My nephew and his wife asked me if I could have a wheelchair on a Sunday when they would come if I would like to go outside, just be wheeled around. I know what everything looks like from the window and I don't need to move around outside."

Restraints

Decisions as to whether or not to restrain an individual and, if so, what type of restraint to use are decidedly of concern in the long-term care of older persons. Yarmesch and Sheafor (1984, 242) suggest that the decision to restrain or not to restrain "is a particularly thorny problem for nurses working with frail elders at risk for falling or with confused individuals who may not only annoy others but sometimes endanger them." One of Bethany Manor's head nurses expressed her views on restraints for ambulatory confused residents:

"Why do we want to tie people in a posey [a type of restraint] and not let them walk? Why take that dignity away from them, why take that independence away from them? It's going to come in time anyway soon enough. So sometimes we get a broken hip, and the person may end up in bed or a chair, but at least they had 40 years of walking versus 20 years tied in a chair." She added, "With restraints you are taking the dignity, you are taking the individuality away, and each of us are individuals and if we have to live in an institution where there had to be a certain amount of general molding, so to speak, so let them have their dignity."

Miss McDermott, an 81-year-old cognitively impaired resident with many physical deficits, commented that her restraints were "just something they use to keep me down." She observed, "I get confused and forget things. I know what I want to say and do but it just doesn't come out right." Many nursing staff members at the Manor said that they disliked the use of physical restraints, but that sometimes it was the only means of protecting the resident or of protecting others from the resident's confused behavior. Falls and the physical abuse of other residents were two concerns raised to validate the use of physical restraint.

Falls

Directly related to the use of restraints in the nursing home is the subject of resident falls, which are a source of concern for staff and family members as well as for the residents themselves. Falls prior to admission to the home were reported for 37 (16%) of the Manor's residents, according to the social history data, and, as noted in Chapter 2, a fall was sometimes the catalyst or critical incident stimulating the move to the nursing home. The import of falls in the nursing home is reflected in the gerontological literature on long-term care, which is replete with discussion of residents' falls and their etiology, sequelae, and prevention. Riffle (1982, 165) states that "accidents are the leading cause of death in older persons, falls are the leading cause of accidental death in the home for older persons, and the mortality associated with falls increases with advancing age." Major causes of falls in the elderly have been identified as "environmental hazards, physiologic changes of age, syncope [fainting], drop attacks [sudden falls without loss of consciousness], orthostatic hypotension [low blood pressure on standing], dizziness or vertigo, neurologic dysfunctions, and drug effects" (Rubenstein and Robbins 1984, 67), and it is suggested that "while results of falls can vary from minor to devastating, even minor falls should be taken seriously, as underlying causes may be dangerous" (Gordon 1982, 117).

Although minimal research has been done on the etiology of falls in the elderly, Louis (1983, 143) reports that one study identified 34% of falls among the elderly as accidental. Several authors suggest that while nursing home falls cannot always be prevented, some risk factors may be identified. These include "the season (from September to November)" and "having more than three unit transfers" at a time (Lund and Sheafor 1985, 38), as found in a study of hospitalized elderly. Significant activities involved in the falls studied by Lund and Sheafor included "Getting in, out of chairs, wheelchairs, toileting" (1985, 38). Studying falls in a Veterans Administration Medical Center, Barbieri (1983, 166) found that the "highest incidence of falls occurred between 6 am and 10 am and 4 pm and 8 pm; and those most affected were over the age of 75." In this study, profiles of high-risk patients revealed "individuals who pride themselves on previous autonomy and who desire to remain independent; individuals preoccupied with life crises; and individuals who do not seek help, have knowledge regarding reasons for falls, and hold the belief that falls are inevitable" (Barbieri 1983, 166). Some suggested ways to reduce the incidence of falls in the nursing home include fall–related "orientation programs for new staff, policies and procedures, inservice, studies, visual aids" (Hernandez and Miller 1986, 100), and safety education classes for residents and staff (Gray-Vickrey 1984, 179).

Many Bethany Manor residents described both falls and the fear of falling. Mrs. Cavanaugh, a five-year resident, reminisced, "I have had 14 falls since I have been here. The first day I was here I went downstairs to breakfast in the main dining room and I used the walker. After breakfast I came back to the elevator, and before I could get on, the door closed on me and knocked me down in the elevator. I didn't break anything but I skinned all my side."

Mrs. Crowley spoke of her fear of falling, noting, "I have certain limitations because I could slip and fall, break something. I can't do much of the activities. I'm not going to try that for fear I'll be the one that's coming down on crutches. You have to set your own limits."

Mr. Franciscus described the difficulty of recouping after a fall: "I haven't got back to what I would call normal yet. I've tried quite a few times to walk, on the street out here where there's the benches. I would start out walking maybe one or two benches, and next week maybe add another bench to it. I did have it so that I could walk down to the street and then I got a spell again. I tried and tried walking. I can see that I couldn't walk like I used to." Mrs. Smithfield explained why she did not try to walk anymore after several falls: "I just look out of the window. That's the safest for me because if I'm going to go out, I'll fall."

Resident falls were also a topic of concern to Bethany Manor staff. One in-service class conducted for the geriatric aides focused on the prevention of falls in the home. Some factors suggested as likely to increase residents' vulnerability to falling included slippery floors, weakness, walking in stocking feet, some types of shoes that were worn by residents, dizziness, unsteady gait, confusion, loss of vision, medication, anxiety, and poor use of wheelchairs and walkers. Some protective measures suggested were to avoid environmental clutter, encourgage residents to wear shoes or slippers, check shoelaces, teach residents to lock wheelchairs, and encourage residents to call for help when needed. The discussion ended with encouragement to staff to try to protect the residents without totally compromising their independence.

Resident Abuse

Elder abuse in general is becoming an area of notable concern in our society. A variety of researchers have defined elder abuse in relation to such factors as physical or emotional neglect or abuse, or not meeting the needs of an elderly person (Floyd 1984). It is suggested that "the multiply impaired frail elder is at high risk for an abuse event" (Fulmer and Cahill 1984, 16). The potential for elder abuse in nursing homes has long been a topic of worry and concern, particularly for family members who are forced to place their loved ones in such a facility. Nursing home resident abuse has been documented by a number of investigators (Vladeck 1980, Moss and Halamandaris 1977, Mendelson 1974). Much of the abuse identified has been caused by poorly paid and little-recognized nurses' aides who, Warner (1982, 28) asserts, "seem to be taking out their own inadequacies on the people in their charge."

No cases of physical abuse against the Bethany Manor residents were observed during the course of the study. A Director of Nursing reported that there had been instances of verbal abuse carried out by one aide; that aide was immediately dismissed. The director, Sister Martha, commented, "Our aides have very little training and sometimes one slips by. If something like this [verbal abuse] happens, we try to catch it right away and I'll fire the aide on the spot. Sometimes it just gets past you, though, until a resident or their family reports it." No study residents or family members reported either physical or verbal abuse in those terms. There were, however, some complaints of residents being left without needed linen change or some other problem for long periods of time. The complaints were difficult to evaluate objectively, however, as the term "long periods of time" had relative and subjective meanings for residents, visitors, and caregivers. Although also not given the label "abuse," occasional verbal and minor physical attacks occurred between residents, usually initiated by a confused or disoriented individual. One wheelchair-bound resident, Mr. Gibbs, was observed being hit lightly by another resident, Mr. Jamison, with his cane. When one of the nursing staff intervened and said she was sure Mr. Jamison had not really meant to hurt Mr. Gibbs, Mr. Jamison replied emphatically, "Yes, I did." Fortunately such disagreements were somewhat controlled by the elderly resident's limited physical strength.

Hospitalization

Hospitalization was often a traumatic occurrence for Bethany Manor residents, who tried to avoid the experience at all costs. Residents generally resisted a hospital trip as long as possible and, the staff feared, might even disguise symptoms in order to avoid even a short-term hospitalization. Thus, such transfers were usually for very serious conditions such as heart attack, fractured hip, or severe respiratory problems.

Although there is much literature on such subjects as relocation of the elderly in the community and transfer trauma within the home (discussed later in this chapter), Feldman (1982) observed that little information existed to prepare the nursing home nurse and the resident for the problems that might accompany emergency transfer from home to hospital. The Bethany Manor nursing staff worried that hospitals did not know how to care for "their" patients. This concern was supported by the assertions of Bossenmaier (1982, 253) that "generally speaking, nurses in acute care settings are less familiar with the special requirements of elderly patients than with the care needs of children and younger adults." The research of Roslaniec and Fitzpatrick (1979, 177), who studied 25 hospitalized individuals ranging in age from 65 to 87 years, found added problems related to the hospitalization. In repeat evaluations of mental status conducted over a four-day period, "statistically significant changes in three components of mental status were found: disorientation increased, level of consciousness declined, and memory improved."

A Bethany Manor nursing supervisor commented, "We send our residents to any one of about six hospitals. We hook up with wherever the doctor wants to send them. Some hospitals do better than others, but it is traumatic for them [the residents] and the hospitals. The hospital staff don't know how to care for elderly nursing home residents, and the residents get real anxious. Some are never the same after a hospital trip."

Psychosocial Deficits Over Time

The physical deficits accompanying the aging process often predispose the nursing home resident to a greater degree of alienation and withdrawal from interaction with others. Progressive decreases in vision, hearing, and mobility begin to limit one in terms both of degree and type of activity. At Bethany Manor one could see the changes as a progressive decrease in interaction with other residents and staff to very little involvement or none at all. Often the first step was discontinuing taking meals in the large first-floor communal dining room and moving to a smaller dining room on one's assigned unit. This could mean that a resident would no longer have to leave his or her floor except for church services on Sunday if desired. The small unit dining rooms were much more easily accessed by wheelchair or walker than the main communal area. A second phase of withdrawal was the move in taking meals on a tray in one's room; this was sometimes necessitated by a physical condition requiring bed rest, and sometimes by the emotional state of the resident. Another sign of withdrawal at Bethany Manor was the move from socializing in the home's front lobby or porch, in clement weather, to visiting and sitting only in the hallways and recreation rooms of one's assigned unit.

One of the Manor's most active and involved residents did just that following her stroke. Miss Martha Butler had been a fixture in the home's front lobby during the early months of the study, greeting visitors and exchanging pleasantries or a bit of grapevine news with anyone who stopped by. Following her illness she was confined to a wheelchair and was left with some residual speech difficulties. Although Miss Butler still liked to sit out in the hall of her unit, where the action was, she reported that she didn't go to the lobby any more because "I don't want people to see me like this." Miss Butler added, "I used to go to more things. The thing I miss the most is walking. I do go to church on Sundays, but what bothers me most is that I can't concentrate. So, mostly now I just stay up here. I like to sit in the hall and see people."

Support of Significant Others Over Time

The current longevity, especially among female elderly, in our society is reflected in the large numbers of nursing home residents in their 80s and 90s, with a few cases surpassing 100 years. The result is that, frequently, the resident's spouse, siblings, and friends, if living themselves, are suffering from similar deficits related to the aging process. They are no longer physically or emotionally able to provide a supportive network for the very elderly resident. A similar case, although not so extreme, may be made for the very old resident's adult children. It is reported that presently, "with four generation families becoming more the rule than the exception, it is not uncommon for the adult offspring of the elderly to be elderly themselves with their own set of functional impairments limiting the amount of caretaking they can provide" (Evans 1985, 130). In a study of 51 elderly individuals who died at an East Coast Veterans Administration Medical Center, Kelly and Ruano (1983, 478) found that "the majority of patients in the study were notably lacking in family and friendship links through whom they could receive emotional support." Although such residents are "abandoned" simply as a result of their being survivors, there is also a more active and direct type of abandonment in which family and friends, after a long period of caring, are drained both emotionally and physically of the resources needed to provide support. Horner (1983, 31, 44), in her view from the inside, speaks very sensitively of this in discussing her housemate and friend, observing in her diary, "Am I going to be able to maintain myself here [in the nursing home] without killing Elizabeth?" She later adds, "I can't take all this from her, it's too hard on her body and mind...this matters to me more than anything."

A Bethany Manor social worker spoke about "abandoned" residents: "I think as the patient deteriorates more, that's when the family support may begin to slack off. There's a feeling of, 'Why is it worth it to come in, what can we talk about? We just sit and look.' Usually they'll come in and maybe bring new clothing. They'll stay five minutes because they find visiting is not productive."

Mrs. Burkholtz described her perception of her family's rationale for not visiting: "They feel I am well taken care of. In fact, they say that I am getting the best of care. I'm off their conscience, so they don't feel obliged to come visit. They've taken care of mother and they can carry on. When they see me, it's, 'How's everything going?' I don't go into details like this with them; it would just bore them."

Another resident who had been single all of her life explained why she had virtually no visitors at the home: "They are so rare I would have to look at them twice. They are gone with the wind. I hear from them once in a while. The landlady is kind enough; she writes occasionally and the girl across the street used to visit. She wrote me. That's all. The rest are dead." A third resident asserted that her lack of visitors was of her own choosing: "I thought it was time to come in here because my children are all grown up and they are all retiring themselves and they all had their lives to plan. They wanted to do some traveling and I thought it was better to let them do that traveling and just stay here."

Other resident comments reflect various types and degrees of abandonment: "I don't have any children, any close relations. Not even a cousin to visit. They have all died." "My brother is wonderful but his wife isn't so anxious to see me, so they don't visit." "Well, I thought I would see more of my children, but I can understand. They've got their own children now."

Whereas a few "abandoned" Bethany Manor residents expressed distress over their lack of visitors, most either accepted or made excuses to justify family members' inability to visit.

Relocation Within the Home

"Transfer trauma," or the traumatic effects of residents' intrainstitutional relocation in long-term care facilities, is a concept that has recently received notable attention in the literature and is being recognized by gerontological caregivers as a variable of concern in nursing home management. Nurses working in long-term care facilities report repeated observations of rapid decline in elderly residents "immediately after their relocation" within the facility (Rosswurm 1983, 632), and Moos et al. (1984, 495) in a study of resident and staff behavior changes following an intrainstitutional relocation, found that residents "restricted their involvement in the new setting. . .spend more time in their bedrooms and less in social spaces and a concomitant increase in passive behavior and a decrease in socializing occurred." Conditions found to mediate the stress of interinstitutional relocation include "degree of environmental change, the quality of the post-relocation environment, the preparation given to the relocation and whether the relocation was voluntary or involuntary" (Mirotznik and Rusking 1985, 127). Some suggestions to promote successful intrainstitutional relocation were identified by Amenta et al. (1984, 360) as provision of information through premove and follow-up discussions with residents, maintenance of communication during the move, and maximization of roommate choice.

Especially traumatic moves for Bethany Manor residents were those away from the first floor (the domiciliary care unit) or to the third floor (the cognitively impaired care area). Miss Loughney related her move to financial concerns: "I am not quite settled in this room because I have only been up here a while. I used to be on the first floor. I didn't like moving from one floor to another, but it's a money problem. It was more expensive." (It was not determined whether this financial concern was based on reality or simply created in the resident's imagination. Quality of care at the Manor does not depend upon the financial resources of the resident.)

Mrs. Eileen Cavanaugh complained about the inconvenience of being up on the fourth floor, where she had lived for five months: "You've got to tackle that darned elevator. That's my hardest thing, riding that elevator. I'm spoiled because I was on the first floor for five years. I haven't been up here very long. I'm still getting settled into my room. Right now, well, it takes time because I can't do things myself. And then the bed is in the way of everything. It's a different shaped room from downstairs, but they couldn't put it like I had it downstairs. I made a print for the man to follow, but the call bell wouldn't fit the way I wanted the bed. And those call bells, of course, are very important. Oh, I am getting along, but I can't entertain like I used to. These two chairs are hard and I used to have them side by side. Then I had the big old clumsy TV. Everybody says, 'Get rid of it,' but I'm not going to get rid of it. I don't watch that much but that belonged to my husband, and those things kind of mean a lot late in life. And I like the chest, being my mother's. All the other furniture I had to give to relatives and friends. You can't expect to have everything when you get over 80."

A Manor social worker reported that on occasion residents absolutely refused to move: "We made some arrangements for some moves last week for two ladies that were having difficult problems with one another. We went to move one last Friday and she absolutely, flatly refused, even after talking with social service, talking with the family, talking with nursing. She absolutely refused, so we couldn't move her." A patient care clinician described a temporary move to the third floor: "This resident from the first floor fell and broke her shoulder. This was a lucid lady, although right on the edge, she is in her 80s, and they put her on the third floor overnight. She was frantic, absolutely frantic. What she did is she broke out. She actually escaped and went back to her first-floor room. She stayed on the first floor."

A move to the third floor was also viewed by some families as traumatic. As one of the social workers observed, "It's like a death sentence to the family that their relative has to go to the third floor. It's such a stigma to have to go to the third floor."

Finally, one of the nurses commented that she had experienced or was aware of the situations in which a resident was so traumatized by a transfer within the home that the resident did not survive long after the move. She gave an example: "I have seen it happen, like we have lost a resident or two because of the move. I recall a couple of years ago they moved one lady. She was moved to another room on the same floor. She was on the blue wing and they moved her to the green wing, and within a week she was gone. Now it could have been coincidental, but we just wondered because she had been in the other room ten years. But they were trying to adjust the patients so that they would be on a more compatible wing."

Summary: A Typology of Long-Term Adaptation to Nursing Home Life

A primary purpose of the in-depth case study of Bethany Manor Nursing Home was to create a composite picture of the elder's long-term adaptation to institutional life. As data were being collected, analysis employing the Glaser and Strauss methodology (1967) for the discovery of grounded theory was initiated. Through this process, an attempt was made to group individual resident attitudes and behaviors into separate categories, which had theoretical meaning in terms of understanding long-term adaptation to nursing home life. Categorical refinement was carried out through comparing properties of individual clusters of resident attitudes and behaviors. Finally a construct or bit of theory grounded in the data emerged and has been labeled "a typology of long-term adaptation to nursing home life." This construct, broadly defined as "the individual's way of experiencing and coping with meaningful life in long-term care," consists of four individual resident types: the "socialite," the "guardian," the "single-room occupant," and the "free-lancer" (See Table 8-1).

Type I: The "Socialite"

Bethany Manor residents identified as "socialites" were those individuals whose attitudes and behaviors were related to positive involvement in almost all aspects of nursing home life. They tended to be concerned about their appearance, to have a number of friendships both within and outside the home, to participate in the majority of home activities, to be other-oriented, and to be in control of their lives (to the degree allowed by the nursing home structure). One such individual was a first-floor resident, Mrs. Armstrong. A 75-year-old who had been at the home for close to five years, Mrs. Armstrong assisted with nursing home committee work, participated in social activities with her group of friends, enjoyed dressing well, and was satisfied with life at the Manor. Mrs. Armstrong had a good handle on the home's grapevine and knew just about everyone at Bethany Manor. She enjoyed meeting and greeting visitors and had her own routine and schedule of daily activities. Mrs. Armstrong was very helpful to the research team in initiating the nursing home study. On one visit she commented, "I enjoy doing this. You can call on me whenever you need help." A Manor social worker, indeed, described Mrs. Armstrong as a "socializer," commenting, "Mrs. A. really gets around this house. She knows everything and

Table 8-1 A Typology of Long-Term Adaptation to Nursing Home Care.

Type I: The "Socialite"	Type II: The "Guardian"	Type III: The "Single-Room Occupant"	Type IV: The "Free-Lancer"
Actively involved in all aspects of nursing home life	Actively directed toward the support of other residents	Activities carried out in the personal space of the nursing home room	Vacillates between active participation in nursing home life and passivity
Attends organized social activities, interacts with other residents, and participates in committee work or small tasks to assist in the running of the home	Assists other residents by pushing wheel-chairs, helping residents get on and off the elevators, and taking residents to meals, church, or social activities	Spends much time in such activities as reading, writing letters, praying, and watching TV	Divides time between involve-ment in social or interactional situations and private activities
Derives pleasure and satisfaction from social and "work" activities	Derives pleasure and satisfaction from helping other residents	Derives comfort from carrying out activities in private	Derives pleasure from the freedom to choose privacy or social interaction as desired
Desires community or "family" involvement in the home	Desires community or "family" responsi-bility in the home	Desires to withdraw from community or "family" involvement in the home	Desires a modified involvement in the home's community
Other-oriented and autonomous	Other-oriented and autonomous	Self-oriented, limited autonomy	Self-oriented autonomous

everybody and she's usually involved in what's happening. Just talk to her if you want to know Bethany Manor's social life."

Type II: The "Guardian"

A number of Bethany Manor residents can be categorized as "guardi-ans." Their observed attitudes and behaviors were directed importantly toward caring for and supporting other residents. Resident guardians took the responsibility for seeing to it that other less able (either physically impaired or cognitively impaired) residents got to such activities as meals, church, or social groups. Mrs. Armstrong, herself a socialite, described a guardian, Miss Angelino, who was observed pushing a fragile-looking woman in a wheelchair: "She always brings her down to meals from the second floor. She calls her 'her baby.' They're roommates and she does everything for her. That's her [Miss Angelino's] job here at the home." A staff nurse commented, "There are some definite buddy systems; they look out for each other. There's some who always push the other person's wheelchair, always go down to programs with the other person. Sometimes we foster that, too. There's a fair number of those, like an informal buddy system."

One of the residents, Mrs. O'Connell, described her "guardianship" of a group of three Manor residents: "I push them to the dining room and settle them at the table. I don't have to. They have a girl that does all that, but she gets busy and I just push them in. I have a lovely group of people eat with me." Another resident commented, "I have a friend who takes care of me. She pushes my wheelchair whenever I want to go somewhere." Some residents, such as Mrs. Julia Crowley, assumed guardian-type activities part-time at the home. Mrs. Crowley confessed, "I don't think I am making too much of a contribution to the patients because I only know a couple of them on this floor. Mrs. Jones—I do errands for her, maybe get a telephone number for her, and then Mrs. Hill down at the end. She is a character. I take her down to Mass." She added, "I would like to read for the blind. There's a lady, maybe you've seen her, Mrs. Paulsen, a delightful old lady and she is very hard of hearing and seeing. She has asked me to read the bulletin for her. I love to do that."

Type III: The "Single-Room Occupant"

Manor residents characterized as "single-room occupants" spent the greater part of the day in their rooms by choice, not out of necessity. That is, they tended to be the more reserved individuals who cherished their privacy and their own very specific schedule and rituals. They reported not being interested in formal social activities, preferring singular pastimes such as reading or watching television. A Recreation Department staff member commented on one such single-room occupant: "I've gone to her room to try and stimulate her to get involved in some recreational activities, but I just got nowhere. I think she's just content to be in that room and nobody's going to get her out. We can't force them."

Miss Ather, a single-room occupant, described her attitude: "I always stay in my room even though they have a lot of entertainment going on. I don't go. They have bingo maybe three times a week, but I don't want to go. The doctor said, 'Why don't you go to whatever they have?' I said, 'I am not interested in ceramics or stuffing rag dolls or things like that, and I don't care to go to any parties.'"

Seventy-eight-year-old Miss Blanchard explained that she would rather be alone in her room: "This is my home now; this room is a part of me. That's all I have." A research data collector described her meeting with a 98-year-old single-room occupant: "Mrs. Hubbard was seated in her own soft armchair in her private room. She had books, religious items set up around her at arm's length. She was reluctant to talk to me at first, but then appeared to enjoy the discussion and talking to me. She asked me to return when I was around. The patient spends time in her room by herself; she only is out of the room for meals. Otherwise she likes to keep to herself. She enjoys her private room and does not initiate contact with other residents at Bethany Manor. She reads in her room and listens to the radio."

Finally, a Manor head nurse described why one of her residents, who had formerly been quite active, became a single-room occupant: "It just recently came up with a resident on this floor. The resident is really alert and rational, so the nurse was trying to make him go to the main dining room and he said, 'I don't want to go. I lived on the first floor and I don't want them to see me in a wheelchair.'"

Type IV: The "Free-Lancer"

Bethany Manor residents identified as "free-lancers" did not fit neatly into any of the preceding three categories, yet they did have an established type of behavior, that being one of alteration between the more social-interactional and the more private types of activity. Free-lancers desired some involvement in the life of the home but retained the right to pull back whenever they wished. Miss Claire O'Rourke and Miss Meg Delaney, both single ladies who had always assumed responsibility for their own lives before admission to Bethany Manor, could be described as free-lancers. Miss O'Rourke had a small circle of friends at the home with whom she periodically interacted, but she also carefully preserved her private time for reading and letter writing. Miss Delaney was basically a "loner," but she attended selected social activities and occasionally visited with staff and other residents. Both Miss O'Rourke and Miss Delaney were strong, independent women to whom control in the scheduling of their activities seemed imperative.

It should be noted that although the typology described here may be used to broadly categorize some adaptive attitudes and behaviors shown by cognitively alert nursing home residents, not all residents fit neatly into any of these categories. For example, whereas a number of residents seemed to make guardianship a primary role, others exhibited this behavior as only one dimension of their overall life-style. It is also assumed that residents may move back and forth among categories depending on their physical or cognitive deficits or the alleviation thereof.

In summary, the constructed typology of long-term adaptation to nursing home life, as well as the descriptive material introduced earlier regarding behavior patterns in the adaptation and care of the institutionalized elderly, is not meant to rigidly categorize or stereotype either the residents, their family members, or the nursing home staff. The study's purpose, as reflected in its title *Anatomy of a Nursing Home*, was to dissect or take apart the home and to examine the structure and function of its individual parts. That was done. This book represents the investigator's attempt to reassemble the dissected structure, interweaving throughout descriptive analyses of its functions and its processes. Through this effort, it is hoped that some new or previously untapped knowledge has emerged that will ultimately contribute to improving the quality of life for elders experiencing long-term care.

References

Amenta, M., A. Weiner, and D. Amenta. 1984. Successful relocation. *Geriatric Nursing* 5(8):356-360.

Barbieri, E.B. 1983. Patient falls are not patient accidents. *Journal of Gerontological Nursing* 9(3):165-173.

Bossenmaier, M. 1982. The hospitalized elderly—a first look. *Geriatric Nursing* 3(4):253-256.

Chung, S. 1983. Foot care. A health care maintenance program. *Journal of Gerontological Nursing* 9(4):213-227.

Clark, H.M. 1985. Sleep and aging. *Occupational Health Nursing* 33(3):140-145.

Department of Health and Human Services. 1980. *Alzheimer's disease. A scientific guide for health practitioners.* Bethesda, MD: National Institutes of Health (NIH Publication No. 81-2251).

Department of Health and Human Services. 1984. *Alzheimer's disease. Report of the Secretary's Task Force on Alzheimer's Disease.* Washington, DC: Government Printing Office.

Evans, L.K. 1985. Over the back fence. *Occupational Health Nursing* 33(3):127-153.

Feldman, A. 1982. Transfer: Nursing home to hospital. *Geriatric Nursing* 3(5):307-310.

Floyd, J. 1984. Collecting data on abuse of the elderly. *Journal of Gerontological Nursing* 10(12):11-15.

Fowler, E. 1982. Pressure sores: A deadly nuisance. *Journal of Gerontological Nursing* 8(12):680-685.

Fulmer, T.T., and V. M. Cahill. 1984. Assessing elder abuse: A study. *Journal and Gerontological Nursing* 10(12):16-20.

Glaser, B., and A. Strauss. *The discovery of grounded theory*. Chicago: Aldine.

Gordon, M. 1982. Falls in the elderly: More common, more dangerous. *Geriatrics* 37(4):117-120.

Gray-Vickrey, M. 1984. Education to prevent falls. *Geriatric Nursing* 5(3):179-183.

Gwyther, L.P., and M.A. Matteson. 1982. Care for the caregivers. *Journal of Gerontological Nursing* 9(2):92-95, 110.

Helfand, A.E. 1982. Avoiding disability: Care of foot problems in the elderly. *Geriatrics* 37(11):49-59.

Hernandez, M., and J. Miller. 1986. How to reduce falls. *Geriatric Nursing* (March/April):97-102.

Hill, D.C., and W.E. Stamm. 1982. Pneumonia in the elderly: The fatal complication. *Geriatrics* 37(1):40-50.

Horner, J.M. 1982. *That time of year*. Amherst, MA: University of Massachusetts Press.

Johnson, J. 1985. Exercise, aging and health. *Occupational Health Nursing* 33(3):137-140.

Kelly, G., and B. Ruano. 1983. Helping the resource poor. *Journal of Gerontological Nursing* 9(9):477-483.

Lonnerblad, L. 1984. Exercise to promote independent living in older patients. *Geriatrics* 39(2):93-101.

Louis, M. 1983. Falls and their causes. *Journal of Gerontological Nursing* 9(3):142-156.

Lund, C., and M.L. Sheafor. 1985. Is your patient about to fall? *Journal of Gerontological Nursing* 11(4):37-41.

McConnell, J. 1984. Preventing urinary tract infections. *Geriatric Nursing* 5(8):361-362.

Mendelson, M.A. 1974. *Tender loving greed*. New York: Alfred A. Knopf.

Mirotznik, J., and A.P. Ruskin. 1985. Interinstitutional relocation and the elderly. *The Journal of Long-Term Care Administration* 13(4):127-131.

Mitchell, C.A. 1986. Generalized chronic fatigue in the elderly: Assessment and intervention. *Journal of Gerontological Nursing* 12(4):19-23.

Moos, R.H., et al. 1984. Coping with an intra-institutional relocation: Changes in resident and staff patterns. *The Gerontologist* 24(5):495-502.

Moss, F.E., and V.J. Halamandaris. 1977. *Too old, too sick, too bad. Nursing homes in America*. Germantown, MD: Aspen Systems.

Palmer, M.H. 1983. Alzheimer's disease and critical care: Interactions, implications, interventions. *Journal of Gerontological Nursing* 9(2):86-91.

Porth, C., and K. Kapke. 1983. Aging and the skin. *Geriatric Nursing* 4(3):158-162.

Quan, S.F., C.R. Bamford, and L.E. Beutler. 1984. Sleep disturbances in the elderly. *Geriatrics* 39(9):42-47.

Riffle, K.L. 1982. Falls: Kinds, causes, and prevention. *Geriatric Nursing* 3(3):165-169.

Roach, M. 1985. Reflection in a fatal mirror. *Discover* (August):76-85.

Rosaniec, A., and J.J. Fitzpatrick. 1979. Changes in mental status in older adults with four days of hospitalization. *Research in Nursing and Health* 2:177-187.

Rosswurm, M.A. 1983. Relocation and the elderly. *Journal of Gerontological Nursing* 9(12):632-637.

Rousey, C.G. 1984. Breaking down the barriers of Alzheimer's disease. *Contemporary Administrator* 7(8):49-50.

Rubenstein, L.A., and A.S. Robbins. 1984. Falls in the elderly: A clinical perspective. *Geriatrics* 39(4):67-77.

Schirmer, M.S. 1983. When sleep won't come. *Journal of Gerontological Nursing* 9(1):16-21.

Spicer, W.A. 1982. Controller infections. *Contemporary Administrator* 5(1):7-10.

Stompor, J.C. 1984. A myth-shattering study: The hatching of decubiti. *Contemporary Administrator* 7(8):28-29.

Tooman, T., and J. Patterson. 1984. Decubitus ulcer warfare: Product vs. process. *Geriatric Nursing* 5(3):166-167.

Vladeck, B.C. 1980. *Unloving care, the nursing home tragedy.* New York: Basic Books.

Warner, S.J. 1982. Preventing patient abuse. *Contemporary Administrator* 5(1):28-30.

Williams, L. 1986. Alzheimer's: The need for caring. *Journal of Gerontological Nursing* 12(2):21-28.

Yarmesch, M., and M. Sheafor. 1984. The decision to restrain. *Geriatric Nursing* 5(6):242-244.

APPENDIX A

The Research Protocol:
Anatomy of a Nursing Home

An overview of the study's aims and basic design is presented in Chapter 1. This appendix details how data were collected and analyzed over the two-year study period.

Method: Gaining Access to the Nursing Home

The Administrator

The first step in undertaking any exploratory effort of an entire institution, such as a nursing home, is to make contact with the significant person in charge, or "gatekeeper," in order to request permission and seek support. Braden et al. (1988, 39) report that in order to initiate research in a nursing home, trust must be established. They assert, "The administrator must feel confident that the disruption in resident care will be minimal and that the approach to residents and staff will be tactful, non-threatening, and non-coercive." After the study protocol had been developed, and following several cursory explorations of the home, the principal investigator requested a meeting with Bethany Manor's sister Administrator, Mother Ann Teresa, to explain the purpose and design of the research. As noted in Chapter 1, relationships had already been established between administrators and researchers through the Teaching Nursing Home Project; however, the request to carry out a case study of the home for publication had certainly not been part of the original Teaching Nursing Home Project protocol. At the meeting, Mother Ann Teresa listened intently to the description of the study, asked a number of questions, shared her opinions about how and where to obtain needed data, and in the end readily agreed to the conduct of the research, pending approval of the Manor's Research and Education Committee. She also offered her support and assistance with any problems that might arise. This administrative stamp of approval proved to be of key importance, as one of the first comments made when the researcher presented the protocol before the Research and Education Committee was, "Of course, Mother Ann Teresa will have to approve the study."

The Research and Education Committee

The Bethany Manor Research and Education Committee was made up of the Director of Nursing, a member of the Department of Social Service, a staff nurse, two university faculty members, and two Manor residents. The committee members provided important input regarding whether other residents would consider a given topic as too intrusive. At the time of the formal protocol presentation, both resident committee members asked numerous questions of the principal investigator and made helpful suggestions for setting up meetings with persons living in the home. The researcher was advised that "most people would probably agree to talk" to her but that appointments must be carefully scheduled. The committee unanimously approved the research.

The Director of Nursing

Although Bethany Manor's Director of Nursing sat on the Research and Education Committee, a separate meeting was scheduled with her to explain specific study details, especially those involving observation of and discussion with the other nursing supervisors, head nurses, staff nurses, and aides. The Director of Nursing, like the Administrator, gave the project her wholehearted support and did not seem at all uncomfortable with the advent of a researcher into the home. She did comment, however, that the staff, especially the nurses' aides, might feel threatened by the presence of an observer while they were carrying out their duties and by researchers' questioning, and added, "They may feel that their jobs are on the line." A suggestion was made that, before the study's initiation, the researcher meet with head nurses, staff nurses, and as many groups of aides as possible to explain the project and answer questions.

The Head Nurses

It was decided that at an immediately upcoming head nurses' meeting the Director of Nursing would play "John the Baptist" and prepare the way by introducing the project to the group and informing them that the principal investigator would come to the next meeting to explain the study and answer questions. At the second meeting very few questions were asked after the researcher's presentation. Several members of the group, however, spoke in support of the study. One head nurse commented, "It will be good to have an outsider look at things that we sometimes get too close to; we cannot see the forest." The session ended on a very positive note, with a plan for the researcher to meet individually with each head nurse in order to identify the residents who might be approached for study participation, and to plan strategies for observation of and discussion with staff working on the care areas.

The Staff Nurses

Although a large staff nurse meeting to discuss administrative issues had been planned at the home, this meeting did not materialize. As a result, most staff nurses (RNs and LPNs) were contacted individually as the researcher began spending time on the nursing care areas. Many staff were inquisitive about the purpose of the research and the background of the investigator, but all were basically supportive of the study. Only one of the nurses approached declined to discuss her observations and attitudes about the home. When informed of the confidential nature of the data they were providing, several respondents gave permission to use their names; however, this was not considered.

The Aides

The home's head nurses offered to set up several scheduled times on the day and evening shifts for the researcher to have brief meetings with small groups of four to five nurses' aides to explain the study. These meetings were organized by individual unit and planned to work around the heavy caregiving activity times. Although the response from some aides was passive or noncommittal, others took an active interest in the project and said that they would like to be part of the study. One of the more verbal members in a second-floor group suggested some possible times when "probably the head nurse could let us talk to you."

In summary, a fair amount of ground work was done with the Bethany Manor staff in order to diminish the impact of an added stressor—that of ongoing research—in the care setting. This preliminary activity proved useful not only for obtaining staff data but also for eliciting the staff members' assistance in locating and scheduling meeting times with residents.

The Sample

Cognitively Aware Residents

After discussion with Bethany Manor staff members and Teaching Nursing Home Project faculty, it was estimated that probably fewer than 70 to 80 residents, or about one-third of the resident population, would have the cognitive, hearing, and speech capabilities to carry on a discussion about life in the home lasting 45 minutes to an hour. Given this estimate, a gerontologist study consultant advised that an attempt be made to meet with every one of the cognitively alert, hearing, speaking residents. The head nurse of each unit was requested to identify those residents who met these criteria; those residents would then be approached for participation in the study. As these meetings were time consuming both to schedule and to carry out, they progressed over approximately an 18-month period. A few of the identified residents became confused or ill during that time, and several died. Ultimately 71 residents were involved in the data collection, some more extensively than others. Discussions ranged from brief sessions of 15 minutes' duration to conversations lasting up to one-and-a-half hours. Only three residents approached declined to participate. No specific reasons for their refusal were documented.

Cognitively Impaired Residents

Initially, it was decided to schedule formal discussions only with cognitively aware residents of the Manor; data about cognitively impaired individuals were to consist of observation only. About halfway through the study, however, a Teaching Nursing Home Project colleague challenged the principal investigator to include formal visits and discussions with cognitively impaired residents as part of the study. Because it was antici-pated that these sessions would be difficult to carry out and require special consent procedures, the decision was made to choose a subsample of 30 residents. One of the home's social workers, familiar with the third floor's cognitively impaired population, was asked to randomly select approxi-mately 30 moderately cognitively impaired residents, whose families would then be approached for permission to visit their relatives. Ultimately 24 cognitively impaired residents participated in the study.

The Families

To identify a subsample of Bethany Manor residents' families for discussions, the assistance of the Social Service Department was again sought. A social worker was asked to randomly select approximately 30 local families who could be contacted about participation in the study. To supplement this group, the study's principal investigator also gave a presentation of the project at several of the home's "Family Circle" gatherings and solicited family members for study participation. To avoid intruding on a family members' visits with their relatives or requesting a second trip to the Manor, most family interactions were conducted by telephone, with handwritten notes taken of the conversation. A successful attempt was made (see Chapter 3) to enlist persons representing a broad range of familial and nonfamilial relationships including spouses, siblings, children, other kin (nieces, nephews, cousins), and friends.

The Staff

As the study design expanded and time went on, it was determined that a specific plan for staff interactions needed to be put in place. Since the Bethany Manor administrative and management staff were relatively small, meetings with all administrative and supervisory staff were planned, with smaller subsamples of direct caregivers involved. The administrative and supervisory group included the Administrator, the Director of Nursing, the Director of Medical Services, the chaplain, the Director of Social Services, the admissions clerk, the Director of the Recreation Department, the Director of Volunteers, the dietitian, and the four head nurses from the resident care areas. Individuals were selected to represent the subgroups: a patient care nurse clinican, a nursing supervisor, several physicians, staff nurses and aides, faculty from the Teaching Nursing Home Project, and a housekeeper. Data were also collected through discussion and interaction with other staff accessible to the investigator, such as Social Service and Recreation Department staff and security personnel. In summary, an attempt was made to speak either formally or informally with all key actors or their representatives involved in the social life of Bethany Manor.

Protection of Human Subjects

All conversations and focused discussions with cognitively aware residents, caregivers, ancillary personnel, volunteers, and family members or significant others were explained to the subject, and the potential respondent's agreement to participate was requested verbally. Anyone not wishing to be involved in the study was free either to decline discussion or to withdraw from participation at any time. All data were coded for anonymity, and neither the facility nor any individual study subject is named in written reports.

The home is labeled with a pseudonym, as are all individuals where naming is warranted. Data for both descriptive and analytic presentations have been carefully treated so that neither the nursing home, nor its residents or staff, nor those tangentially involved in the study (e.g., families and volunteers) can be identified. During the course of the study, Bethany Manor had several changes in personnel in the roles of Administrator, Director of Nursing, admissions clerk, and chaplain. Thus, individual comments by persons holding those titles can be presented with no breach of anonymity. However, for three other positions, namely, the Medical Director, the Director of Volunteers, and the Teaching Nursing Home Project Director, the incumbent did not change. Thus, data provided by those respondents are presented under the anonymous labels (which could refer to other staff members) of physician, recreational therapist, and Teaching Nursing Home Project faculty member. In the few situations where more detailed accounts of a residents' behavior or life in the home are presented, some descriptive details such as age, sex, ethnicity, or length of time in the home have been changed to guarantee the subject's anonymity and confidentiality.

As focused discussions were of a conversational nature and no intrusive procedures were utilized, the study was considered as fitting the criteria for documentation of informed consent, section 46,117 of the Code of Federal Regulations [45 CFR 46], Protection of Human Subjects which reads as follows: "That the research presents no more than minimal risk of harm to subjects and involves no procedures for which written consent is normally required outside of the research context" (National Institutes of Health 1983, 10). General ethical guidelines for the protection of elderly subjects were employed in the conduct of the research (National Institutes of Health 1977).

In order to visit and hold discussions with a subpopulation of cognitively impaired residents, formal third-party written permission was obtained from the identified significant other or guardian. (The cover letter and consent form are found among the study instruments reproduced in Appendix B.) This process is discussed in more detail in Chapter 2. Each cognitively impaired resident was also asked if he or she would be willing to participate in the project, and a brief explanation of the research was given. Tape recorders were not used with this group. Data were preserved through the method of handwritten "process recordings."

Data Collection Procedures

The Key Informant

To assist with initiation of data collection activities with cognitively alert residents, one Bethany Manor resident was identified as a "key informant" (Whyte 1943). The study's key informant was a person who had lived at the Manor for over five years, was actively involved in the life of the home, and provided advice on such topics as appropriate days and times to schedule meetings with residents, where to meet with residents, and how best to explain the research so as to make it understandable to the subjects. The key informant also met with several study data collectors and took them on informal tours of the home, introducing them to staff and residents.

Discussions With Cognitively Aware Residents

In a discussion on "Interviewing Older Adults," Harbert and Ginsberg (1979, 100) assert that "perhaps the most important principle in interviewing is knowing why the interview is being held." Because of concern for the possibility of short-term memory loss among some of the Bethany Manor residents, data collectors were instructed to explain the purpose of the study, and how the data would be used, at the beginning of a visit, at an estimated midpoint in the discussion, and again following conclusion of the interaction. The discussions were focused by the data collectors, who carried a set of cards containing broad foci directed to such topics as demographic data, reason for admission to the home, personal interests, relationships within and outside the home, visitors, activities, sleep and rest, power, religion, interaction with caregivers, and death (see Cognitively Aware Resident Discussion Guide in Appendix B).

After the initial consent procedure was carried out, the resident was asked if the discussion could be tape recorded. Most residents agreed, although a few preferred that their comments not be tape recorded; in such cases handwritten notes were taken. Residents who agreed to tape recording their remarks were informed that should they wish the recorder turned off or anything erased at any time, it would be done immediately. On the suggestion of a gerontologist consultant, the tape recorder was placed near the resident, who was instructed how to stop the machine if he or she desired.

Of course, residents were told that they were free to decline to discuss any topic raised. Although data collectors did make an effort to focus or redirect certain topics according to the Glaser and Strauss methodology (Glaser and Strauss 1967), the discussions generally flowed conversationally, with a number of residents leading the way on certain issues. As noted in Chapter 7, the topic of death, an area recognized as needing great sensitivity in discussions, was more often than not raised by the resident. A final point of satisfaction to the researchers was the fact that many residents invited their data collectors to come back so they could "talk some more." Because, as noted earlier, the study's principal investigator needed help to carry out the expanded methodology, a cadre of student nurses, primarily master's students, was enlisted to visit residents. This proved fortunate for the research. The students enjoyed the residents and the residents enjoyed the students. The age gap was a positive rather than a negative force in the interactions.

Discussions With Cognitively Impaired Residents

Schmidt (1975, 546) suggests that two common misconceptions exist in regard to interviewing the "old old": first, that "a person who is out of touch with some things is necessarily confused about everything," and second, that "all instruments require a perfectly oriented respondent." She adds, "Often persons who do not know where they are are perfectly clear about how they feel. How they feel may be what the researcher wants to know." How the cogntively impaired residents at Bethany Manor felt was indeed what the researchers wanted to know! The researcher's interest was in whether they existed in a world of fantasy, whether fantasy and reality appeared to overlap, and, more importantly, whether the confusion caused pain or suffering to the cognitively impaired resident.

Following the advice of two gerontological consultants, a very brief (five-item) focused discussion guide was developed to direct conversations (see Cognitively Impaired Resident Discussion Guide in Appendix B). It was suggested that the items be short and direct so that a moderately impaired respondent might be able to focus on a few words rather than have to integrate a lengthy sentence into higher consciousness and formulate a response. One consultant, who had much experience interviewing the confused elderly, suggested that if a resident did not respond to the first or even the second topic on the list, the data collector should continue through all the items, and attempt to stimulate cognition on the part of the respondent, a practice that had worked well for the consultant.

Because of the difficulty of communicating with the older cognitively impaired person, a master's-prepared psychiatric-mental health nurse who had considerable experience in the area was hired to carry out the meetings. One of her first strategies was to make preliminary visits, before the formal discussion session, to members of the sample group to assess the degree of the resident's impairment and also to introduce herself, in hopes of being recognized at the next meeting.

Streib (1983, 41) observes that new ways of obtaining data must be considered in working with the frail elderly. Discussions with the Bethany Manor cognitively impaired group were carried out in a variety of ways: while visiting in the resident's room, while going outside for a walk, and while sitting in the front lobby. Regarding one 87-year-old resident who tended to drift in and out of sleep most of the day, the nurse researcher wrote, "Before talking with Miss Clark, I took her down to the lobby for a change of scenery." Some residents wandered about during the discussion; the researcher wandered with them. One resident said she was flattered to be asked to participate in the study but was "wondering if [she] would be able to help." After the questions were read to her, she responded that she "felt better."

Discussions With the Families

Family discussions, as noted earlier, were conducted primarily by telephone. These interactions were directed toward an understanding of family perceptions and needs related to having a loved one residing at Bethany Manor. The discussions were directed toward such areas as the difficulty of the resident's being admitted to the home (for both the resident and the family member); the reasons for nursing home placement; interference with family life or plans; physical and cognitive expectations for the resident; ways of supporting residents; and interaction with nursing home staff. The Family Discussion Guide used is reproduced in Appendix B.)

Discussions With the Staff

Staff discussions had to be scheduled carefully to prevent the study from intruding upon the business of the nursing home, that of providing care for its residents. For more senior or supervisory staff specific appointments were made; for some of the other staff, data collectors "hung around," observing or collecting resident data, until the individual could manage a break. Staff conversations ranged in length from approximately 15 minutes to an hour, depending often on the time constraints of the respondent. Topics of discussion included duties as a geriatric caregiver, interaction with residents, morale, rewards and frustrations of work, coping with chronicity, and coping with death. (See Caregiver Discussion Guide in Appendix B.)

Observations

To inform the initial observational phases of data collection with some degree of direction and structure, observation guides were developed to focus data collectors' activities on topics of interest. These tools included a Family Observation Guide, a Caregiver Observation Guide, a Nursing Home Environment Observation Guide, and a Nursing Home Social Life Observation Guide. These observation guides are reproduced in Appendix B.

The foci of these instrument were as follows: The Family Observation Guide addressed the composition of Bethany Manor families (children, siblings); the age ranges of family members; the type and degree of support provided to residents (e.g., frequency of visits, calls, letters); relationships with residents; and relationships with staff and volunteers. The Caregiver Observation Guide focused on demographic data; appearance; activities and responsibilities; morale; staff education; staff rotation; turnover; attitudes toward the elderly; communication among staff; interaction with residents; interaction with family members; coping with confused patients; and coping with death. Foci of the Nursing Home Environment Observation Guide included population description; administration; admission routine; medical staff; external quality control; internal quality control; staff education and development; atmosphere of the home; philosophy of care; and quality of care. Finally, the Nursing Home Social Life Observation Guide focused on the physical environment of the facility; the social environment; formal activities; informal interactions; language; and nonverbal communication. Categories in the Nursing Home Social Life Observation Guide were derived partly from suggestions for observational data collection presented by Patton (1980).

One of the final qualitative tools, the Management of Nursing Home Patient Care Observation Guide (reproduced in Appendix B) was developed to evaluate specifically the interactional power and authority relationships among and between different levels of staff (head nurses, charge nurses, staff nurses, aides); the planning and carrying out of patient care assignments; and nursing shift transitions at 3 p.m., 11 p.m., and 7 a.m.

Quantitative Data

Data from assessment of Patient Progress forms were coded directly from patient charts onto coding sheets constructed to conform to the instrument's format; social history coding cards were also created to organize social history data of interest from patient records.

Data Processing

All tape-recorded data and handwritten observational data were transcribed onto 4 x 6 cards for analysis. In addition to descriptive data derived from formal meetings with residents, staff, and family members, theoretical, methodological, and observational notes were recorded according to the process described by Schatzman and Strauss (1973, 99-101).

Theoretical Notes

Theoretical notes record concepts that represent the investigator's interpretation of a meaningful observation or experience. For example:

1. *Paradox of insecurity versus security.* Many residents commented that they came to the home for reasons of security and physical safety, the fact that someone is there to care for them if they need it, and so on, yet they are now faced with a different type of insecurity, as they must become dependent on strangers rather than on themselves, their family, and their friends.

2. *Aloneness in groups.* Although the home often organizes group interactions through social service, recreation, and volunteer organizations, these group interactions may be superficial. Some residents, because of fatigue, apathy, depression, or cognitive impairment, attend activities in a group but appear to remain alone in the group.

Methodological Notes

Methodological notes record significant or serendipitous procedural variables to be considered as the study is going on. For example:

1. *Respect the residents' time.* Although a resident may appear to be only "sitting," it is important to ask if they have time for a discussion. Many residents report having busy schedules in the nursing home. It is necessary to have respect for their personal time.

2. *Researcher presence.* In a study such as this one, there is no substitute for the researchers' presence in the home for a considerable period of time, as this is the only way of meeting many people and really getting a feel for the world of the nursing home.

Observational Notes

Observational notes are data obtained through direct or participant observation in the study setting. For example:

1. *Reluctance to express criticisms.* Patients seem to have reticence or anxiety with regard to making any negative comments about the nursing home care, often prefacing remarks with: "I probably shouldn't be saying this, but..." or "I don't really want to get anybody in trouble, but..." or "You'd better not say I told you this, but...."

2. *Touch.* Patients respond to and initiate touch. They will often reach out and touch or grasp a researcher's hand, or even kiss it when the researcher is leaving.

Data Analysis

Data were analyzed on both a descriptive and a theoretical level. A descriptive categorical schema to impose upon the data was constructed, undergirded theoretically by the Loomis social system model. Data were broadly organized and cross-related according to classificatory labels for data sources and topics. Data sources included residents, family members, medical and nursing caregivers, and ancillary caregivers. Data topics included beliefs, sentiments, goals, norms, status roles, rank, power, sanctions, and the facility. On the theoretical level, qualitative study data were also analyzed according to a modification of the methodology articulated by Glaser and Strauss (1967) for the discovery of grounded theory. Through this method, individual resident and staff attitudes and behaviors were clustered into meaningful categories that might have theoretical input in evaluating nursing home life.

Categories emerging from resident data were related to such topics as social activities, interaction with other residents, interactions with caregivers, life goals, and personal autonomy. As the initial categories became more clearly defined through comparing the properties attributed to a group, the analysis progressed to the stage of integrating the categories and delineating a construct or bit of theory. For example, this analytic process was used to construct the resident typology of long-term adaption to nursing home life (Chapter 8), which typologized residents into the categories of the socialite, the guardian, the free-lancer, and the single-room occupant.

References

Braden, B.,C. Smith, and N. Bergstrom. 1988. Paving the way to research in nursing homes. *Geriatric Nursing* 9(1):38-41.

Glaser, B., and A. Strauss. 1967. *The discovery of grounded theory*. Chicago: Aldine.

Harbert, A.S., and L.H. Ginsberg. 1979. Interviewing older adults. In *Human services for older adults: Concepts and skills*. Belmont, CA: Wadsworth.

National Institutes of Health. 1977. *Protection of Elderly Research Subjects, Summary of the National Institute on Aging Conference*, July 17-19, 1977. Washington: Government Printing Office.

National Institutes of Health. 1983. *OPRR Report*. Washington: Government Printing Office.

Patton, M.Q. 1980. *Qualitative evaluation methods*. Beverly Hills, CA: Sage.

Schatzman, L., and A. Strauss. 1973. *Field research*. Englewood Cliffs, NJ: Prentice Hall.

Schmidt, M.G. 1975. Interviewing the "old old." The *Gerontologist* (December):544-547.

Streib, G.F. 1983. The frail elderly: Research dilemmas and research opportunities. *The Gerontologist* 23(1):40-4

Whyte, W.F. 1943. *Street corner society. The social structure of an Italian slum.* Chicago: University of Chicago Press.

Study Instruments

Cognitively Aware Resident Discussion Guide

Demographic Data

1. Name:

2. Age:

3. Sex:

4. Religion:

5. Marital status:

6. Length of time in the home:

    First admission to a long-term care facility?

7. Ward:

8. Physical disability (problem):

9. Former profession/occupation:

Discussion Foci

10. A. Reason for coming to the home.

    What happened to previous home? (what about furniture, personal possessions?)

    B. Ability to maintain previous relationships (friendships) with persons outside the home. How?

C. Ease/difficulty of developing new friendships in the nursing home.

11. Desire to get news of the outside world. Former profession. Home. Former colleagues.

12. Ability to maintain former (lifelong) interests in: politics; world affairs; professional interests; hobbies; recreational activities.

Territoriality

13. Presence of "personal space" or privacy: Is room a single? double? on a ward? Personal things in room? What?

   Choice (decision-making) regarding what personal items kept in room.

14. Ease/difficulty of sharing a room. (New or different experience for resident?)

15. Ability to keep up appearances. Hair; clothes; weight; grooming (cleanliness). (For women): Makeup.

   Ability to choose what clothes to wear.

16. Ability to make/receive telephone calls. To/from whom? When? How frequently? Who calls whom? Are telephone calls an important part of resident's life in the home?

Resident's Visitors

17. Who are resident's visitors? When do they come? How often? How important are visitors in resident's life at the home?

Resident's General Activities

18. How does resident usually spend his/her day at the home? Do the days pass quickly or slowly? Why?

19. With whom does resident interact most at the home? Where? At what times of the day?

Resident's Relationships in the Home

20. Importance of having friends at the home. Kinds of things friends do together. How many friends does resident have?

Resident's Activities in the Home

21. Does resident take walks around the home? Where? With whom?

    Does resident go "visiting" in the home? When? Whom does resident visit?

    Does resident read? watch television?

    What does resident do for recreational therapy? occupational therapy?

22. Does resident have any special "jobs" here? Are they personal or related to the home? For example: taking care of room; keeping clothes clean; serving on nursing home committees; helping other residents.

23. Where does resident spend most of day? Room? Hall? Front lobby? Variety of places?

Trips Outside the Home

24. Does resident take trips outside the home? Where does resident go? When? How often? With whom (relatives, friends, staff)?

    How important are trips outside the home?

Sleep and Rest

25. How well does resident sleep at night? How long?

    Does resident take naps during the day? When? How Long?

Entertainment

26. What kind of formal entertainment does resident experience? enjoy?

    In the home: television, card games, bingo, anything else?

    Outside the home: movies, concerts, picnics?

    Does resident prefer doing things alone or with others?

Meals

27. Where does resident eat? With whom? When? What does resident like/dislike about the food; the eating arrangement; the time for meals?

28. Is there an opportunity to select food preference?

    Is the food at the home "good" (from resident's perspective)?

Holidays

29. Are the holidays important and meaningful? Birthdays? Are they time of joy? or depression?

    How does resident celebrate special days in the home?

Decision-Making in the Home

30. Is resident involved in any decision-making in the home?

    Is resident involved with any resident groups? Research Committee, etc.?

    Are there norms of behavior in the home for residents? Are there any positive or negative sanctions for behavior?

Religion

31. What are resident's religious beliefs?

Who supports resident's religious interest? Home chaplain? priest? rabbi? minister? church?

Can resident select own pastoral caregiver? go out of the home for church services?

How important is religion in resident's life now?

Time

32. Does time pass quickly or slowly in the home? Are there activities which break up the day? Is there something to look forward to in the morning? afternoon? evening?

Major Changes Resulting From Living in a Nursing Home

33. Does resident feel he/she still has independence? is more or less active physically? socially? depressed?

    Have physical habits changed?

    Do family and friends visit less?

    Are there any plans for leaving the home or is this a permanent arrangement?

Routine

34. Does resident have to stick to the schedule of the home?

    Is change or movement of room-site difficult to deal with?

Resident's Attitude Toward Life in a Nursing Home

35. How does resident feel about living predominantly among elderly people?

    Is there any sense of stigma to living in a nursing home?

    Who has power/control over residents' lives (the residents? caregiver? administrator?)

Resident's Attitude Toward Fellow Residents

36. Is there a sense of camaraderie among residents?

    Do residents have fun together? help each other? share good and bad news?

    Are there "cliques"? Are some residents excluded?

    Are there social classes based on education? money? health?

    Do some residents feel others receive preferential treatment?

37. Does resident become upset or depressed seeing other residents becoming confused? debilitated?

Social Interaction of Residents

38. What are the formal social activities in the home? Informal activities?

    How does the staff interact with residents? Formally or informally?

    Are withdrawn residents looked after? encouraged to participate?

Resident's Attitude Toward Family and Friends

39. Does resident feel that family members and friends are still interested in him/her? Do they visit often enough? How often?

    Who is most frequent visitor?

    Have family and friends' attitudes changed since resident has been in the nursing home?

Resident's Attitude Toward Caregivers

40. Are staff supportive of both physical and emotional needs?

    Is resident respected?

Are caregivers well trained? adequately educated to do their job?

Does resident feel free to voice complaints about the staff?

Does resident have an advocate?

Death and Dying

41. How does resident feel about experiencing death of friends at the home?

    Does resident ever attend funerals at the home?

    Do deaths of others make resident think about his/her own death?

Closing

42. What are some of the good things about living at Bethany Manor? the staff? the other residents? the sisters?

    What are some negative or bad things about the home?

43. How does resident envision the future?

Family Discussion Guide

1. Difficulty of [family member] (mother, father, brother, sister, etc.), Mr./Mrs./Ms. ____, coping with admission to the nursing home.

    Difficulty of your coping with his/her admission to the nursing home.

2. Changes in family roles and role responsibiliites because of your [family member] being admitted to the nursing home.

3. Effect of nursing home regimen on family plans or activities.

4. Kinds of problems [family member's] illness condition and institutionalization cause in terms of family relationships.

5. Kinds of expectations you have for [family member] in terms of ADL; social activities; church activities; participation in family activities.

6. Degree to which [family member's] condition brought the family closer together or made sharing and interaction more difficult.

7. Difficulty of family coping [family member]'s condition as the length of time in the nursing home increase.

8. Things family does to be supportive [family member] to help him/her cope with life in the nursing home.

9. Kinds of things medical caregivers (i.e., nurses, physicans, technicians, social workers) could do to help [family member] and you in coping with the nursing home situation.

10. Close relationships established with medical caregivers during the course of [family member's] nursing home care.

11. Religious faith as an element in helping to cope with [family member's] condition.

12. Hardest thing about having someone you care for in a nursing home.

13. Degree to which major family goals have been changed or modified because of [family member's] admission to the nursing home.

14. Difficulty of [family member] in coping with nursing home life over time.

15. Any good or positive benefits for your family because of [family member's] admission to the nursing home.

Caregiver Discussion Guide

Demographic Data

1. Age:

2. Sex:

3. Degree (or technical training):

4. Position (head nurse, aide, etc.):

5. Type of unit (where respondent works):

6. Length of time in the nursing profession:

7. Length of time working with the elderly:

8. Length of time working in this nursing home:

9. Duties as a geriatric caregiver primarily physical (technical); psychological (resident support); or sociological (resident and family adaptation)?

10. Important qualities in a geriatric caregiver (e.g., technical skill, empathy, caring).

11. Involvement with residents: Do you ever see or talk to residents outside of work hours? Have any of the residents become your friends? Is it difficult to care for elderly patients because of their uncertain futures?

12. Ability to cope with deaths of residents you have gotten close to?

13. Establishment of relationships with residents' families or significant others. In what context or setting do you see these persons? Do they come to depend on you? call on you for advice?

14. Frequency of being a geriatric caregiver getting depressing or boring. Do you get tired of working with the same patients? Do you ever feel burned out?

15. Ability to talk about feelings with other geriatric caregivers. Is this done formally in meetings or informally during breaks or outside of work?

16. Morale among the staff at your unit.

17. Primary role seen as administrator; counselor; teacher; (patient) technician? All of these? Other? If you have several roles, which is primary? Why?

18. Burnout: Do you get to the point where you just don't want to be involved with geriatric patients?

19. Your treatment by nursing home residents: as a professional; servant; other.

20. Aspects of geriatric work that are most frustrating; most rewarding.

21. Personal comments about role as a nursing home caregiver.

Family Observation Guide

1. Who are the "families"? Significant others of the nursing home residents? Siblings? Children? Kin? Friends? Lawyers?

2. Are families of nursing home residents themselves elderly or middle-aged?

3. Do families experience guilt or relief regarding the admission of a loved one to a nursing home?

4. How frequently do families keep in touch with residents? How? By telephone? visits? letters? Do patterns of interaction change over time?

5. Do families experience anger from their resident relative because of admission to the nursing home? Does this vary depending upon whose decision the nursing home admission was?

6. Who are the resident's outside visitors? Family/friends? Organized volunteer groups? Religious caregiver (priest, minister, rabbi)? Churchmembers? Lawyers?

7. *Family Involvement in the Home*

   Is there evidence of encouragement for family to visit? Planned activities for family? Residents?

   Are staff members available and open to family members' needs for advice? comfort?

Can family members offer criticism and be listened to without staff becoming defensive or angry?

Do family members feel they can depend upon staff to provide the best care? How do they rate the caregiver?

8. *Volunteers at the Home*

Who are the nursing home volunteers? Routine or periodic?

Activities?

What is the meaning of the "volunteering" to the volunteers? the resident? the nursing home staff?

Caregiver Observation Guide

1. *Staff Population Description*

Number of staff, age range, SES [socioeconomic status] education, length of time working at the home

Nursing and nonnursing personnel

Number of RNs (MSN, BSN, AA, diploma)

Number of LPNs; aides; social workers; dietary staff; OTs; PTs; RTs

Number of physicians

2. *Staff Appearance*

Presentation of self: Professional? Warm, friendly? Distant?

Grooming: Uniforms, etc.

3. *Activities and Responsibilities of Staff*

Nurse and nonnurse: Role descriptions/responsiblilities

4. *Observation of Home's Activity Program*

Occupational therapy? physical therapy? music therapy? recreational therapy?

Where? When? What? Who?

Opportunity for nongroup therapies?

5. *Social Services Activities*

Who carries out patient admissions? patient transfers? patient discharge? family support ("Family Circle" groups)?

6. *Staff Attitudes: Morale (About the Job)*

Do staff manifest a sense of pride in their work? Do staff feel the work is rewarding? Do they feel they are adequately compensated? Is there a sense of harmony among differing levels of staff? What is the work atmosphere? Do some staff feel they are being discriminated against by having to care for more confused residents? What is the chance for career advancement?

7. *Staff Education*

Is there staff in-service education at the home? How often? Quality?

Is there evidence of staff interest in learning more about care of the elderly?

Is there an adequate staff orientation?

8. *Staff Rotation*

Do caregivers rotate shifts? If so, does this add to the confusion of those residents already possessed of cognitive deficits?

Do staff get pulled from one unit to another? How frequently?

9. *Staff Tunover*

What is the degree of staff turnover in the home? If low, why? If high, why?

10. *Staff Attitudes (Towards the Elderly)*

Do the attitudes of staff reflect respect for the elderly as person entitled to consideration of their rights and needs? Does this attitude differ among levels of staff?

Do staff attitudes reflect the home's basic philosophy?

11. *Communication Among Staff*

Are there regular staff meetings? What is discussed?

Are those lower on the career ladder listened to? Is their advice sought?

What is the atmosphere in these meetings? Are members free to air their grievances?

12. *Mental Health Services*

What services are provided? Who are the mental health workers? How available and interested are they? Is there communication between mental health workers and staff? follow-up? therapy groups? remotivation groups?

13. *Staff and Confused Patients*

Do staff encourage the more confused patients to use their mental faculties? Are clocks, calendars, etc., visible and used to orient patients? Are the confused encouraged to join in or are they isolated? Do they have regular caregivers or are there frequent changes?

14. *Staff and Depressed Patients*

Are staff aware that depressed patients may often be mistaken for senile? Are signs/symptoms of depression known and looked for in confused patients? What is done to help these patients? Groups? Indivdiual psychotherapy?

15. *Staff and Deaths of Residents*

How do staff handle residents' deaths? expected deaths? unexpected deaths?

Nursing Home Environment Observation Guide

1. *Population Description*

Who are the residents of Bethany Manor ($N = 230$)?

Age; sex; race; religion; marital status; socioeconomic status (education, former occupation); physical functioning; cognitive functioning; usual length of stay.

2. *Admission*

   A. How do residents get admitted to the home (physician referral, hospital reserval, family referral)?

   B. What are criteria for admission (physical condition, psychosocial condition, religion, age, race, financial status)?

   C. Observe a resident being admitted to home: resident-family interaction; resident-family-staff interaction; resident emotional state; etc.

   D. What personal items (i.e., clothes, television, books, furniture) can residents bring to the home when admitted?

3. How is the nursing home care financed? Private payments? Medicare/Medicaid? Charity?

4. *Medical Staff*

   A. Who is (are) the nursing home physician(s)?

   B. How frequently do physicians visit the residents? Do residents have a choice of a physician?

   C. What are the linkages with local facilities for hospital care if needed?

5. What types of cae does the nursing home provide?

   Skilled? ($N = ?$) Domiciliary? ($N = ?$) Intermediate ($N = ?$)

6. *External Quality Control*

   What type of accreditation does the home have? Who carries out quality assurance inspections?

7. *Internal Quality Control*

   What type of internal quality controls does the home provide (chart audits, resident care conferences, etc.)?

8. *Staff Development*

   What type of staff development programs does the home provide (in-service)? For whom? HNs/RNs? LPNs? Aides?

9. *Physical Layout of the Facility*

Floors: What facilities/services on each floor?

Grounds? Parking? Architectural barriers for disabled? Safety factors?

10. *Atmosphere of the Home*

Entrance/main lobby: How is one greeted by staff?

Cleanliness: What is the first impression upon entering the home?

Institutional vs. home environment

11. *Physical Environment*

Privacy?

Well lit? cheerful?

Adequate communal area?

Secure environment: Can residents move about safely? Security guards?

How are the residents divided up? Are the more active segregated from the more dependent? the more alert from the more confused?

12. *Territoriality*

Where is the resident's private space? Where is the staff's private space?

Residents' rooms: Are these private? Who has entrée? Must staff knock or can anyone just walk in? Does this differ on different floors?

13. What is the philosophy of care of the nursing home?

Is there a philosophy of care which can be objectively observed in the quality of nursing care given to the residents?

14. What is the relationship of administration with residents? with staff? with families?

15. Is there a sense that the religious orientation of the home provides a spiritual support for the residents?

Nursing Home Social Life Observation Guide

Observation Categories

1. *Physical Environment*: The facility—visualization of the physical area (color of walls; furniture; pets; number of persons in setting; equipment; lighting; space; odors; noises; etc.).

2. *Social (Human) Environment* (supportive, rigid, free): How people organize themselves into groups and subgroups; patterns of interaction; the direction of communication patterns (from staff to participants and participants to staff); changes in these patterns.

   Characteristics of residents (sex, race, age); decision-making patterns (how open are decisions; who initiates). Who has power in the nursing home? Who is in control?

3. *Participants' Formal Activities*: Sequence of activities: Physical care (ADL); PT; OT; recreation (formal and informal); work. What is done? What is said? How do behaviors and feelings appear to change in the sequence of activities? Closure points: When is activity ended? How? Signals? ("Units" of activity and "patterns" of activity.)

4. *Informal Interactions and Uplanned Activities:*

   Waiting periods

   Emergency situations (resident's illness becomes critical; death)

   Surprise visits from relatives and/or friends

5. *Language*: Language of the residents and staff; words used to describe problems and/or characteristics of nursing home life. Key words and phrases; connotations and symbolism involved in the words used by actors in the setting.

6. *Nonverbal Communication* : Ways to get attention—fidgeting; moving about; complaining; dress (or undress); physical space (territoriality). Physical contact among residents and/or staff.

Cognitively Impaired Resident Discussion Guide

1. How are you?

2. What is it like living here?

3. What do you do all day?

4. Whom do you talk to here?

5. Is there anything you need?

Management of Nursing Home Patient Care Observation Guide

Observation/Interview

Times: Nursing Shift Transition
Times: (Suggested Times)
7:00-3:00 (6:00-8:00 a.m.)
3:00-11:00 (2:00-4:00 p.m.)
11:00-7:00 (10:00 p.m.-12:00 midnite)

General Observation

1. What type of education/training do the staff members have? How many in each nursing category, for example, RN, LPN, aide, etc.?

    (a) Number: RNs ____LPNs ___; Medical Aides ___;

    Aides ____.

    (b) RN education type, for example, diploma, AA, BSN:

LPN education type, for example, eighteen-month course:

Aide education, for example, six weeks training:

Comments:

2. Persons in authority (shift going off and shift coming on)?

3. Who seems to have most power (control), for example, charge nurse; staff nurses; aides?

4. Are there informal relationships among staff, for example, friendships, cliques?

5. Do there seem to be any observable stresses between or within the staff group or the two transitioning shifts, for example, frustration if someone has called in sick; anger about work not done on a prior shift, etc.?

6. Who makes patient care assignments?

7. Are patient care assignments made by the charge nurse alone or in consultation with the staff?

8. On what basis are assignments made, for example, patient classification?

9. What is the patient care assignment ratio, for example, 1:10, 1:5, 1:3? Does this vary for patients regarding classification?

10. Patient classification system

Patient Activity Type

Activity	Independent	Assistance Needed	Dependent
A. Mobility Transfer Bed/chair Wheelchair Walker Cane Alone			
B. Nutrition Spoon-feeding Minimal assistance Alone			
C. Elimination Incontinent totally Incontinent occasionally Normal			
D. ADL Grooming (hair, nails) Dressing Bathing			

11. Are there "choice" or "favorite" patient assignments? Are there "undesirable" patient assignments?

12. How frequently do patient care assignments change? For example, daily, weekly, monthly?

13. Are patient care assignments made by patient or by floor wing?

14. What differences are observable among transition times on the three shifts—day, evening, night?

15. Other comments:

Letter to Significant Other of a Cognitively Impaired Resident

Dear

For the past two years I have been working with the Bethany Manor Nursing Home residents and staff as a faculty member serving on the _____ University School of Nursing–Bethany Manor Teaching Nursing Home Project. The project's aim is to try and improve care and general quality of life for nursing home residents. In my role as project researcher I have spent the past year and a half observing and talking with staff members and residents about their problems, needs, and lives in general, in order to assist us in planning future nursing care activities.

One group of residents with whom I have not worked are those persons who have some cognitive impairment or confusion as I felt that it might not be possible for them to totally understand my study. However, we do not want to neglect these residents as they also can often express their needs and fears if given the opportunity.

I would like to request your approval to conduct a simple conversation of approximately 15-20 minutes with _____. The discussion will involve five basic questions:

1. How are you?

2. What is it like living here?

3. What do you do during the day?

4. Whom do you talk to here?

5. Is there anything you need?

plus any additional comments which the residents wish to share. All information will be confidential and no resident will ever be identified by name or unique characteristics which might lead to identification by other residents or staff. If the resident should not wish to talk or wishes to terminate the conversation at any time, this will of course be honored.

If you agree that your resident be included, would you kindly sign the attached form and return it in the enclosed stamped, self-addressed envelope. Thank you very much for your assistance. If you have any questions, please feel free to call me: 202/635-5400 (work) or 301/864-4831 (home).

Sincerely,

Mary Elizabeth O'Brien, RN, PhD
Associate Professor, Doctoral Program

Informed Consent Agreement

I agree to allow Dr. Mary Elizabeth O'Brien, RN, PhD, of _____
University to converse with _____ in the conduct of a study
entitled "Anatomy of a Nursing Home: Behavior Patterns in the
Adaptation and Care of the Nursing Home Resident." I understand that
all information will be confidential and no resident will ever be
identified by name.

Name

Relation to Resident

Date

INDEX